Latin American and Arab Literature

Edinburgh Studies in Modern Arabic Literature
Series Editor: Rasheed El-Enany

Writing Beirut: Mappings of the City in the Modern Arabic Novel
Samira Aghacy

Women, Writing and the Iraqi State: Resistance and Collaboration under the Ba'th, 1968–2003
Hawraa Al-Hassan

Autobiographical Identities in Contemporary Arab Literature
Valerie Anishchenkova

The Iraqi Novel: Key Writers, Key Texts
Fabio Caiani and Catherine Cobham

Sufism in the Contemporary Arabic Novel
Ziad Elmarsafy

Gender, Nation, and the Arabic Novel: Egypt 1892–2008
Hoda Elsadda

The Arabic Prose Poem: Poetic Theory and Practice
Huda Fakhreddine

The Unmaking of the Arab Intellectual: Prophecy, Exile and the Nation
Zeina G. Halabi

Egypt 1919: The Revolution in Literature and Film
Dina Heshmat

Post-War Anglophone Lebanese Fiction: Home Matters in the Diaspora
Syrine Hout

Prophetic Translation: The Making of Modern Egyptian Literature
Maya I. Kesrouany

Nasser in the Egyptian Imaginary
Omar Khalifah

Conspiracy in Modern Egyptian Literature
Benjamin Koerber

War and Occupation in Iraqi Fiction
Ikram Masmoudi

Latin American and Arab Literature: Transcontinental Exchanges
Tahia Abdel Nasser

Literary Autobiography and Arab National Struggles
Tahia Abdel Nasser

The Libyan Novel: Humans, Animals and the Poetics of Vulnerability
Charis Olszok

The Arab Nahḍah*: The Making of the Intellectual and Humanist Movement*
Abdulrazzak Patel

Blogging from Egypt: Digital Literature, 2005–2016
Teresa Pepe

Religion in the Egyptian Novel
Christina Phillips

Space in Modern Egyptian Fiction
Yasmine Ramadan

Gendering Civil War: Francophone Women's Writing in Lebanon
Mireille Rebeiz

Occidentalism: Literary Representations of the Maghrebi Experience of the East–West Encounter
Zahia Smail Salhi

Sonallah Ibrahim: Rebel with a Pen
Paul Starkey

Minorities in the Contemporary Egyptian Novel
Mary Youssef

edinburghuniversitypress.com/series/smal

Latin American and Arab Literature

Transcontinental Exchanges

Tahia Abdel Nasser

EDINBURGH
University Press

Edinburgh University Press is one of the leading university presses in the UK. We publish academic books and journals in our selected subject areas across the humanities and social sciences, combining cutting-edge scholarship with high editorial and production values to produce academic works of lasting importance. For more information visit our website: edinburghuniversitypress.com

Edinburgh University Press Ltd
The Tun – Holyrood Road
12 (2f) Jackson's Entry
Edinburgh EH8 8PJ

First published in hardback by Edinburgh University Press 2023

Typeset in 11/15pt Times New Roman by
Cheshire Typesetting Ltd, Cuddington, Cheshire

A CIP record for this book is available from the British Library

ISBN 978 1 3995 0712 7 (hardback)
ISBN 978 1 3995 0713 4 (paperback)
ISBN 978 1 3995 0714 1 (webready PDF)
ISBN 978 1 3995 0715 8 (epub)

Contents

Series Editor's Foreword vi
Acknowledgements ix
Note on Transliteration and Translation xiii

Introduction: Cultural Exchange between Latin America and the Arab World 1
1 Transcontinental Literature: Gabriel García Márquez and Héctor Abad Faciolince 23
2 The African Shore: Rodrigo Rey Rosa and Alberto Ruy Sánchez in Morocco 57
3 Children of Scheherazade: Gabriel García Márquez in Arabic 78
4 Che Guevara's Diaries, Miguel Littín's Adventures: Latin American Iconography in Arabic Literature 114
5 Dreams of Jorge Luis Borges, Nightmares of Carlos Fuentes: Arabic and World Literature 135
Epilogue: The Legacy of Transcontinental Ties 159

Notes 165
Bibliography 180
Index 204

Series Editor's Foreword

Edinburgh Studies in Modern Arabic Literature is a unique series that aims to fill a glaring gap in scholarship in the field of modern Arabic literature. Its dedication to Arabic literature in the modern period (that is, from the nineteenth century onwards) is what makes it unique among series undertaken by academic publishers in the English-speaking world. Individual books on modern Arabic literature in general or aspects of it have been and continue to be published sporadically. Series on Islamic studies and Arab/Islamic thought and civilisation are not in short supply either in the academic world, but these are far removed from the study of Arabic literature qua literature, that is, imaginative, creative literature as we understand the term when, for instance, we speak of English literature or French literature. Even series labelled 'Arabic/Middle Eastern Literature' make no period distinction, extending their purview from the sixth century to the present, and often including non-Arabic literatures of the region. This series aims to redress the situation by focusing on the Arabic literature and criticism of today, stretching its interest to the earliest beginnings of Arab modernity in the nineteenth century.

The need for such a dedicated series, and generally for the redoubling of scholarly endeavour in researching and introducing modern Arabic literature to the Western reader, has never been stronger. Among activities and events heightening public, let alone academic, interest in all things Arab, and not least Arabic literature, are the significant growth in the last decades of the translation of contemporary Arab authors from all genres, especially fiction, into English; the higher profile of Arabic literature internationally since the award of the Nobel Prize in Literature to Naguib Mahfouz in 1988; the growing number of Arab authors living in the Western diaspora and writing both in English and in Arabic; the adoption of such authors and others by mainstream, high-circulation publishers, as opposed to the academic publishers of the past; and the establishment of prestigious prizes, such as the International Prize for Arabic Fiction, popularly referred to in the Arab world as the Arabic Booker, run by the Man Booker Foundation, which brings huge publicity to the shortlist and winner every year, as well as translation contracts into English and other languages. It is therefore part of the ambition of this series that it will increasingly address a wider reading public beyond its natural territory of students and researchers in Arabic and world literature. Nor indeed is the academic readership of the series expected to be confined to specialists in literature in the light of the growing trend for interdisciplinarity, which increasingly sees scholars crossing field boundaries in their research tools and coming up with findings that equally cross discipline borders in their appeal.

The cultural encounter between Latin America and the Arab world goes back to the late nineteenth century and early twentieth, when waves of migrants, particularly Syro-Lebanese, escaping Ottoman tyrannical rule, economic hardship and religious strife, settled diversely in both North and South America. The migrants brought with them their language, culture and literature, allowing a thriving literary movement to emerge in diaspora in the first half of the twentieth century. This movement, which literary historians later labelled as *Adab al-Mahjar*, or emigrant literature, while rooted in the Arabic language and its heritage, also bore the fruit of the influence of the new environment, the geographic distance from Arab lands and the freedom from restraints of tradition that continued to exercise their power back home. Such was the grace and beauty of their literary imagination, they became from their distant lands of exile a modernising influence on Arabic literature back in their land of birth. In the postcolonial period from the 1950s onwards, political and diplomatic ties were fomented between newly independent Arab nations and their counterparts in South America, generating a parallel interest in the literature of the continent, which was also beginning to make its international mark through some of its giant figures in poetry and fiction, such as Pablo Neruda and Gabriel García Márquez, to name but two. Much of Latin American literature began to make its way into Arabic through translations, with literary techniques such as magical realism, popularised in Latin American fiction, filtering among other evidence of cultural interaction into Arabic writing.

Such a strong literary connection with a long history and a burgeoning present has been waiting to have a scholarly book dedicated to its examination. This is what Tahia Abdel Nasser, who has previously contributed to this series a volume on *Literary Autobiography and Arab National Struggles*, undertakes in the work to hand, bringing a welcome comparative approach to the subject with interest extending to studies of world literature and the global South, particularly the South-South exchange.

Rasheed El-Enany,
Series Editor,
Emeritus Professor of Modern Arabic Literature,
University of Exeter

Acknowledgements

This book has grown out of an enduring interest in connections between Latin America and the Arab world and more than a decade of conversations with friends, scholars and writers. Thank you, first and foremost, to Rasheed El-Enany for including the book in the Edinburgh Studies in Modern Arabic Literature series and his editorial advice. It has been a great pleasure to work with him. I am deeply grateful for his immensely helpful comments. Many thanks to Nicola Ramsey and Emma House at Edinburgh University Press for their enthusiasm and support. I also wish to express my deepest gratitude to Louise Hutton, Isobel Birks, Eddie Clark and Caitlin Murphy at Edinburgh University Press for their gracious editorial help and smooth production. I am grateful to the two generous anonymous reviewers who offered thoughtful feedback.

It is a great pleasure to thank the friends who guided me in Cuba, which was an inspiration for my research. I am especially grateful to Tania Aguiar Fernández for the warm welcome in Cuba. In Havana, I warmly thank Maria Cristina Lopez Riviera and Daniela Sardiñas Rodríguez who welcomed and guided me and shared materials.

I had the pleasure of meeting Héctor Abad Faciolince who was so gracious and helpful. Lina Meruane generously shared her books and interviews. I warmly thank Elias Khoury for his warm and humorous conversations and thoughtfully sharing materials with me. I am grateful to Jabbar Yussin Hussin for kindly sharing his short stories and insights. I thank Hassan Blasim who answered my questions. I am also grateful to Ibrahim Abdel Meguid and Sayed Mahmoud who promptly responded with help. I was fortunate to have conversations with the late Radwa Ashour, Mourid Barghouti and Mahmoud Darwish that inspired me. I am immensely grateful to Susanne Klengel for her warm welcome at the Latin Amerika Institute in Freie Universität Berlin, where I was a visiting scholar in 2014 and 2017, and Alexandra Ortiz Wallner for the knowledge she shared. I am deeply grateful to Georges Khalil for his generous help with introductions and the opportunity to present at a workshop on Encounters in ArabLatinAmerican Literatures at the Europe in the Middle East–The Middle East in Europe (EUME) Forum Transregionale Studien in Berlin. It was a great pleasure to present with Ottmar Ette at the workshop. I thank the participants: Elias Khoury, Susanne Klengel and Friederike Pannewick.

I am most grateful to Víctor Mahana Nassar for permission to use his beautiful artwork on the cover of the book.

This project has been funded with support from the European Commission. This book reflects the views only of the author, and the Commission cannot be held responsible for any use which may be made of the information contained therein. An Erasmus Mundus Scholarship and Eramus+ grant at Freie Universität Berlin generously supported my research in 2014 and 2017. A sabbatical leave from the office of the provost at the American University in Cairo (AUC) in 2019–20 helped me to complete the manuscript. A research grant from AUC allowed me to travel to the Gabriel García Márquez archive at the Harry Ransom Center at the University of Texas, Austin, in 2016. A writing fellowship from AUC's School of Humanities and Social Sciences offered me time to research and write the book in the spring of 2018.

I warmly thank dear friends for advice and conversations: Reem Abou-El-Fadl, Reem Bassiouney, Sharif Elmusa, Ferial Ghazoul, Lina Meruane and Mounira Soliman. I am grateful to Mahmoud El Lozy, may he rest in peace, for his advice and camaraderie. Catalina Constain shared so much knowledge with me of Colombia and Latin America. I thank Ferial Ghazoul, Christina Civantos, Ira Dworkin, Haytham Nawar, Hasna Reda Mikdashi, Shadi Rohana, Amro Sabeh and Bahia Shehab for passing along materials. I am grateful to Mona Baker for her helpful comments on a portion of the Epilogue.

At AUC, I thank my colleagues in the Department of English and Comparative Literature. Ferial Ghazoul has been a generous mentor, colleague and friend. Many thanks to Yvette Isaac for her thoughtful support. I am thankful to Wafaa Fahmy, Peter Philps and Lamiaa ElNakib at the AUC library for their generous help. I also thank the librarians and archivists at the Harry Ransom Center at the University of Texas, Austin. Special thanks to Miguel Angel Araujo and Araceli Noquez from Dirreción General de Bibliotecas of Universidad Nacional Autónoma de México.

Thank you, also, for invitations to present at conferences: Stephanie Fleischmann, Susanne Klengel, Jorge Locane, Benjamin Loy, Gesine Müller, Robert Myers, Ana Nenadović, Kamran Rastegar and Ignacio M. Sánchez Prado. I am grateful to interlocutors who offered feedback on portions of the manuscript at conferences. Hoda El Shakry and Sophie Esch offered excellent suggestions for Chapter 4. The anonymous readers for an article in *Comparative Literature Studies* offered helpful comments. I thank Lila Abu-Lughod, Ussama Makdisi, Rania Said and Stephen Sheehi for fruitful conversations. I thank students in Susanne Klengel's PhD Colloquium, particularly Camila Gonzatto, and in my courses on Arab Latin American literature at AUC.

Portions of the manuscript were presented at annual meetings of the Modern Language Association, the American Comparative Literature Association, the University of Oslo, Freie Universität Berlin, Köln University and the EUME Forum Transregionale Studien in Berlin. In 2015 and 2018, I convened panels on Latin America and the Arab world at annual meetings of the Modern Language Association in Vancouver and New York. Part of Chapter 3 appeared in *Comparative Literature Studies*, 52, no. 3 (2015), 91–113. Chapter 2 appeared in *Re-Mapping World Literature: Writing, Book Markets, and Epistemologies between Latin America and the Global South* (De Gruyter, 2018). Portions of Chapter 4 appeared in *América Latina – África del Norte – España: lazos culturales, intelectuales y literarios del colonialismo español al antiimperialismo tercermundista* (Iberoamericana/Vervuert, 2020) and *A Companion to African Literatures* (John Wiley & Sons Ltd, 2021). I am grateful for permission to reprint and expand portions here.

Thank you to my family; my parents, Khaled Gamal Abdel Nasser and Dahlia Fahmy, have always been so generous and supportive. Though my father passed away more than a decade ago, I draw inspiration from him. He always appreciated and supported my love of literature with love, kindness, generosity and enthusiasm. Thank you also to my parents-in-law who have been so thoughtful and supportive. Ahmed Fahmy and our daughter, Nadine, were delightful company as I laboured on the book. Profuse gratitude to them, with love.

Note on Transliteration and Translation

I adopt the standard system of transliteration from Arabic to English used by IJMES (*International Journal of Middle Eastern Studies*). Personal names with spellings that have become standard in English are rendered in the forms known to an anglophone audience (for example, Gamal Abdel Nasser). The names of Arab authors whose works have been translated into English are transliterated upon first mention, and appear thenceforth in the conventional English spellings (for example, Mahmoud Darwish). The names of Arab authors writing in English, Spanish and French are rendered in the most common and preferred spelling.

All references to Arabic and Latin American literature are to the original. I use existing translations of works that have been translated from Arabic, Spanish or French to English. Unless otherwise noted, all translations are my own.

Introduction
Cultural Exchange between Latin America and the Arab World

I know of Egypt and Niger,
Of Persia and Xenophon, no less.

José Martí, *Versos sencillos*

On 16 September 1881, José Martí (1853–95), the Cuban revolutionary and poet, living in exile in New York (1881–95), penned a chronicle on the ʿUrābī revolution in Egypt. Shortly thereafter, the chronicle appeared in his regular column in the Caracas newspaper *La Opinión Nacional*. In 'La revuelta en Egipto. – Interesante problema' ('The Revolt in Egypt. – An Interesting Problem'), Martí praises the 1881 popular revolution against British and French imperialism, led by the Egyptian nationalist Colonel Aḥmad ʿUrābī Pasha, and acknowledges its swift victory.[1] His impassioned chronicle begins: it is no 'simple foreign news' ('una simple noticia extranjera'), but 'a serious event that moves Europe and convulses Africa' ('un grave suceso que mueve a Europa, estremece a África') (14: 113).[2] Though he had never been to Egypt, he describes the country as 'heady and rebellious like its steeds' ('airoso y rebelde como sus corceles') (14: 116). In his column 'Escenas Europeas' (European Vignettes), his chronicle's picturesque scene is a 'diorama' that conjures the event with rhetorical flair: the Egyptian colonel on his horse, brandishing his sword, surrounded by rebellious officers.[3] He hails ʿUrābī, who speaks 'a picturesque Arabic' ('un pintoresco árabe') and exudes 'gallant courtesy' ('gallarda cortesía'), as 'a robust colonel, with immense popularity, full of the Egyptian spirit, Muslim and independent' ('un robusto coronel, dotado de condiciones populares, lleno del espíritu egipcio, muslímico e independiente') (14: 114). Fittingly, Martí, the Apostle of Cuba's independence, extols the hero of the 'Urābī revolution. His treatment of a geographically remote and contemporary event is deeply telling of connections between Latin America and the Arab world that would be deepened in the mid-twentieth century.

Besides Martí's attention to the 1881–82 'Urābī revolution, his oeuvre shows an enduring interest in the Arab world. Surprisingly, there is little scholarship on Martí's relationship to the Orient.[4] In *Versos sencillos* (Simple Verses, 1891), the speaker declares: 'I know of Egypt . . .' ('Yo sé de Egipto') (25).[5] There are several allusions to the Moor in *Versos sencillos*.[6] His poems are sprinkled with a constellation of Arab themes: his early dramatic poem *Abdala* (1869), where a bold African warrior defends Nubia, his patria (homeland), from invaders, has been read as 'an allegory of Cuban independence' (Allen 2002: 3). In *Abdala*, the valiant warrior (whose name means 'slave of God' in Arabic) brandishes a scimitar on his noble steed. The evocation of 'Urābī, the Egyptian nationalist, in his chronicle harkens back to *Abdala*, the African warrior. In *Ismaelillo* (Little Ishmael, 1882), a collection of poems dedicated to his son, the theme of the Arab recurs. The title of *Ismaelillo* is a diminutive of Ishmael, the son of the Prophet Abraham and Hagar, an Egyptian slave. Several allusions to the Moor and the Arab world remind us of the expulsion of the Moors from Spain and Spanish colonialism in Cuba. In *Ismaelillo*, Oriental details accrue and the speaker addresses his playful son as 'Ismaelillo – árabe!' (14: 30) ('Ismaelillo, Arab!').[7]

Critics have debated Martí's Orientalism and international solidarity, but his 'Orient' rests on his interest in the Arab world and anti-colonialism. Martí's Orient – evoked through anti-imperialism and revolution in the Arab world in 'La revuelta en Egipto' and *Abdala* – and the Cuban War of Independence are intimately intertwined.[8] In 'Los moros en España' (1893), Martí expresses support for the revolt in the Rif against Spanish colonialism in northern Morocco. His famous declaration 'Seamos moros!' expresses a solidarity with the Moors who were subjected to Spanish rule in Muslim Iberia: 'Seamos moros: . . . nosotros, que moriremos tal vez a manos de España . . . Pero seamos moros!!' ('Seamos moros: Let us be

Moors . . . we who will probably die by the hand of Spain . . . But let us be Moors!') (5: 334).[9] Moreover, 'Seamos moros!' celebrates a Moorish heritage and acknowledges a common struggle against Spanish colonialism. Martí's Orient is telling in that both the Moor and the 1881–82 revolution in Egypt, in a column about European imperialism, become emblems of anti-colonialism.

Martí's international solidarity would be revived in the 1950s and 1960s with Cuban internationalism. During the Cold War, Latin American countries engaged with Third World decolonisation movements and established diplomatic and historical ties with the Arab world. Soon after the 1959 Cuban Revolution, Che Guevara travelled to Egypt on his tour of Bandung countries in June 1959, arrived in Algeria in July 1963, and travelled again to Egypt on 11 February 1965 on his way to the Congo. Cuba admired Egypt's stand in the 1956 Israeli-British-French attack and armed the Algerian War of Independence (1954–62) in the 1960s.[10] Cuba's solidarity with anti-colonial movements in Africa and historical ties to the Arab world in the 1950s and 1960s redrew transcontinental routes. The relationship of Latin America to the Arab world in the 1950s and 1960s grew out of revolutionary movements and transnational solidarity. In the mid-twentieth century, Latin America and the Arab world shared a common struggle against imperialism which was central to Third Worldism from Bandung in the 1950s to the Tricontinental in the 1960s.

This book makes visible linkages in Arab and Latin American cultural production within the legacy of Third World projects in the mid-twentieth century. The relationship of Latin America to the Arab world extends from Martí's engagement with the Arab world, which grew out of shared political struggles, to cultural exchange in the twentieth and twenty-first centuries. However, settler colonialism in Cuba and other Latin American countries, which gained independence in the nineteenth century, differed from the colonial history of the Arab world where decolonisation began in the mid-twentieth century. The literary ties between Latin America and the Arab world extend from Orientalism to international solidarity in the sense of a Hispanic Orientalist tradition and Arab and Latin American shared struggles. They encompass a relationship to colonialism and imperialism in Latin America and the Arab world and encounters that have extended from Orientalism to migration to translation. The Arab Orient attracted Latin American writers, poets and chroniclers in the nineteenth century. Since the late nineteenth century, Arab immigrants migrated to Latin America from the Ottoman Empire. In some cases, Oriental themes in Latin American literature were an extension of a history of Arab migration to Latin America. The travel of 'Boom' literature in the Arab world, in turn, inspired Arab writers in the twentieth century. These routes have shaped literary ties and direct networks that extend from Cuba to Egypt and from Iraq to Argentina.

A new cadre of Latin American and Arab writers fostered ties in novels, chronicles, travelogues, memoirs and poems. In *La ciudad letrada* (*The Lettered City*), Ángel Rama traces the rise of what he calls 'the lettered city', 'a nexus' of lettered culture, the state and urbanism, and argues that men of letters or *literatos*, a 'lettered' elite, who authored documents, reports, chronicles, edicts, correspondence and records, were closely linked to the state and the city in the former Spanish and Portuguese empires (the 'lettered' extended thereafter to the literate in society) (Chasteen 1996: vii). Arab and Latin American writers and poets have revived the ties created by revolutionaries, statesmen, dignitaries, diplomats and functionaries. I argue that Arab and Latin American cultural exchange cemented historical, cultural and diplomatic ties of the mid-twentieth century.[11] Lettered encounters may be read through the cultural production of writers from Cuba, Colombia, Guatemala, Mexico, Egypt, Lebanon and Iraq.[12]

Arab Latin American connections are most visible in Latin American Orientalism, the legacy of Arab migration to Latin America, cultural encounters in Arabic and Latin American literatures, and the translation and circulation of Latin American literature in the Arab world. We will turn to several Arab Latin American encounters in novels, chronicles, travelogues, memoirs and poems. Cultural encounters in Latin American and Arabic literatures encompass Arab immigrants in Colombia, a Colombian in Cairo, Mexican and Guatemalan travellers in Morocco, Che Guevara's iconography in 1960s Egypt and Oman, Gabriel García Márquez's novels in Egypt and Lebanon, and reading Jorge Luis Borges and Carlos Fuentes in Iraq. We will examine the circulation of literature and the legacies of transcontinental ties in Latin America and the Arab world.

Arab Latin American ties will help advance new comparative models that draw on transcontinental solidarities, trace ties to the Third Worldism of the mid-twentieth century, and broaden the category of world literature. They can contribute to new comparatisms through a model that restores the importance of historical links and direct connections between Latin America and the Arab world. Examining cultural exchange between Latin America and the Arab world can offer a fruitful model for the comparative study of two regions with historical, cultural and literary ties. My intent in examining cultural exchange between Latin America and the Arab world is two-fold: first, to examine the relationship between Latin American and Arabic literatures and the circulation of literature across continents with historical, cultural and literary ties; and second, to contribute to scholarship in the field of Comparative Literature on new comparatisms that extend beyond institutional, disciplinary, ideological and geographic borders by recovering largely overlooked internationalist networks and a broader history of South-South exchanges.

This book examines a body of Arabic and Hispanic literature that brings together two literary spheres and proposes new comparatisms based on direct networks and comparative methodologies beyond continents. I frame my comparative study of Latin American and Arabic literatures in the legacy of internationalist networks that were formed in the 1960s. These connections have been eclipsed in postcolonial studies. Besides the relationship between Latin America and the Arab world in the mid-twentieth century, I consider shared political struggles in a longer history from Martí to the twenty-first century. Drawing on a history of the unique relationship of Latin America to the Arab world and the legacies of Third Worldist networks, the book explores new avenues for comparative study.

Why Latin America and the Arab World?

Latin American and Arab Literature: Transcontinental Exchanges contributes to a growing, albeit small, field on connections between Latin America and the Arab world. There is wide interest in the routes between Latin America and the Arab world in history, politics, anthropology and literature. Both regions share a long history of solidarity, alliances and convergences that extend to Third Worldist networks of the mid-twentieth century and formal cooperation in the mid-2000s.[13] Arab migration to Latin America has produced a rich body of literature that encompasses the cultural production of the Syro-Lebanese *Mahjar* (emigré) poets and pre-eminent Latin American writers who have explored Arab themes and drawn on the legacy of al-Andalus and a fascination with the Orient. Latin American and Arab writers have obliquely and directly drawn on historical and cultural ties. As we shall see, the effects of Latin American literature on Arabic literature have produced important connections.

Connections between Latin America and the Arab world extend from the Cuban revolutionary José Martí at the end of the nineteenth century to the early twenty-first century. Martí's chronicle on the anti-imperial revolt in Egypt in the 1880s, which is situated within his struggle for Cuba's independence from Spanish rule, shows not only early connections with the Arab world that extended beyond Orientalism, but also that engagements with the Arab world anticipated the close political and diplomatic ties between Cuba, Egypt and Algeria that began in 1959. Moreover, the direction of Martí's engagement anticipated the scope of transcontinental literature. Of course, Arab Latin American solidarity was a project of leftist politicians and revolutionaries in the 1950s and 1960s, interrupted by right-wing governments and Cold War superpowers. Similarly, Arab Latin American ties resurfaced during the Pink Tide with the rise of the new left governments in Latin America in the mid-2000s, followed by the conservative wave in the twenty-first century.[14] The Left's engagement with the Palestinian struggle in Latin America affords another example of the solidarity networks that prevailed in the late twentieth century and extended to the literary sphere.[15] Cuba expressed solidarity with the Palestine Liberation Organization (PLO) in 1964 (Stites Mor 2014: 189) and there were strong ties between the Sandinistas in Nicaragua and the PLO.

Most scholarship on Arab and Latin American literary ties has focused on Arab migration to Latin America.[16] Arab migration to Latin America began in the 1860s, and immigrants settled mostly in Brazil, Argentina and Chile (Civantos 2006: 6). Since the late nineteenth century, waves of Arab immigrants from the Levant (Syria, Lebanon, Jordan and Palestine) arrived in Latin America, settling in Argentina, Brazil, Chile, Mexico,

Cuba, Colombia and Honduras (Zabel 2006b: 2).[17] In 1870–1947, Syro-Lebanese immigrants arrived mostly in Brazil and Argentina (Fadda-Conrey 2006: 25). Further waves of Arab migration arose from the Lebanese Civil War (1975–90). Arab immigrants were mostly peddlers and merchants and would go on to play an important role in economic, political and cultural spheres in Latin America. Migration from Syria, Iraq and Palestine resumed in the twenty-first century during political upheavals in the Arab world such as the 2003 US invasion of Iraq and the Syrian Civil War in 2011.

The routes of migration from the Arab world to Latin America show multi-directional linkages, networks and influences. The *Mahjar* (emigré) poets who emigrated to the Americas in the late nineteenth and early twentieth century such as Iliyā Abū Māḍī and Nasīb ʻArīḍa played a central role in the development of modern Arabic poetry. The southern *Mahjar* began early networks of Arabic cultural production in South America and founded *al-ʻUṣba al-Andalusiyya* (the Andalusian League), a literary society, in Brazil in 1933 and *al-Rābiṭa al-Adabiyya* (the Literary Union) in Argentina in 1949. The Syro-Lebanese poets who settled in South America were forefathers of the modern literary ties with South America. As Robyn Creswell has noted:

> Brazil and Argentina were centers of the southern *mahjar*, a lively intellectual community that sprang up during the last two decades of the nineteenth century in South America. Levantine identity, the role of literature in civic life, and calls for Syrian or Lebanese independence were the common topics of debate in this milieu, which was closely in touch with intellectual currents in the homeland. (2019: 58)

M. M. Badawi describes the name of the literary society *al-ʻUṣba al-Andalusiyya* as ʻclearly harking back to the Arab past and designed to establish a link with traditionʼ (1975: 181). Clearly, *al-ʻUṣba al-Andalusiyya* invokes an Arab-Iberian heritage in al-Andalus.

Latin American interest in and travel to the Arab Orient produced a tradition of Orientalist literature.[18] Encounters with the Orient in the cultural production of Latin America offer forms of South-South Orientalism that do not fit within Edward Said's *Orientalism*. Scholars have examined

Argentine Orientalism and 'alternative' or 'peripheral' Orientalism.[19] In *Between Argentines and Arabs*, Christina Civantos links the Orientalist practices of Euro-Argentine and Arab Argentine writers to the formulation of Argentine national identity from the mid-nineteenth to the mid-twentieth century. In *Alternative Orientalisms in Latin America and Beyond*, Ignacio López-Calvo problematises Latin American Orientalism by drawing attention to the colonial history of Latin America. Although there is a long tradition of Eurocentric Orientalism in Latin America, Latin American Orientalism is largely different in that there is no cultural or racial superiority in South-South exchanges (López-Calvo 2010a: 5). Waïl Hassan has explored what he calls 'Brazilian Orientalism' (or 'Carioca Orientalism') as distinct from French, British and US Orientalism. The Brazilian variety celebrates 'Amerindian, African, and "Oriental"' cultures (Hassan 2020: 123).

The Arab Orient attracted Latin American writers whose works are Orientalist or evince an ambivalent Orientalism that is part of a long tradition of Latin American Orientalism and, unlike works from the late twentieth century, share no direct relationship to Arab migration, internationalist networks or colonial history.[20] There are two groups of Latin American writers: first, those who travelled to the Orient; and second, those who drew on the Orient and *The Thousand and One Nights* but had no direct knowledge of the Arab world. Argentine writer Jorge Luis Borges (1899–1986) drew on the Orient and *The Thousand and One Nights* in his magical realism. Latin American writers travelled to the Arab Orient from the late nineteenth century: Argentine writer Domingo Faustino Sarmiento's *Viajes por Europa, África y América* (Travels in Europe, Africa and America) recounts his travels to Algeria.[21] Nicaraguan poet Rubén Darío, the founder of *modernismo*, made a brief trip to Tangier in 1904. Argentine writer Roberto Arlt's Orientalist 'Aguafertes marroquíes' (Moroccan Etchings) in *Aguafuertes españolas* (Spanish Etchings, 1936) recounts his travels to Tangier. Guatemalan writer and chronicler Enrique Gómez Carrillo (1873–1927) recounted his travels to Egypt in the partly Orientalist *La sonrisa de la esfinge: sensaciones de Egipto* (The Smile of the Sphinx: Sensations of Egypt, 1913) and travelled to Morocco and Palestine at the turn of the twentieth century.[22]

Cuban Guillermo Cabrera Infante and Severo Sarduy travelled to Tangier (Aidi 2017: 21).

In the 1950s and 1960s, the relationship of Latin America to the Arab world grew out of transnational solidarity with Third World liberation movements. Solidarity networks with pan-Africanism, the Bandung Conference and the Non-Aligned Movement extended to the Arab world. The relationship of Latin America to the Arab world began in 1959 with the Cuban Revolution and internationalist solidarity with Third World liberation movements in the 1960s. Christine Hatzky and Jessica Stites Mor, writing of Latin American transnational solidarities, note the development of solidarity networks that extended to the Arab world:

> From the mid-1950s, the influence of pan-Arabism, pan-Africanism, aboriginal rights movements, and events in Asia, such as the Bandung Conference, which would eventually lead to the Non-Aligned Movement, similarly influenced the way in which regional solidarities would be configured. What these movements shared with the ideas of Martí is that they each in their own way articulated a vision of the 'poor' and the 'colonized' as a common 'third force' in the bi-polar conflict of the Cold War. (2014: 134)

In 1960, Cuba joined the Non-Aligned Movement, begun in 1955 in Bandung by formerly colonised countries that sought to maintain neutrality in the Cold War. This was the onset of a relationship of Latin American anti-imperialism to African and Asian liberation struggles (Stites Mor 2019: 47). The 1960s and 1970s saw the Latin American Left's engagement with the Arab world. For example, the relationships of Cuba with Egypt, Algeria and Palestine in the 1960s created political, historical and diplomatic ties between Cuba and the Arab world.

Cuba's relationship to Egypt began with the Cuban Revolution. In 1959, Che Guevara toured Egypt, Gaza and Damascus (Vélez 2016: 75). In July 1960, Raúl Castro arrived in Cairo on the anniversary of Egypt's 1952 Revolution. The historic meeting of Gamal Abdel Nasser and Fidel Castro in Harlem for the United Nations General Assembly in New York on 25 September 1960 was symbolic of Egyptian-Cuban ties and Third World solidarity networks.

Cuba's involvement with Algeria began in 1961. After Algeria gained its independence in July 1962, then-Prime Minister Ahmed Ben Bella travelled to Cuba from New York in October 1962 during the Cuban Missile Crisis. The trip began a deep friendship between Cubans and Algerians. This was due in part to the parallel between the Cuban Revolution and the Algerian War of Independence (Gleijeses 1996: 162–3). Cuba supported the Algerian War of Independence, lent military assistance to the Algerian National Liberation Front (FLN), trained Algerian troops, and sent medical missions to postindependence Algeria (Gleijeses 1996: 159, 182). A medical mission arrived in Algeria in May 1963 (Gleijeses 1996: 165). Che Guevara visited Algeria in July 1963 on the occasion of the anniversary of Algerian independence (Gleijeses 1996: 167). In December 1964, he went on a trip to Africa that lasted to 14 March, visiting Algeria and Egypt twice (Gleijeses 1996: 188). Che Guevara's frequent trips to Algeria from 1963 to 1964 show close ties between Cuba and Algeria and the centrality of the Algerian friendship to Cuban internationalism in Africa.

Arab Latin American ties were nurtured from Bandung to the Tricontinental. Egypt's links with the Tricontinental are unexplored.[23] In April 1955, representatives of twenty-nine newly independent nations from Africa and Asia met at Bandung to promote non-alignment with the United States or the Soviet Union during the Cold War and cooperation against imperialism.[24] Cuba was invited to attend the Bandung Conference. Robert J. C. Young notes that the declaration of Bandung countries 'for closer economic, cultural and diplomatic links between the countries of Africa and Asia' was 'the first public statement of the creation of an independent transcontinental political consciousness in Africa and Asia' (2016: 191). The Bandung Conference and the Non-Aligned Movement began what Young has called 'tricontinentalism' (2016: 5) – an expression of Third World solidarity and anti-imperialism that would become central to transcontinental alliances.

In January 1966, the Tricontinental Conference, convened in Havana, Cuba, gathered delegates from liberation movements in Africa, Asia and Latin America. The Tricontinental (the Organization of Solidarity of the Peoples of Africa, Asia, and Latin America) (Organización de Solidaridad de los Pueblos de África, Asia, y América Latina) (OSPAAAL) expanded the Afro-Asian People's Solidarity Organization (AAPSO), founded in Cairo in 1957, to Latin America (Padilla and Palieraki 2019: 412). As Young has noted: 'It was at Havana that for the first time the three continents of the South – the Americas, Asia and Africa – were brought together in a broad alliance to form the Tricontinental. In contrast to Bandung, the Havana Tricontinental marked the formal globalization of the anti-imperial struggle' (2016: 192). The *Tricontinental Bulletin*, founded by OSPAAAL in 1966, featured the writings of fellow African, Asian and Latin American theorists and intellectuals. As Young observes: 'In the pages of the *Tricontinental* we find for the first time the conjunction of tricontinental social, theoretical and cultural political thought' (2016: 213). The *Tricontinental* magazine, published from 1967 to 1990 and 1995 to 1998, featured in its pages Amilcar Cabral, Frantz Fanon and Gabriel García Márquez (Young 2018: 532, 535). The cultural production of the Tricontinental – films, posters and journals such as the *Tricontinental Bulletin* – appeared in English, Spanish, French and Arabic (Mahler 2018: 3).[25] Anne Garland Mahler notes that the Tricontinental was an 'extension into the Americas of the well-known Afro-Asian movement begun at the 1955 Bandung Conference', which also serves as 'an originary moment for the field of postcolonial studies' (2018: 3, 247). The relationship of Latin America to the Arab world was unique among the otherwise Asian and African countries that were involved in Bandung and the Tricontinental, spanning the 1959 Cuban Revolution and the Latin American Left's solidarity with Palestine.

The Third Worldist networks of the mid-twentieth century set the framework for forms of cultural exchange between Latin America and the Arab world. The cultural production of Arab writers that draws on Latin American literature, directly or obliquely, revives the Third Worldism of the mid-twentieth century and the literary ties created thereafter. Cultural journals in Latin America and the Arab world ran in parallel and tell the same story of cultural cold war.[26] Arab Latin American cultural encounters in Latin American and Arabic literatures draw from shared struggles and a parallel history from the Cold War to the present. The result is direct links that are deeply rooted in shared political struggles in the global South.

The historical ties between Latin America and the Arab world extended to the literary sphere in the twentieth century. Latin American writers of Arab ancestry have produced a body of Hispanic literature. There are a number of Latin American writers of Arab origin: Chileans Miguel Littín (b. 1942), Diamela Eltit (b. 1947) and Lina Meruane (b. 1970); Colombian Luis Fayad (b. 1945); Brazilians Milton Hatoum (b. 1952), Raduan Nassar (b. 1935) and Alberto Mussa (b. 1961).[27] In the twenty-first century, the frequent travels of Latin American writers to North Africa appeared to be patterned on nineteenth-century journeys to the Orient. In 2000, Colombian novelist Héctor Abad Faciolince travelled to Egypt and wrote a fictional travelogue *Oriente empieza en El Cairo* (The Orient Begins in Cairo, 2002). In the late twentieth century, Mexican writer Alberto Ruy Sánchez, who travelled to Essouira, and Guatemalan writer Rodrigo Rey Rosa, who travelled to Tangier, produced novels that explore routes between Mexico and Central America, on the one hand, and North Africa, on the other.

The translation and circulation of Latin American literature in the Arab world introduced Arabic literature to formal innovations and postcolonial and New World aesthetics. Latin American literature enjoyed popularity in the Arab world and circulated in Arabic. The Iraqi poet Badr Shakir al-Sayyab (Badr Shākir al-Sayyāb) (1926–64) published poems by Pablo Neruda in a collection of his own translations, *Qaṣa'id mukhtāra min al-shi'r al-'ālamī al-ḥadīth* (*Anthology of Modern World Poetry*, 1955) (Creswell 2019: 40). Edward Said has noted that Arabic translations of major novels by the Mexican novelist Carlos Fuentes, Colombian writer Gabriel García Márquez and Guatemalan novelist Miguel Angel Asturias appeared in the 1970s (2000: 322). Lebanese novelist Elias Khoury (Eliās Khūrī) oversaw the translations at a Lebanese publishing house. Thus, translation played a central role in the circulation of Latin American literature in the Arab world and cultural exchange. Arabic translations of Argentine novelist Ernesto Sábato were published by the state-sponsored press Dār al-Ma'mūn in Iraq in the 1970s and 1980s (Jacquemond 2009: 15). Kalima, a translation programme begun in 2007 by the Abu Dhabi Authority for Culture and Heritage, has published Arabic translations of Borges, Honduran Augusto Monterroso and Uruguayan Carlos Liscano.

There has been a steady increase in direct translations of Latin American literature, from Spanish into Arabic, most recently of post-Boom writers such as Héctor Abad Faciolince.[28] In 2014, Abad's memoir *El olvido que seremos* (*Oblivion: A Memoir*, 2006) was translated into Arabic. Over the past decade, the translation of Latin American literature has flourished in the Arab world, with numerous translations of contemporary new writers.

The flow of Arabic-Spanish translation is multi-directional. Spain is a large consumer of Arabic literature in translation. The new series *Turner-Kitab* is devoted to the translation of International Prize for Arabic Fiction novels into Spanish (Fernández Parrilla 2013: 99). While the translation of Arabic literature into Spanish has burgeoned in Spain, Arabic literature in translation has appeared in Latin America. A Spanish translation of Naguib Mahfouz's *Zuqāq al-midaqq* (*Midaq Alley*) was reissued with the Mexican cinematic adaptation *El callejón de los milagros* (The Alley of Miracles).

The cultural and historical ties extending from the nineteenth century to the 1950s and 1960s animate new directions of comparative study, as I will outline.

Transcontinental Literature

Latin American and Arab Literature proposes a comparative model that arises from contact and exchange between Latin America and the Arab world. It adopts comparative methodologies that have been eclipsed by postcolonial studies and area studies. Arabic and Latin American literatures are rarely read together through Third Worldist networks. Cultural exchange between Latin America and the Arab world has deep roots in the Third Worldism and transnational solidarity of the 1950s and 1960s. These connections can help scholars propose comparative frameworks that recover overlooked links in the global South. Direct encounters in Arabic and Latin American literatures may be read through the legacy of Third Worldism and the Cold War as well as through shared political struggles in the global South. On the other hand, as I will show, leftist Arab writers express a sense of kinship with Latin American writers as a legacy of Third Worldism.

Scholars have shown a growing interest in interconnections between two fields that have long been separated by area studies and have pursued theoretical directions that connect Arabic and Latin American literatures within several frameworks. In the groundbreaking collection *ArabAmericas: Literary Entanglements of the American Hemisphere and the Arab World*, Ottmar Ette and Friederike Pannewick trace important connections between the Americas and the Arab world that have set a framework of comparison of Arab and Latin American literatures: Arab migration to the Americas; Latin American writers of Arab ancestry; Latin American writers' interest in *The Arabian Nights* and Arabic poetry; and Arabic reworkings of Latin American literature.[29] Ette and Pannewick examine 'transfer, exchange and interaction' between Latin American and Arab literatures (2006a: 12). In recent years, there have been several efforts to explore connections between Latin America and the Arab world within a frame of the Americas and the Middle East or direct relations between Argentina, Brazil or Mexico and the Arab world.[30]

Expanding scholarship on the multifaceted connections between Latin America and the Arab world has opened up avenues for comparative study. Most scholarship has attended to the Arab heritage and cultural production of Latin American writers of Arab origin.[31] Scholars have extended interconnections between Latin America and the Arab world to Spain's *convivencia* (coexistence). Miguel de Cervantes's Don Quixote's adventures, purportedly written by Cide Hamete Benengeli, an Arab historian, and extemporised from Arabic into Spanish by a Morisco interpreter, are intimately intertwined with Spain's Moorish heritage. Ella Shohat reads the 'two 1492s' – the Spanish *Reconquista* and Columbus's conquest of the Americas – as a 'Sephardi/Moorish Atlantic' that enabled the traffic of Iberian Orientalist conceptions of the Moor and Jew to the Americas (2013: 52–3). Shohat's examination of the multi-directional routes of 1492 draws attention to the historical ties between Latin America and the Arab world through Spain, specifically Moorish history in the Iberian Peninsula and its transfer to the New World. The Latin American celebration of a Moorish past created further connections. Carlos Fuentes's 'celebration of Mexico's "buried mirror"' (Shohat 2013: 54) refracts Latin America's cultural heritage through

Europe: 'Iberian, and through Iberia Mediterranean, Roman, Greek, and also Arab and Jewish' (1999: 9).

The past decade has seen a surge in scholarship on Latin America and the Arab world. They were hitherto rarely compared and, more often than not, within a tradition of Latin American Orientalism. While scholars have examined connections among the Americas and the Arab world, scholarship is rarely devoted to Latin American and Arabic literatures. Little has been written on Latin American writers' relationship to the Arab world and the effects of Latin American literature on Arab cultural production. Expanding the study to Arabic literature, while examining direct links between Latin America and the Arab world, can help us propose a new model of horizontal comparatism.

The comparative study of Latin America and the Arab world is underexplored largely because of a divide between Latin American and Arabic scholarship. Most comparatists study Arabic literature within the frame of Middle East studies and postcolonial studies, producing scholarship that focuses on the effects of colonialism and East-West encounters, and Arabic literature is routinely compared with anglophone and francophone literatures. Likewise, Latin American literature is often compared to North American and European literatures. Few scholars have the necessary language skills in Spanish and Arabic to undertake comparative study between Latin American and Arabic literatures. Furthermore, English and French are the languages most accessible to comparatists from Arabic Studies and Latin American Studies. However, direct comparisons yield the fruitful understanding of two regions that share a history of solidarities and common struggles that are otherwise overlooked (but that do not fit within a fully postcolonial framework). Exchanges between Latin America and the Arab world can animate the fields of comparative literature and the global South.

There is no book-length study of Arabic and Latin American literatures within Third World internationalist networks.[32] No scholarship has focused on how the historical links of Latin America and the Arab world have shaped connections between Arabic and Latin American literatures. There are no comparisons of Latin America and the Arab world that consider a comparative model drawn from Third Worldist networks beyond a South-South model that connects two literatures.[33] Critics of world literature have challenged the field's emphasis on North-South comparisons. For example, Ette and Pannewick have offered a transnational framework for reading literatures from the Americas and the Arab world.

Comparisons in the South have been overlooked or obfuscated by ideological, disciplinary and institutional borders. As Silvia Spitta and Lois Parkinson Zamora observe: 'Comparative literature departments and programs in the U. S. were engendered by the tectonic shifts occasioned by World War II and the cold war' (2009: 196). Mahler notes the limits of postcolonial studies: 'Equally significant is the way in which Cold War decolonization discourses would become preserved within the academic field of postcolonial studies, a field that has had a contentious relationship with Latin Americanism and that has tended to emphasize an experience of colonization rather than a horizontalist ideological project' (2018: 17).

Critics such as Robert J. C. Young have revisited postcolonialism through 'tricontinentalism' as the origin of postcolonial theory. Young uses the term 'tricontinentalism' to refer to 'the geographical, locational and cultural description of the "three continents" and the "tricontinental" (i.e. Latin America, Africa, and Asia)' after the 1966 Havana Tricontinental (2016: 5). For Young, the term 'tricontinental' highlights the internationalist relationships of postcolonialism (2016: 5).

Young's reassessment of postcolonialism as 'tricontinentalism' is central to the study of historical and literary ties between Latin America and the Arab world. Latin American encounters with the Orient draw from a history of Arab migration to Latin America and Third Worldism, albeit under the guise of Orientalism, as I argue in Chapter 1. A comparative model that focuses on the relationship of Latin America and the Arab world has been overlooked in postcolonial studies. Directions that attend to horizontal links are important for recovering networks between Latin America and the Arab world. My intent is not to claim that all Arab and Latin American writers are engaged with the politics of the Tricontinental movement or offer examples of solidarity. Borges was interested in the Islamic world and García Márquez's novels are rooted in a multi-ethnic Caribbean with a history of Syro-Lebanese migration. Although in some cases writers belong to a generation far removed from the 1950s and 1960s, they engage Latin American literature as part of a legacy of Third World solidarity networks that promoted new literary ties in the Arab world.

Mahler traces the roots of the post-Cold War global South to the transnational solidarity formed in the Tricontinental movement.[34] The 'global South' is a term that has replaced the terms 'Third World' and 'postcolonial' and, as a critical concept, as Mahler notes, encompasses 'horizontalist models' of comparative study and shared struggles (2018: 4, 6) . The global South has been read as an extension of postcolonial theory beyond continents and nation-states as frameworks of comparative study (Lee and Mahler 2020: 201–2). Mahler, in *From the Tricontinental to the Global South: Race, Radicalism, and Transnational Solidarity*, notes that 'our amnesia around the Tricontinental movement' (2018: 4) has obscured models of comparison in the global South. As Mahler has rightly noted, the Tricontinental's transnational solidarity is 'largely forgotten' (2018: 4) and has been eclipsed by the focus on colonial relationships in postcolonial studies. I read Latin American and Arabic literatures through what Mahler has described as a revival of 'Tricontinentalism . . . in horizontalist critical approaches' (2018: 244).

Critics have challenged the Eurocentrism that has dominated comparative literature. In 'Rethinking Comparativism', Gayatri Chakravorty Spivak argues that an 'epistemic change' (2009: 616) is necessary to redress the lack of parity among established and neglected languages in the field of comparative literature towards a more even comparatism. Meanwhile, a centre-periphery model has circumscribed practices of world literature. In his world-systems theory, Franco Moretti has argued that 'movement from one periphery to another (without passing through the center) is almost unheard of; that movement from the periphery to the center is less rare, but still quite unusual, while that from the center to the periphery is by far the most frequent' (2003: 75–6). Moretti's theory largely concerns inequality in the mobility of literatures – which is more often than not the case – but also precludes any movement in the periphery. Of course, there are many limitations on the movement of literatures and admission into world literature. One impediment in the study of connections between Latin America and the Arab world is language. David Damrosch highlights ways by which a work gains the status of world literature through translation and circulation 'into a broader world beyond its linguistic and cultural point of origin' (2003: 6); therefore, world literature is 'a mode of circulation and of reading' (2003: 5). Scholars have sought to redress the centre-periphery model by focusing on the circulation of cultural production between the Middle East and the Americas.[35] They consider transnational networks that compare minor literatures, along with comparisons of minor and major literatures.[36] Cultural exchange between Latin America and the Arab world allows us to trace new theoretical frameworks between continents in the global South.

Scholars have advanced models for South-South comparison beyond North-South and centre-periphery relationships (Klengel and Ortiz Wallner 2016: 11). Susanne Klengel and Alexandra Ortiz Wallner's *Sur/South* posits a framework of South-South comparison that departs from the asymmetries and hierarchies of North-South and centre-periphery models. A South-South comparative framework recovers neglected networks. This book contributes to South-South comparison by examining Arab and Latin American exchange through internationalist networks and the relationship of Latin America and the Arab world.

Latin American and Arab Literature traces connections between Latin America and the Arab world and proposes a model of exchange that draws on 'transcontinental literature'. Borrowing from Shaden Tageldin's description of anti-colonialism and reinscription of Africa in postcolonial theory – a form of 'transcontinentalism' bequeathed by pan-Africanisms – beyond Africa, this book is concerned with exchanges that are 'transcontinental' (2014: 320). Tageldin notes a 'transcontinental anticolonialism' in her reinscription of Africa into postcolonial theory in the sense of pan-Africanisms that promote a '*transcontinental anti-imperialism*' over time (2014: 319, emphasis in original). Drawing on Tageldin's theory of 'transcontinental literature', this book reads the effects of Arab Latin American contact through Andalusian Spain, Arab migration from the Ottoman Empire to Latin America, Latin American Orientalism and travel to North Africa, and the Arabic translation of Latin American literature. These connections extend Tageldin's theory to the nexus of Latin America and the Arab world and draw on a transcontinentalism inherited from Third World transnational solidarity.

Employing a comparative framework based on direct networks and the relationship of Latin America and the Arab world from the mid-twentieth century, my book builds on scholarship through several unexplored connections and focuses on exchanges between Latin America and the Arab world and routes of comparison that have been obscured by the models of postcolonial studies and area studies. Whereas scholars have focused primarily on the cultural production of Latin American writers of Arab ancestry, this book explores Arab themes in Latin American literature and the effects of Latin American literature on Arabic cultural production. This model builds on Mahler's extension of Tricontinentalism to horizontalist comparative approaches.

Latin American and Arab Literature examines new routes of comparison between Latin America and the Arab world from the late twentieth to the twenty-first century. The cultural encounters in Latin American and Arabic literatures explore the relationship between Latin America and the Arab world. My book attends to transcontinental relationships in these two literatures. Chapters 1 and 2 focus on Arab themes in Latin American literature. The remainder of the book explores the effects of Latin American literature in the Arab world: direct Arabic reworkings of García Márquez's novels, Che Guevara in Arabic literature, and intertextual ties in Arabic. I adopt comparative methodologies based on direct networks and shared struggles. Chapter 1 examines forms of 'transcontinental literature' produced by encounters with the Orient in Colombian literature in the twentieth and twenty-first centuries. Analysing links to the Arab world in Gabriel García Márquez's *Crónica de una muerte anunciada* (*Chronicle of a Death Foretold*, 1981) and Héctor Abad Faciolince's *Oriente empieza en El Cairo* (The Orient Begins in Cairo, 2002), I argue that they offer forms of 'transcontinental literature' that involve movement and connections along peripheral or semi-peripheral circuits. The two works are unique examples that offer a new perspective on Arab Latin American ties. García Márquez's novel *Crónica de una muerte anunciada* draws upon a history of Arab migration to Latin America and Latin American Orientalism, while Abad's travelogue-novel *Oriente empieza en El Cairo* offers a Latin American traveller's *voyage en Orient*. García Márquez's novel is rarely read with a focus on links to the Arab world, nor has Abad's work been the subject of critical study. They share literary ties to the Arab world: García Márquez mirrors the multi-ethnic community of the Caribbean coast, and his fellow Colombian Abad recounts his trip to Egypt. In Chapter 1, I argue that the cultural encounters in *Crónica de una muerte anunciada* and *Oriente empieza en El Cairo* show multidirectional routes between Latin America and the Arab world from the nineteenth to the twenty-first century.

Central American and Mexican literature transports us to Morocco. In the twentieth century, Latin American writers explored the relationship of Latin America to North Africa. Chapter 2 traces contact between Latin America and North Africa in Central American and Mexican literature through a parallel relationship vis-à-vis Iberian colonisation. This chapter focuses on connections between Latin America and North Africa in Guatemalan writer Rodrigo Rey Rosa's *La orilla africana* (*The African Shore*, 1999) and Mexican writer Alberto Ruy Sánchez's *Los nombres del aire* (*Mogador: The Names of the Air*, 1987). The Orientalist novels of Rey Rosa and Ruy Sánchez explore cultural contact and direct routes between Latin America and North Africa. Rey Rosa explores connections between Latin America and Morocco vis-à-vis Spain, while Ruy Sánchez highlights the Arab-Iberian heritage of Mexico and Morocco.

Latin American literature travelled to the Arab world and spurred Arabic cultural production in the late twentieth century. Chapter 3 examines direct reworkings of Gabriel García Márquez's novels in Arabic literature. The chapter focuses on the Arabisation of the genre of magical realism and a rewriting of a Latin American novel by comparing two sets of novels of the second half of the twentieth century: *Cien años de soledad* (*One Hundred Years of Solitude*, 1967) by Colombian writer Gabriel García Márquez and *Layālī alf layla* (*Arabian Nights and Days*, 1982) by Egyptian writer Naguib Mahfouz (Najīb Maḥfūẓ); and García Márquez's *Crónica de una muerte anunciada* and Elias Khoury's *Majma' al-asrār* (*The Assembly of Secrets*, 1994). In this chapter, I examine the ways in which Mahfouz's *Layālī alf layla*, a modern Arab adaptation of *The Thousand and One Nights*, reworks the style of magical realism popularised by García Márquez in his masterwork *Cien años de soledad* and Khoury's reworking of García Márquez's *Crónica de una muerte anunciada* in *Majma' al-asrār*. The intertextuality in Khoury's novel has been characterised as 'transcontinental' (Ette 2006: 244) and contributes to connections between Latin America and the Arab world. While Mahfouz's Arabisation of magical realism and Khoury's Lebanese Civil War novel focus on local contexts, they show engagements with Latin American literature and foreground shared political struggles.

Chapter 4 examines the effects of the circulation of Latin American literature and political iconography in the Arab world. In this chapter, I trace how Latin American iconography and literature travelled in the 1960s–80s in Arabic during Third World revolutions and through the legacy of Tricontinentalism. Chapter 4 focuses on *Warda* (2000) by the Egyptian novelist Sonallah Ibrahim (Ṣun' Allāh Ibrāhīm) and *Laḥaẓāt gharaq jazīrat al-ḥūt* (*Memories of a Meltdown: An Egyptian Between Moscow and Chernobyl*, 1998) by the Egyptian writer Mohamed Makhzangi (Muḥammad al-Makhzanjī). In *Warda*, Che Guevara's diaries play a central role in the notebooks of an Arab woman revolutionary in the Dhofar revolution in 1960s and 1970s Oman. In *Laḥaẓāt gharaq jazīrat al-ḥūt*, Makhzangi experiments with literary reportage, a form adopted in García Márquez's *Relato de un náufrago* (*The Story of a Shipwrecked Sailor*, 1970) and *La aventura de Miguel Littín: clandestino en Chile* (*Clandestine in Chile: The Adventures of Miguel Littín*, 1986). Drawing on Third Worldist networks, the chapter examines how intertextuality and rewritings extend Arab Latin American ties and transnational solidarity to the twenty-first century.

Chapter 5 analyses intercultural exchange and international networks that open up new directions in Arabic literature in the twenty-first century by focusing on the relationship of the Iraqi writers Jabbar Yussin Hussin (Jabbār Yāsīn Ḥusayn) and Hassan Blasim (Ḥassan Blāsim) to Carlos Fuentes and Jorge Luis Borges. In this chapter, I examine Arabic short stories that directly engage with Fuentes and Borges: Hussin's 'Yawm Bwinus Ayris' ('The Day in Buenos Aires', 2000) and Blasim's 'Kawābīs Kārlus Fwintis' ('The Nightmares of Carlos Fuentes', 2009). Blasim's 'Kawābīs Kārlus Fwintis', a short story about migration, adopts a style that he calls 'nightmare realism'. Hussin's 'Yawm Bwinus Ayris' reworks Borges's short story 'La busca de Averroes' ('Averroes's Search', 1947).

In his story, Ibn Rushd's dream of Borges in Buenos Aires focuses on intercultural contact and a shared heritage of the Arab world, al-Andalus and Latin America. Blasim's and Hussin's rewritings, I argue, recontextualise Latin American literature in the Arab world in the twenty-first century. Both Borges and Fuentes epitomise intercultural exchange that extends beyond exile and migration, the central themes of the stories. Hussin and Blasim draw comparisons and produce original stories that open up further directions for Arabic literature and Arab Latin American ties. Thus, we begin to note the new relevance of Arab Latin American literary ties to themes of migration and neo-colonialism in Arabic literature in the twenty-first century. Hussin's philosophical parable and Blasim's experimental short story prove to be examples of some of the most original Arab cultural production and are widely available in translation.

The Epilogue turns to the circulation of Latin American literature in Arab popular culture and Latin American writers' further engagements with the Arab world. These connections highlight longstanding ties and materialise in Latin America and the Arab world in the twenty-first century. Turning further away from Orientalism, they serve as a model that is already clear in Martí's Orient. They have resurfaced in the 2011 Arab revolutions and drawn on historical and political ties between Latin America and the Arab world. I argue that peripatetic exchange has burgeoned in the twenty-first century and opens up further routes of circulation of cultural production between Cuba and Egypt, Palestine and Chile.

1

Transcontinental Literature: Gabriel García Márquez and Héctor Abad Faciolince

On the eve of 2000, Colombian novelist Héctor Abad Faciolince (b. 1958) travelled to Egypt, where he spent two months and began composing a fictional travelogue *Oriente empieza en El Cairo* (The Orient Begins in Cairo, 2002).[1] *Oriente empieza en El Cairo* focuses on a Colombian traveller's *voyage en Orient* in the twenty-first century. Abad models a tour of the 'Orient' (read Egypt) on the nineteenth-century travel literature of French Orientalists Gustave Flaubert and Gérard de Nerval. Like his fellow Colombian Gabriel García Márquez, he explores interactions between Latin America and the Arab world and represents the Orient, albeit more directly.

Abad's *Oriente empieza en El Cairo* travels to another continent in the global South. Other Latin American writers have drawn on the routes of migration from the Arab world to Latin America in the nineteenth century. Thus, there is a sizeable literature that explores the effects of Arab migration and settlement in Latin America. García Márquez's novels, from *La mala hora* (*In Evil Hour*, 1962) to *Cien años de soledad* (*One Hundred Years of Solitude*, 1967), have obliquely drawn on the history of Arab migration to Latin America. In his famous novel *Crónica de una muerte anunciada*, García Márquez draws upon the effects of Arab migration to Colombia and the Orientalist imagery characteristic of Latin American Orientalism. *Crónica de una muerte anunciada* centres on an Arab character in 1950s Colombia and, in his masterwork *Cien años de soledad*, Arabs form part of the mythical town of Macondo.

Crónica de una muerte anunciada and *Oriente empieza en El Cairo* belong to a growing body of Latin American literature that focuses on interrelations between the Arab world and Latin America. García Márquez's *Crónica de una muerte anunciada* and Abad's *Oriente empieza en El Cairo* explore two transcontinental encounters by focusing on Arab immigrants in Colombia and a Colombian traveller in Egypt. The Colombian traveller's Orient, however, is steeped in another legacy. Abad's *Oriente empieza en El Cairo* explores the Arab Latin American nexus through Orientalism and 1960s Third Worldism in the twenty-first century. Both *Crónica de una muerte anunciada* and Abad's *Oriente empieza en El Cairo* trace exchanges between Latin America and the Arab world that help scholars to propose new frameworks of comparison that are rooted in migratory and Third Worldist networks.

García Márquez and Abad share several interests and themes. First, both are Colombian writers whose works are unique in exploring the relationship of Latin America to the Arab world, and this particular connection in García Márquez's novels and Abad's *Oriente empieza en El Cairo* is underexplored. *Crónica de una muerte anunciada* and *Oriente empieza en El Cairo* offer examples of different relationships to the Orient and routes between the Arab world and Latin America such as Arab migration to Latin America and Latin American travel to the Arab world. Second, Abad has been compared to García Márquez and his novel *La oculta* (*The Farm*, 2015) and memoir *El olvido que seremos* (2006) contain echoes of García Márquez's *Cien años de soledad* and *Crónica de una muerte anunciada* respectively. Although the two works are different in terms of genre, *Oriente empieza en El Cairo* is a metafictional travelogue that purports to be fiction.

This chapter examines forms of 'transcontinental literature' produced by Colombian encounters with the Orient in the twentieth and twenty-first centuries and the circulation of literature between Latin America and the Arab world. My purpose in focusing on *Crónica de una muerte anunciada* and *Oriente empieza en El Cairo* is to examine the relationship of Latin American literature to the Arab world as part of comparative literary study that contributes to growing scholarship concerned with decentralising world literature by underscoring interactions between semi-peripheral and peripheral literatures. This uncovers some of the affinities already existing, though under-researched, in the global South. García Márquez's *Crónica de una muerte anunciada* and Abad's *Oriente empieza en El Cairo*, I argue, offer new avenues for South-South exchanges that draw on direct relationships and historical links. This model of comparative study between semi-peripheral and peripheral literary spheres extends beyond inequality and asymmetry. In what follows, the chapter examines how two pre-eminent Colombian writers read the Orient through Arab migration to Colombia and a trip to Egypt. After a brief survey of recent scholarship on directions in world literature, I consider how the two works show semi-peripheral engagement with the Arab world.

Models of World Literature

Scholarship on world literature has been dominated by a framework of centre and periphery that has eclipsed the study of connections between peripheral and semi-peripheral literatures and horizontal comparatism in the global South. In *Modern Epic*, Moretti examines a new world literary system made up of what he calls 'writers from the semiperiphery' – German, American, Irish and Latin American (1996: 217). As he notes, 'powerful literatures' and 'peripheral literatures' represent the inequality of the world literary system (1996: 221). As Moretti has amply noted, the movement of literatures in the world literary system is largely between centre and periphery and is thus characterised by inequality (2000: 56). He rethinks the canon through a world literary system made up of the 'semi-periphery', but notes that 'movement from one periphery to another' is rare (2003: 75). Though the possibility of exchanges and contact among semi-peripheral literatures is fully accounted for by Moretti's world-system, connections between Latin American and Arabic literatures attest to more frequent movement between the semi-periphery and periphery. Moretti's system allows little movement between semi-peripheral literary spheres, does not account for equal and multi-directional exchange in the periphery, nor makes room for South-South exchanges. Nonetheless, these direct exchanges in the global South advance a model of literary relations that has been overlooked in comparative literary study.

While Latin American literature has been read as world literature, with Jorge Luis Borges, Gabriel García Márquez and Pablo Neruda admitted into the canon, there have been few attempts to trace connections with different linguistic traditions. Indeed, as Aijaz Ahmad observes in his rebuttal of Fredric Jameson's controversial theory of Third World literature, 'Neruda, Vallejo, Octavio Paz, Borges, Fuentes, Marquez *et al.* (i.e. quite a few writers of Latin American origin) *are* considered by the American academy as major figures in modern literature' (1987: 15–16, emphasis in original). Latin American novels have been not only canonised but also appropriated as European novels. Franco Moretti reads García Márquez's *Cien años de soledad* as a novel that decentres Europe through magical realism, which transports us to Latin America and creates a world literary system, and reaches Europe (1996: 233). Noting the enthusiasm of the reception of García Márquez's *Cien años de soledad* by the Old World, he maintains that 'In García Márquez, however, [magic] belongs *to the future*: to the West, to the core of the world system' (1996: 249, emphasis in original). He equates magic to Western technology because García Márquez has enchanted the cinema and the telephone, sent from Europe to Macondo, and his novel travels to Europe to recount a hundred-year history magically (1996: 250).

Recent scholarship has outlined minor networks that depart from hegemonic models of world literature. Françoise Lionnet and Shu-mei Shih read transnational minor-to-minor networks through interrelations among different minority cultures in cultural production. They are concerned with 'minor-to-minor networks that circumvent the major altogether' besides the minor's 'productive relationship' to the major (Lionnet and Shih 2005a: 8). 'But it isn't until Frantz Fanon traveled from the Caribbean to Algeria, which is to say from one minor space to another, that we can begin to see . . . a minor transnational intellectual linking spaces and struggles laterally,' they note (Lionnet and Shih 2005a: 3). Thus, they theorise minor networks for the travel of literature across the global South. In *Minor Transnationalism*, exchanges and interactions among minority cultures and minor literatures are plausible and frequent.

Latin American and Arabic literatures are less commonly compared in scholarship in English, Arabic or Spanish. Nonetheless, there is growing scholarship on comparisons of Arab and Latin American cultural production.[2] In recent years, scholars have explored Arab Latin American ties, but there is little scholarship on relationships to the Arab world in Latin American literature. There is little study of direct networks between Latin America and the Arab world or the legacies of Third Worldist networks. Nor does scholarship focus on the effects of Latin American literature on Arabic cultural production. Waïl Hassan has proposed 'one network in which Europe and the United States do not play a primary role' – the connection between Arabic and Latin American literatures – that is overlooked by world literature and has noted that 'South-South connections' can expand frameworks of world literature (2012: 395, 403). Directions in world literature can be animated by exploring ties between Latin American and Arabic literatures within Third Worldist or migratory routes.

The circulation of literature between the semi-periphery and periphery can offer a new model of world literature in which connections between semi-peripheral and peripheral literatures do not only show the existence of cultural contact between two southern zones but also focus attention on a form of transcontinental literature based on direct networks and historical ties. The study of exchanges with the Arab world in Latin American literature contravenes the centre-periphery model and draws attention to direct contact in the semi-periphery and the centrality of further historical and political links to horizontal comparisons.

The Orient in Latin America

The Arab Latin American literary ties in *Crónica de una muerte anunciada* and *Oriente empieza en El Cairo* are rooted in Arab migration to Latin America and a tradition of Latin American Orientalism. Arab migration to Colombia had an effect on the north of the country where immigrants settled from the mid-nineteenth century. By the 1950s, Arabs had settled on the Caribbean coast and assimilated to Colombian culture. In the 1860s, when Arabs began to migrate to Latin America, Latin American writers such as Sarmiento had already travelled to the Orient. Abad, however, frames his Orient in a nineteenth-century European Orientalism and a history of Third Worldism.

Many Latin American writers were often more interested in the Far East than the Arab world. Therefore, it is important to distinguish between the different Orients invoked by Latin American writers. Both García Márquez and Abad belong to a tradition of Latin American Orientalism and interest in the Arab world. Latin American literature has offered different forms of Orientalism, from Borges's fiction to García Márquez's novels. Borges borrowed from *The Thousand and One Nights* and the Islamic world. In *Orientalism in the Hispanic Literary Tradition*, Julia Kushigian traces longstanding Hispanic Orientalism that is characterised by 'veneration and respect for the Orient' and a relationship of 'dialogue and exchange with the East' (1991: 3) in contrast to Western European Orientalism. Kushigian's study, however, is limited to three elite Latin American writers: Jorge Luis Borges, Octavio Paz and Severo Sarduy. In her study, Kushigian examines the relationship of Borges to the Islamic world, Paz to India, and Sarduy to China. She concentrates on the mysticism of the Orient and Oriental themes in Spanish American literature (Kushigian 1991: 7–8). However, her study does not represent the totality of Latin American Orientalism. Furthermore, classic Eurocentric Orientalism abounds in Latin American literature and cultural production.

Encounters with the Orient in Latin American cultural production offer forms of South-South Orientalism that do not fit within Edward Said's *Orientalism*. Said's *Orientalism* focuses on British, French and post-World War II American domination of the Orient. Said has observed that the Orient is 'one of [Europe's] deepest and most recurring images of the other' and Orientalism is 'a Western style for dominating, restructuring, and having authority over the Orient' (1978: 1, 3). Unlike European Orientalism, Latin America has no colonial relationship to the Orient and, therefore, departs from the colonialism and imperialism characteristic of Said's Orientalism. Camayd-Freixas has noted that Latin American Orientalism, 'in the periphery', where there is no relationship of domination of the Orient, is practised by the colonised (2013a: 3). Moreover, Latin American cultural production draws attention to interactions between semi-peripheral and peripheral literatures (López-Calvo 2010a: 5). Araceli Tinajero has focused on the exotification of the Far East in

Latin American literature that differs from imperial domination of the Orient in European Orientalism.[3]

Critics have examined Orientalism in Latin America and the Caribbean with a focus on the Latin American relationship to the Far East. The relationship between Spanish America and the Orient emulates the characteristics of European Orientalism. Nonetheless, Latin American Orientalism departs from the colonialism and imperialism of its European counterpart. Christina Civantos has focused on a *criollo* Orientalism in Argentina and examined the Orient in Argentine letters within 'the legacy of the Spanish *Reconquista* and European Orientalisms' (2006: 3). In other words, she notes the historical background that differentiates Argentine Orientalism. Civantos notes that 'an Orient assembled through readings in Orientalist academic studies and literature produced in Europe and through travels in the Middle East . . . was already a presence in Argentina' since 1845 before the arrival of Arab immigrants around 1860 (2006: 2) and that the relationship of South America to the Arab world was intertwined with Arab Spain (2006: 25). López-Calvo's 'alternative Orientalisms' explore 'Oriental exoticism', 'cultural inferiority' and a sensual Orient in Latin America literature (2007: x–xi). South-South Orientalism is not mediated by Europe (López-Calvo 2012: 1). On the other hand, Waïl Hassan has argued that the relationship between Brazil and the Arab world is 'mediated by the "northern" discourse of Orientalism' (2018: 274) in what he calls 'carioca Orientalism'. In other words, the Brazilian variety of Orientalism is at once derivative and different (Hassan 2018: 275).

There are several characteristics of Latin American Orientalism. First, Said has noted that the Orient is a European invention. While Latin American Orientalism reworks a 'Western style' and is, therefore, derivative, it departs from hegemony and domination of the Orient. Second, critics have traced the particularity of Latin American Orientalism to the interchange between Latin America and the Arab world through Spain's vexed relationship with the Orient, a legacy of the Arab presence in the Iberian Peninsula for eight centuries. Therefore, an Arab Iberian heritage distinguishes Hispanic Orientalism (Camayd-Freixas 2013a: 9). García Márquez's *Crónica de una muerte anunciada* and Abad's *Oriente empieza en El Cairo* offer two unique examples of Latin America's relationship to the Orient.

Arabs in Colombia

The presence of Arab Levantine immigrants who settled in Colombia along the Caribbean coast from the nineteenth century echoes in García Márquez's novels. A flow of Syro-Lebanese Arabs migrated to Colombia between 1880 and 1930, settling in the north where they contributed to industrial and commercial activities (Posada-Carbo and Fawcett 1998: 58). By the 1870s, Levantine immigrants played a central role in the Caribbean coast of Colombia (Klich and Lesser 1998b: xi). Arab immigrants, mostly from Lebanon, settled in Colombia where 45 per cent of the population of Barranquilla, Cartagena, Maicao and Santa Marta are of Arab origin.[4] Currently, the Arab population in Colombia is around 200,000 (Hudson 2010: 92–3). Colombia's ethnic make-up is a mixture of indigenous, creoles, *mestizos* and immigrants which distinguishes Colombia, for instance, from Argentina, which exterminated its indigenous population and promoted immigration from Western Europe. Thus, Latin American Orientalism, in the case of Colombia, bears Iberian influences, while Argentina draws from French and British Orientalisms as well as the Iberian past.

García Márquez (1927–2014) makes several allusions to Arab immigrants in Latin America in his masterwork *Cien años de soledad*. *Cien años de soledad* contains references to Arabs in Macondo, especially the 'Calle de los Turcos' ('Street of the Turks') (Ette 2006: 227). In *Cien años de soledad*, Macondo changes into 'un pueblo activo, con tiendas y talleres de artesanía, y una ruta de comercio permanente por donde llegaron los primeros árabes de pantuflas y argollas en las orejas, cambiando collares de vidrio por guacamayas' (53) ('a town with stores and workshops and a permanent commercial route over which the first Arabs arrived with their baggy pants and rings in their ears, swapping glass beads for macaws' (39)).[5] The changes in Macondo evoke historical developments in Latin America with the migration of Arabs from the provinces of the Ottoman Empire, but also the magical-fictional world where the Arabs arrived with wondrous inventions. In his biography of García Márquez, Gerald Martin notes the 'makeshift modernity' of Barranquilla, which was full of foreign business, including 'Arab stores' (2008: 63). In *Cien años de soledad*, the Arabs, called *turcos* because they migrated with Ottoman travel papers, are peddlers, traders and store owners who are part of Macondo. García Márquez chronicles a history of Arabs in Macondo that integrates Arab immigrants in Latin American culture: for example, the Hotel Jacob is built by Arabs; the Street of the Turks is a landmark of Macondo; and the local theatre projects images of actors who appear to be Arab in one film or another. Allusions to Arab migration to the Caribbean coast include 'los ojos árabes de José Arcadio Segundo' (372) ('the Arab eyes of José Arcadio Segundo' (317)) in Melquiades's workshop; Petra Cotes, 'el único nativo' ('the only native') with 'corazón de árabe' (395) ('an Arab heart' (337–8)), to imply her perseverance; and Úrsula's 'antiguos collares de árabes' (397) ('old Arab necklaces' (339)) worn on her deathbed. In the end, Macondo's modernisation is set against the decline of the Arab community:

> La antigua Calle de los Turcos era entonces un rincón de abandono, donde los últimos árabes se dejaban llevar hacia la muerte por la costumbre milenaria de sentarse en la puerta, aunque hacía muchos años que habían vendido la última yarda de diagonal, y en las vitrinas sombrías solamente quedaban los maniquíes decapitados. (480)

> (The old Street of the Turks was at that time an abandoned corner where the last Arabs were letting themselves be dragged off to death with the age-old custom of sitting in their doorways, although it had been many years since they had sold the last yard of diagonal cloth, and in the shadowy showcases only the decapitated manikins remained.) (409)

The repetition of descriptions of the Arabs who swap 'de chucherías por guacamayas' (74) ('knick-knacks for macaws' (57)) – an incantation that forms part of the magical world of Macondo – draws attention to the presence of Arabs in Latin America, or the fictional world of *Cien años de soledad*.

While *Cien años de soledad* is populated by Arabs, founders, peddlers and traders in Macondo, García Márquez's 1981 novel *Crónica de una muerte anunciada* centres on a character of Arab origin and highlights the immigrant Arab community in Colombia. The novel appeared at the pinnacle of García Márquez's popularity and in the shadow of his magical realism popularised by *Cien años de soledad*. Inspired by an honour killing in Sucre, Colombia, García Márquez's hometown, in 1951 (Pelayo 2001: 111–12), *Crónica de una muerte anunciada* refocuses on an Arab immigrant.

A simple plot is told through an elaborate narrative structure. *Crónica de una muerte anunciada* centres on the son of a local wealthy Arab family, Santiago Nasar, in a fictional Colombian town. Santiago Nasar is accused of deflowering Angela Vicario who is returned to her family after her wedding to Bayardo San Román, a newcomer in the town, when he discovers that she is not a virgin. Angela names Santiago Nasar as her lover whereupon the duty falls on her twin brothers Pedro and Pablo Vicario to avenge her honour. The death is clearly foretold in the town through rumours, hearsay and warnings, but the Vicario twins kill Santiago Nasar in front of his house. Years later, the narrator-chronicler returns to his hometown to reassemble the event from reports, testimonies and confessions.

The title of the novel alludes to the long and established tradition of the *crónica* in Spain and Latin America, which extends beyond the *crónicas de conquista*, a form made known by the Spanish conquistadors of the New World. The *crónica* flourished in early-twentieth-century post-revolutionary Mexico (Corona and Jörgensen 2002: 1; Monsiváis 2002: 31). *Crónica de una muerte anunciada* draws on the form of the chronicle in a fictional reworking of events to assemble the mystery of a death foretold. While *Crónica de una muerte anunciada* takes the form of the *crónica* to report and investigate the death, the novel, on the other hand, features García Márquez's family.

Crónica de una muerte anunciada belongs to a body of Latin American novels that explore connections between Latin America and the Arab world. The novel opens with an announcement of the death of Santiago Nasar, a Colombian of Arab ancestry with Hispanic and Arab names.[6] To date, most scholarship on *Crónica de una muerte anunciada* has focused on the honour killing, the structure of the chronicle, and detective fiction, while Santiago Nasar's Arabness, Arab culture and Orientalism have been the subject of little attention.[7] Scattered references to the Arabness of Santiago Nasar in the novel call attention to the cultural and ethnic heterogeneity of a coastal Colombian town. Curiously, an early manuscript of *Crónica de una muerte anunciada* with corrections shows García Márquez's inclusion of an Arab-named character: revisions of the manuscript show deletions of Santiago's last name and the addition of his Arab surname 'Nasar'.[8] It is unclear from the typescript why García Márquez chose to add an Arab character to his novel except that the fictional Colombian town seems to mirror the multi-ethnic Caribbean coast of Colombia, with which García Márquez was familiar, and a history of Arab migration to South America. The most likely explanation – García Márquez's in his memoir *Vivir para contarla* (*Living to Tell the Tale*, 2002) – is that 'many years later', after the murder in his hometown, he had a 'providential' ('providencial') (384) encounter at the airport in Algiers:

> Y entró un príncipe árabe con la túnica inmaculada de su alcurnia y en el puño una hembra espléndida de halcón peregrino, que en vez del capirote de cuero de la cetrería clásica llevaba uno de oro con incrustaciones de diamantes. Por supuesto, me acordé de Cayetano Gentile, que había aprendido de su padre las bellas artes de la altanería . . . (462)

> (An Arab prince came in wearing the immaculate tunic of his lineage, and carrying on his fist a splendid female peregrine falcon that instead of the leather hood of classic falconry wore one of gold encrusted with diamonds. Of course I thought of Cayetano Gentile, who had learned from his father the fine arts of falconry . . .) (383)

Cayetano Gentile, his friend in Sucre whose murder inspired *Crónica de una muerte anunciada*, is the antecedent of Santiago Nasar who learns from his Arab father the arts of falconry. The accretions in the typescript, however, show the process of writing the novel in which Oriental details seem to have accrued, becoming central to the novel's underlying themes.

Santiago Nasar's ethnic background is central to *Crónica de una muerte anunciada*. Santiago Nasar and his fate invite a variety of readings of Orientalism in the novel. Ottmar Ette reads the fear of Arab reprisals for the murder as a sign of 'existing multicultural faults and fractures'

(2006: 230). After the murder, the Arab immigrants are described as 'roused-up' (48). Heba El Attar observes that the portrayal of Santiago Nasar is 'typically Orientalist', though the nuances of the novel challenge Eurocentric Orientalism and allow the reader to 'acknowledge the absurdity' of his death (2013: 254). Christina Civantos, on the other hand, reads 'an ambiguous relationship' with '"The Orient"', noting 'that the attitude toward the Arab world . . . is one of ambivalence' (2018: 169, 172). Civantos reads this ambivalence in the narrator-chronicler's awareness of the townspeople's prejudice and, on the other hand, his description of the Arab community as 'peaceful' and 'hardworking' (2018: 173). While there are instances of criticism of Orientalism, as Civantos notes, ethnic tensions and Orientalist imagery persist in *Crónica de una muerte anunciada*.[9] Though the narrator-chronicler ruminates on the history of Arab migration and assimilation to Latin American culture in Colombia, and within the drama of Santiago Nasar disproves the suspicions of revenge and ethnic tensions with the Arab immigrant community, invoking its 'pastoral spirit' (82) ('su espíritu pastoral' (95)),[10] descriptions of Santiago Nasar and some of the townsfolk's xenophobia are characteristic of Orientalism.

Crónica de una muerte anunciada abounds with Orientalist descriptions of Santiago Nasar that have been overlooked by scholarship on the novel: 'era esbelto y pálido, y tenía los párpados árabes y los cabellos rizados de su padre' (13) ('he was slim and pale and had his father's Arab eyelids and curly hair' (5)). Arab eyes and curly hair are common features of Arab ethnicity in Latin American literature, and the appearance of commonplace Oriental attributes draws attention to Santiago's cultural difference. The description of Santiago Nasar evokes José Arcadio Segundo's 'Arab eyes' that makes Arabs a fixture of Macondo in *Cien años de soledad*. Though references to the Arab community imply the assimilation of immigrants in Colombia, descriptions of Santiago Nasar accentuate his otherness. His father Ibrahim Nasar 'came with the last Arabs [los últimos árabes] at the end of the civil wars' (9) and settled on the Caribbean coast.[11] Santiago Nasar inherits a cattle ranch from his father who instructs him in the arts of falconry and horsemanship, which are important practices of Arab heritage and culture:

> De su padre aprendió desde muy niño el dominio de las armas de fuego, el amor por los caballos y la maestranza de las aves de presa altas, pero de él aprendió también las buenas artes del valor y la prudencia. Hablaban en árabe entre ellos, pero no delante de Plácida Linero para que no se sintiera excluida. (13–14)
>
> (From his father he learned at a very early age the manipulation of firearms, his love for horses, and the mastery of high-flying birds of prey, but from him he also learned the good arts of valor and prudence. They spoke Arabic between themselves, but not in front of Plácida Linero, so that she wouldn't feel excluded.) (6)

The consensus is that Santiago Nasar was 'alegre' ('merry'), 'pacífico ('peaceful'), 'de corazón fácil' ('openhearted') (14; 6) and popular in the town. The novel draws attention to conceptions of the *turco* in the Colombian town through references to Arab migration to Latin America and the Arab ancestry of Santiago Nasar. The name 'Nasar' evokes Nazareth (Pelayo 2001: 130), or Christian Arabs for arabophone readers who know the name of the city in Arabic (*al-Nāṣira*) (while *turcos* conflates Arabs with Muslims from the Ottoman Empire). The fictional name of Santiago Nasar, named for the narrator's mother and his godmother Luisa Santiaga, appears to be a composite of Luisa *Santiaga*, also the author's real mother, Nazareth, and the surname of the sweetheart of Santiago Nasar's real-life counterpart (Nydia Naser).[12] The name of an Arab immigrant, closely related to the Colombian narrator-chronicler, brings together Latin American and Arab cultures. In an epilogue in an early draft of the manuscript, García Márquez observes: 'Se llamaba Santiago Nasar, y era alegre y gallardo, y un miembro prominente de la comunidad árabe del lugar' ('his name was Santiago Nasar, and he was merry, gallant, and a prominent member of the Arab community'), but he is also seen as 'immoral' and 'exotic'.[13] Bernard McGuirk, echoing a character's prejudice against the wealthy Arab, alludes to the otherness of Santiago Nasar: 'Santiago Nasar is the outsider, "just like all Turks"' (1987: 179). Bell-Villada, commenting on García Márquez's reworking of true events, notes in passing the ethnic background of Angela's alleged lover: 'Santiago's Arab origins, for one, make him additionally remote and exotic' (2010: 207). Bell-Villada's comment affirms the novel's ambivalent Orientalism. In my view, though Santiago Nasar is integrated in the Colombian town, he is exoticised in the novel.

The evocation of the Arab community in *Crónica de una muerte anunciada* differs from Macondo's Arabs. Amid the town's fears of reprisals by the Arabs, the narrator notes the assimilation of Arab immigrants to Colombian culture:

> Los árabes constituían una comunidad de inmigrantes pacíficos que se establecieron a principios del siglo en los pueblos del Caribe, aun en los más remotos y pobres, y allí se quedaron vendiendo trapos de colores y baratijas de feria. Eran unidos, laboriosos y católicos. Se casaban entre ellos, importaban su trigo, criaban corderos en los patios y cultivaban el orégano y la berenjena, y su única pasión tormentosa eran los juegos de barajas. Los mayores siguieron hablando el árabe rural que trajeron de su tierra, y lo conservaron intacto en familia hasta la segunda generación, pero los de la tercera, con la excepción de Santiago Nasar, les oían a sus padres en árabe y les contestaban en castellano. (95)

> (The Arabs comprised a community of peaceful immigrants who had settled at the beginning of the century in Caribbean towns, even in the poorest and most remote, and there they remained, selling colored cloth and bazaar trinkets. They were clannish, hard-working, and Catholic. They married among themselves, imported their wheat, raised lambs in their yards, and grew oregano and eggplants, and playing cards was their only driving passion. The older ones continued speaking the rustic Arabic they had brought from their homeland, they maintained it intact in the family down to the second generation, but those of the third, with the exception of Santiago Nasar, listened to their parents in Arabic and answered them in Spanish.) (81–2)

García Márquez evokes a history of assimilation to Colombian culture and a Caribbean coast teeming with different ethnicities. However, the death of an Arab highlights ethnic tensions between Arabs and the Colombian town. The communal network of the Arab community in the Colombian town is more fully developed in *Crónica de una muerte anunciada* where they are no longer the stock characters of knick-knack-swapping Arabs. The community is further strengthened by marriages. Santiago Nasar accepted an engagement to Flora Miguel, the daughter of an Arab immigrant, Nahir Miguel, who appears in 'la chilaba de beduino que trajo de su tierra, y que siempre usó dentro de la casa' (129) ('the bedouin caftan he had brought from his homeland and which he always wore at home' (115)). Nahir Miguel offers him, in Arabic, refuge and firearms for protection. Yamil Shaium, a store owner, 'uno de los últimos árabes que llegaron con Ibrahim Nasar . . . y seguía siendo el consejero hereditario de la familia' (118–19) ('one of the last Arabs who had come with Ibrahim Nasar . . . and was still the hereditary counselor of the family' (104)), warns Santiago Nasar when he learns of the rumour of the Vicario twins' revenge.[14] He and Santiago Nasar exchange puns in Arabic before Santiago Nasar turns the corner of the square and walks to his death. *Crónica de una muerte anunciada* designates the Arabs as immigrants, challenging the view that they have fully assimilated to Latin American culture. They have formed an Arab community that preserves its own culture through intermarriage and commercial activities. Nonetheless, the assimilation of the community is shown in the loss of language: while immigrants retain a rustic Arabic, third-generation Colombians, with the exception of Santiago, answer their Arabic-speaking parents in Spanish.

Crónica de una muerte anunciada culminates in Santiago Nasar's massacre by the Vicario twins in a scene in which he is exoticised and Orientalised. Just before his murder, Santiago is warned by a non-Arab who refers to him as a *turco*: 'Por ahí no, turco, por el puerto viejo' (131) ('Not that way, Turk; by the old dock' (117)). Ette observes that Santiago returns to the '*turco*' or 'Oriental' immigrant before his murder and the 'Saracen, an Arab' upon his death (2006: 238–9). While Santiago Nasar clutches his entrails, his 'rostro de sarraceno con los rizos alborotados estaba más bello que nunca' (136) ('Saracen face with its headstrong ringlets was handsomer than ever' (122)). Exoticised, a tragic hero returns to his origins. Here, the image of his 'ringlets', circling back to that of his 'Arab eyelids and curly hair', and his Saracen face are filtered through Orientalist imagery. In death, Santiago Nasar is Orientalised, the matter of honour reinforcing his origins.

In *Crónica de una muerte anunciada*, the representation of the Arab community helps us to understand the tensions in the Colombian town. Ironically, the town's network helps rumours to circulate but forestalls assistance. Events and developments reinstate the Arabs' otherness and amplify Orientalist stereotypes. The representation of the characters and the death of Santiago Nasar is Orientalist, and some of the townsfolk's xenophobia, anti-Arab sentiment and complicity suggest that Santiago Nasar may have been killed because he is an Arab Other. Notes and emendations in an early draft of *Crónica de una muerte anunciada* show the accretions and revisions that made Santiago Nasar's cultural and ethnic origins central to the novel, which may seem incidental from García Márquez's observation about the Arab prince but have roots in Colombia's multi-ethnic Caribbean coast.

Cien años de soledad has an ambivalent relationship with the Orient in that the Arab traders of Macondo are stock characters. In both *Cien años de soledad* and *Crónica de una muerte anunciada* there are direct references to Arab immigrants and a congeries of images of the Orient. The Arab has settled in Macondo, a fictive utopia, or a fictional Colombian town – a founder, trader, labourer, cattle-ranch owner. *Cien años de soledad* references 'the Orient' without being there, the Arab an exotic character from *The Thousand and One Nights*. The fictional town in *Crónica de una muerte anunciada*, modelled on García Márquez's hometown, is shaken by the death of the Arab, an immigrant and Colombian. Abad's Orient, in turn, is a discursive Orient, drawn from Gérard de Nerval, Gustave Flaubert and Mark Twain, to which he travels with Orientalist assumptions at the turn of the millennium.

The Orient in Cairo

Héctor Abad Faciolince is one of the foremost Colombian post-Boom novelists, best known for *Basura* (Garbage, 2000), a novel that metafictionally examines literary influences through the centrality of the author's compatriot Gabriel García Márquez to the fictional writer (Quesada 2013: 215–16). In his well-known *El olvido que seremos* (*Oblivion: A Memoir*, 2006), a chronicle of his father Héctor Abad Gómez, a physician, professor and former president of the Antioquia Human Rights Defense Committee, who was murdered by the Colombian paramilitary, his father quotes García Márquez in a letter. Like García Márquez, Abad's novels are suffused with Colombian history such as La Violencia (1948–58), the civil war between Liberals and Conservatives, the guerrillas and paramilitary in his novel *La oculta* – a family saga set on La Oculta (literally 'hidden' or 'the hideaway'), a utopian farm in the mountains of Antioquia amid guerrilla and paramilitary violence, hailed as a hyperrealist *Cien años de soledad* – and drug trafficking. In interviews, Abad has confessed that writers of his generation no longer write in the shadow of García Márquez and observed a relationship to the Nobel laureate characterised by an 'implicit influence' (Polit Dueñas 2013: 148).[15]

Abad's *El olvido que seremos* offers another example of his kinship to García Márquez. The last pages of *El olvido que seremos* in which his father's death is recounted contain echoes of the final chapter of *Crónica de una muerte anunciada*. Abad reconstructs the family tragedy from conversations, reports and an investigation of the crime on 25 August 1987. His father was shot at the funeral of a murdered teachers' union leader by paramilitary hitmen. One reviewer, describing *El olvido que seremos* as a 'chronicle of Colombia's violence', draws parallels with *Crónica de una muerte anunciada*: 'The future murder hangs over Abad's book from the very start.'[16] Twenty years later, Abad assembles the fateful moments of his father's murder and how his family came to know of the tragedy: 'Lo que pasó después yo no lo vi, pero lo puedo reconstruir por lo que me contaron algunos testigos, o por lo que leí' (242) ('What happened afterwards I didn't see, but I can reconstruct it from what various witnesses told me, or from what I read' (228)) of the investigation.[17]

Abad's name and *Oriente empieza en El Cairo* invite speculation about his Arab origins (which he never denies in spite of his uncertainty).[18] Abad has frequently made an etymological note of his Arabised surname:

> Because of my surname, Abad, when I enter the United States, they ask me if I am of 'Middle Eastern origin,' and I say yes, that I am of all origins. I am invited to conferences of Arab writers and to participate in anthologies of Jewish writers, and I always say yes, because I feel as Jewish as I do Arab; I feel myself to be a foundling descendant of

> the mortal sin of the mother superior of a convent. A bastard. Many great Spanish-American writers were or are . . . hybrids: . . . the mulatto Garcia Marquez, and the Anglo-Lusitanian Jorge Luis Borges as well. (2014a: 80)

In the introduction to the Arabic translation of *El olvido que seremos* (*Al-Nisyān* in Arabic), Abad parses the etymology of his name: it is possible that his name is derived from Arab roots; his ancestors came from Spain (or he is descended from Moriscos, *conversos* or Spaniards, or all of them at once) (2014d: 3); or his name is derived from the word 'el abad' ('abbot') from monasteries in the Eastern Mediterranean.[19] Elsewhere, he has frequently invoked a hybrid origin and multi-ethnic history.[20] He remarks upon *El olvido que seremos*'s translation into Arabic: 'And now finally it is published in one of the most important and widely spoken Eastern languages, Arabic' (2014d: 3).[21] In his introduction, he shares his delight and surprise at the translation of his memoir into Arabic, the source of some of the most beautiful words in Spanish ('Almohada' (*al-makhadda*, 'pillow'), 'Alcázar' (*al-qaṣr*, 'palace') and 'Álgebra' (Algebra)) (2014d: 5).

Abad has travelled to the Arab world and shown interest in *The Thousand and One Nights*.[22] There are no Arab themes or echoes of Orientalism in his novels, except for *Fragmentos de amor furtivo* (Fragments of a Furtive Love, 1998) whose structure he borrows from *The Thousand and One Nights*. Set in 1990s Colombia, *Fragmentos de amor furtivo* adopts the frame tale of *The Thousand and One Nights* in the story of two lovers, Susana and Rodrigo, who sit out the violence of Medellín on the hills. Like Scheherazade, Susana postpones Rodrigo's departure by telling him a story of her former lovers every night over several months.

Abad was commissioned to write a travelogue by then-Italian publishing house Mondadori as part of the series *Año O* (2000),[23] a collection of travelogues written by renowned world authors about different cities at the start of the millennium (Hubert 2012: 43).[24] The series was part of an effort to promote intercultural exchange and the global circulation of Spanish literature. In 2014, Abad undertook another trip to Cairo on the occasion of the publication of the Arabic translation of his memoir *El olvido que seremos*.[25] Abad's *El olvido que seremos* thus circulates in an Arab book market. Interviews with the author and reviews of translations of *El olvido que seremos* and *Oriente empieza en El Cairo* into Arabic have appeared in the Egyptian press and introduced him to an Arabic readership.

Oriente empieza en El Cairo is unique among Abad's well-known novels and memoir *El olvido que seremos*.[26] Abad belongs to the post-Boom generation that revolted against and overthrew the legacy of magical realism and wrote during the violence that plagued Colombia, whose effects he felt intimately with the murder of his father. His experimental and multi-genre novels are located in a tradition of post-Boom literature and have experimented with new forms that refract Colombia's violence.

The Orient begins and ends in *Oriente empieza en El Cairo*. Abad's travelogue is characterised by the humour and parody that have flourished in his novels from *Asuntos de un hidalgo disoluto* (*The Joy of Being Awake*, 1994), a humorous metafictional parody of the Spanish picaresque novel, to *Basura*, a 'parody of his compatriot Gabriel García Márquez'.[27] Similarly, Polit Dueñas notes Abad's portrayal of characters in *Angosta* by his 'humor, affection, irony' (2013: 153). *Oriente empieza en El Cairo* is a fictional travelogue by a Latin American writer whose descriptions of his trip to Cairo demystify the Orient and trace Third World commonalities between Colombia and Egypt.

Oriente empieza en El Cairo recounts the adventures of a Colombian traveller in Cairo in December 1999 and January 2000. The Colombian traveller wishes to flee from guerrillas, paramilitaries, massacres and kidnappings in his country. Flaubert wrote: 'the Orient begins in Cairo' and the Colombian traveller's choice falls upon Egypt. With the humour characteristic of Abad's novels, the fictional narrator undertakes a trip to Cairo with his two wives, A and C (Abad's wife Ana and sister Clara were his fellow travellers on his trip to Egypt), with the Orientalist assumption that polygamy is a common Islamic practice in the Arab world, and that thus he will be able to blend in in the 'Orient'. Though the traveller purportedly prepares for his trip by perusing books, he is befuddled by Cairo. Ensconced in the famous Shepherd Hotel, described by Mark Twain in *The Innocents Abroad*, he and his co-wives explore the environs of Cairo. The traveller embarks on an assiduous study of Cairo's cafés, women,

men's relations with women, the pyramids and mosques, following in the footsteps of Gustave Flaubert, Gérard de Nerval and Mark Twain.

Set in Cairo at the start of the millennium, *Oriente empieza en El Cairo* invokes mythical and contemporary images of the Orient together with the 'Third World'. Orientalist and contemporary Cairo evokes mythical and 'real' Medellín. For the narrator, Egypt offers a reprieve from guerrilla kidnappings and paramilitary massacres in Colombia. Egypt was the start of an Oriental tour for nineteenth-century European travellers and, naturally, for the Colombian traveller, the point of entry to the Orient. *Oriente empieza en El Cairo* abounds with allusions to Gérard de Nerval and Gustave Flaubert in a parody of the nineteenth-century *voyage en Orient*. While Abad employs parody as imitation and subversion of Orientalist travel literature, his travelogue recounts the misadventures of the Third World traveller, from Medellín to Cairo. *Oriente empieza en El Cairo* explores the modern Orient, conjuring the 'Third World' as distinct from the rigidly drawn borders of the 'First World' – the US and Europe – that the Colombian travellers cross on the journey. Through the interplay of Cairo and Medellín, *Oriente empieza en El Cairo* focuses on cultural encounters between Latin America and the Arab world and de-exoticises the Orient. Parodying Orientalist exoticism, the narrator continually revises his assumptions of an exoticised Orient as he expresses a 'Third World' solidarity.

Oriente empieza en El Cairo emulates European Orientalists and departs from them. There are almost no references to Latin American authors who travelled to the Orient with the exception of fellow Colombian Andrés Holguín's *Notas egipcias* (Egyptian Memoirs, 1982). It is curious that Abad makes almost no intertextual allusions to Latin American Orientalists in North Africa but rather to the voyages of fellow European and American travellers to the Orient.[28] In fact, he follows the writers of Latin American *modernismo* who inherited the exoticism of French Orientalism from Nerval and Flaubert.[29] The Orientalist literature he draws on, in a list appended to *Oriente empieza en El Cairo*, features Gustave Flaubert's *Notes de voyage* (1910), Juan Goytisolo's *Crónicas sarracinas* (1982) and Edith Wharton's *In Morocco* (1920). Like Nerval and Flaubert, Abad reads mostly European Orientalists to prepare for his trip. He depends on Euro-American Orientalism with which he compares his Orient: Gérard de Nerval's *Voyage en Orient* (1851), Gustave Flaubert's *Notes de voyage*, Mark Twain's *Innocents Abroad* (1869), Rudyard Kipling's *Letters of Travel* (1892–1913) and William Makepeace Thackeray's *Notes on a Journey from Cornhill to Grand Cairo* (1845). He reads about Old and modern Cairo, Muslims, Non-Aligned countries and the Arab-Israeli wars. *Oriente empieza en El Cairo* parades images of the Arab world that revise Sarmiento's stereotypes, reproduce Nerval's and Flaubert's Orients, and trace Third World ties.

Abad's trip to Egypt recalls the travels of renowned Latin American writers such as Argentine statesman and writer Domingo Faustino Sarmiento. Unlike Abad, Sarmiento, in *Facundo o Civilización y barbarie* (*Facundo or Civilisation and Barbarism*, 1845), evokes the Orient, which he read about (Civantos 2006: 32). Sarmiento, in *Facundo*, characterises the gaucho as barbaric by comparing him to the Arab Bedouin and the Oriental in the service of Argentine nationalism (Spence 2007: 182). In *Viajes por Europa, África y América 1845–1847* (Travels in Europe, Africa and America, 1849), Sarmiento wrote about his trip to Algeria and showed interest in the 'gaucho and the Arab' but wrote ambivalently of North Africans, 'the barbarian Other', who is also 'noble' and 'elegant' (Civantos 2006: 42–3). His Orientalist characterisation equates the Argentine gaucho to inferiority, barbarism and alterity in opposition to the European (Spence 2007: 183). In *Oriente empieza en El Cairo*, the narrator's Orientalism is markedly different from the European form: he does not speak through an 'imperial' or 'asymmetrical' relation to the Orient.[30] As Axel Gasquet has noted, Latin American writers express a peripheral form of Orientalism.[31] Before his trip, the narrator locates himself in the Occident vis-à-vis the Orient because he writes in a 'Western' (occidental) language whose culture, he also acknowledges, colonised New Granada (Colombia), inscribing himself in a dichotomy of ours/Occidental-foreign/Oriental (14). Nevertheless, he goes on to acknowledge humorously a Third Worldness that separates 'us' (Third World passport holders) from 'them' (the United States and Europe) when he undergoes the rigorous inspections of border control in the United States en route to Egypt.

For Abad, the Orient is no different from Latin America, unlike Edward Said's description of European Orientalism, and a topos that does not conform to the narrator's Orientalist expectations of beauty, decadence and sensuality. *Oriente empieza en El Cairo* begins with *The Thousand and One Nights* and Flaubert: that often 'en los relatos hilvanados de *Las mil y una noches*' (13) ('in the spinning stories of *The Thousand and One Nights*'), one of the characters is possessed by wanderlust, prepares his caravan, charges a vizier with his affairs, and begins his journey.[32] As the narrator tells us, 'Un viajero curioso, Gustave Flaubert, hace dos siglos, nos lo dijo: "Oriente empieza en El Cairo"' (14) ('Two centuries ago, a curious traveller, Gustave Flaubert, tells us, "the Orient begins in Cairo"'). *Oriente empieza en El Cairo* takes its title from a letter by Flaubert to his mother in which he writes that the Orient begins in Cairo. Before the Colombian narrator's trip, the Orient is 'irreal' ('unreal') (27) – a patchwork of images: 'de dioses, templos, pirámides, dinastías y faraones . . . los mamelucos, Mahoma, Cleopatra, Saladino, *El libro de los muertos*, el Corán, el canal del Suez, *Aída*, los pachás, Moisés, Nasser, Sadat, los No Alineados, la Hermandad Musulmana, Mahfuz' (27) ('of gods, temples, pyramids, dynasties, pharaohs . . . Mamluks, Mohamed, Cleopatra, Saladdin, the Book of the Dead, the Qur'an, the Suez Canal, *Aida*, pashas, Moses, Nasser, Sadat, the Non-Aligned countries, the Muslim Brotherhood, Mahfouz'). For the narrator, the 'Orient' is an amalgam of nineteenth-century European literature and historical-political fragments. Said defines the Orient as the European Orientalist's congeries of images. Instead, the Orient here is the Third World traveller's wherein lies the difference. The narrator's evocation of his trip is steeped in *The Thousand and One Nights*: 'La magia del vuelo hace realidad el cuento de Aladino: se le pide el espíritu de la lámpara maravillosa que nos transporte a la ciudad de las mezquitas y los alminares, y antes de poderlo siquiera pensar bien, ya estamos ahí' (24) ('The magic of flying makes Aladdin's tale come true: we ask the genie of the magic lamp to transport us to the city of mosques and minarets, and before we know it, we are there'). Ancient Egypt beguiled Herodotus, Plato, Alexander the Great, Julius Caesar, Marc Antony and Napoleon. The irreality of the Orient is further shown in the contrast between the narrator's imaginary Orient, on the one hand, and a 'real' Cairo in which he arrives, on the other.[33] Likewise, a Cairo-Medellín nexus runs through *Oriente empieza en El Cairo*: the one dusty and the other humid, an arid desert and a lush jungle, the Sahara and el Chocó.

In Cairo, the narrator comments on common Orientalist assumptions, from the Arabic language to the sensuality of the Orient:

> El idioma árabe, en español, es una algarabía. Sólo la ignorancia y el prejuicio antiislámico hacen que esa lengua bellísima haya llegado a ser, en nuestros oídos torpes e inexpertos, un sinónimo de ruido. Sé que durante un mes me acompañaran, como una música de fondo que no entiendo, esas jotas recias, esas eles insistentes y el abierto predominio de una vocal: la a. En Colombia, para imitar el sonido de la lengua árabe, decimos una frase a toda velocidad, dos veces: 'Bajalajaulajaime, baja-la-jaula-jaime.' (25)

> (The Arabic language, in Spanish, is una algarabia. Only the ignorant and the anti-Islamic would make of a beautiful language that has been hard on our awkward and inexpert ears a synonym of noise. For a month, these hard 'J's, persistent 'L's and the dominant open vowel 'A' will accompany me like a soundtrack that I don't understand. In Colombia, to imitate the sound of the Arabic language, we rush through a phrase twice: 'Bajalajaulajaime, baja-la-jaula-jaime' [Bring down the cage, Jaime, bring down the cage, Jaime].)

The *arabismo* 'algarabia', a derogatory word, duplicates the sound of Arabic in Spanish. The nonsense phrase 'Bajalajaulajaime, baja-la-jaula-jaime' (transliterated in the Arabic translation) mimics Arabic for Colombian ears. Later, the narrator interweaves the Cairene idiom in his travelogue as he traverses Cairo's cultural and linguistic labyrinths. Inherited from Arabic, 'Ojalá' is widely used in Spanish, like the Muslim '*inn sha' Alah*' (150) ('God willing'). Like Nerval, the narrator wields *mots clefs* in Arabic, '*tayyeb*', ever-useful, ideal, evocative of the magical 'abracadabra', a modern-day 'Open Sesame' – like 'fine', 'perfect', an emphatic 'yes', a modest assent or unequivocal agreement – and the eternal '*shukran*' ('thank you') to express gratitude, 'yes and no' (172). As Said notes, Nerval moves through the 'labyrinths' of the Orient, 'armed – Nerval tells us – with two Arabic words, *tayeb*, the word for assent, and *mafisch*, the word for rejection' (1978: 182).

In *Oriente empieza en El Cairo*, the Colombian narrator both confirms and challenges the common Oriental tropes popularised by his predecessors Flaubert and Nerval. Said notes that the Orient is a topos rather than an actual, real space:

> In the system of knowledge about the Orient, the Orient is less a place than a topos, a set of references, a congeries of characteristics, that seems to have its origin in a quotation, or a fragment of a text, or a citation from someone's work on the Orient, or some bit of previous imagining, or an amalgam of all these. (1978: 177)

When he set his eyes on the shores of Egypt in 1848, Flaubert wrote: 'I had my first sight of the Orient through, or rather in, a glowing light' (1972: 28). Said notes that the 'Orient impressed him [Flaubert] with its decrepitude' (1978: 185). Like Flaubert, the Colombian traveller's first impressions of Cairo dispel his romantic Orient. Upon his arrival, he remarks upon the Orient's decrepitude. While Flaubert would go on to note the decay of the Orient and his travel notes are steeped in his *ennui*, the Colombian narrator encounters an anachronistic decay upon arrival. Cairo seems faded, dusty and contradictory to the Orientalist imagery that enhances his imaginary Orient. His Orient is exoticised, borrowed from his fellow scholarly French and American travellers. Flaubert's Orient exudes exoticism, excess and grotesquerie in his notes and letters. Abad's Orient is exhausted, modelled on Flaubert's, but inflected by his own Third Worldism. When Flaubert arrived in Cairo, he wanted to return to Normandy. The Colombian narrator's repulsion by the dust, smoke, noise and poverty upon arrival echoes Flaubert. Humour runs through his contact with the Orient. Curiously, Cairo makes him homesick for Medellín, from which he seemed all too eager to depart for a reprieve from the paramilitary and guerrillas.

The narrator interweaves Orientalist tropes and motifs inherited from Nerval. Like Nerval, the narrator notes: 'Querida ciudad de El Cairo: déjame quitarte tus velos de uno en uno' (26) ('Dear Cairo: let me raise your veils one by one'). The trope of Cairo-the-Oriental-woman that echoes Nerval is evoked in jest. The narrator is naive and ironic, Orientalist and Third World, antiquated and modern. Upon his arrival in Cairo, he comments on the Orient he dreamed about when he began his trip and the contrast of his encounter: 'Querida ciudad de El Cairo: me gustaba más tu cara antes de conocerte. De tu cuerpo no puedo decir nada todavía porque te cubre de arriba abajo una densa y opaca vestidura de polvo' (26) ('Dear Cairo: I liked your face better before I met you. I can't say anything about your body yet because you are clothed in a thick, opaque veil of dust from top to toe'). In *Voyage en Orient*, Nerval devotes attention to the women of Cairo: 'Mais l'Égypte, grave et pieuse, est toujours le pays des énigmes et des mystères; la beauté s'y entoure, comme autrefois, de voiles et de bandelettes' (2020: 88) ('Egypt, serious and devout, is still the land of enigmas and mysteries. There, beauty surrounds itself, as it has ever done, with veils and coverings' (2013: 5)). The apostrophe by Abad's narrator (cited above) plays upon Nerval's comments on the veil in Cairo: 'Arrêtons-nous, et cherchons à soulever un coin du voile austere' (2020: 88) ('Rather let us stay and try to raise a corner of that austere veil' (2013: 5)). But the Colombian narrator employs the trope to explore the mystery with which – as Nerval puts it – the Orient 'enshrouds itself' ('s'enveloppe') and Cairo gradually 'unveils' ('dévoile') its mysteries (2013: 6). For Nerval, the ubiquitous veil in Cairo betokens beauty and sexuality; he notes of the veil with which half of the Orient enshrouds itself that Cairo is 'le pays des rêves et de l'illusion' (2020: 73) ('indeed the country of dreams and of illusions' (2013: 6)). More than a century before Abad, however, Nerval found the Orient wanting, compared to the Orient he had read about and expected when he travelled to Egypt. Nerval's narrator is discouraged by nineteenth-century Cairo, befuddled by 'the city of the Thousand and One Nights' (2013: 6). In contrast, Abad's narrator goes on to undo his own Orientalist assumptions modelled on Nerval.

His evocation of the unveiling of Cairo is, in fact, a parody of Nerval. For Bakhtin, parody undermines the authority of a previous text. Bakhtin, drawing from Paul Lehmann on medieval parody, describes parody as 'appropriation', 'reworking' and 'imitation' of 'another's language, another's style, another's word' (1981: 69). The relationship of parody to the parodied text ranges 'from reverent acceptance to parodic ridicule – so that it is often very difficult to establish where reverence ends and ridicule begins' (Bakhtin 1981: 77). Linda Hutcheon defines parody in the twentieth century thus: 'Parody . . . is a form of imitation, but imitation characterized by ironic inversion, not always at the expense of the parodied text' (1989: 87–8). As she further notes, 'Its range of intent is from respectful admiration to biting ridicule' (1989: 97). Abad's parody dovetails imitation and subversion of Flaubert and Nerval in the apostrophe cited above. His parody is imitation and irony, whose effect is playful and subversive. The Colombian traveller, who has travelled through the richer continents and endured Third World ordeals at border inspections, and has recently arrived from violence-ridden Medellín, is steeped in nineteenth-century Orientalism and about to be enlightened in Cairo at the turn of the millennium. For the Colombian narrator, the Orient, he notes humorously, is far from sensual.

The unveiling of Cairo, a trope that echoes Nerval, helps him to demystify the Orient. He concludes that evocations of women in Nerval's *Voyage en Orient* and *The Thousand and One Nights* are invented and undertakes to uncover the truth of his encounter with women in Cairo in his tongue-in-cheek humour: the sensuality of the Orient is a misconception. Instead, the Orient is full of prohibitions for women and taboos for men. The narrator notes the famous sensuality of the Orient and contravenes the Orientalist imagery so characteristic of Nerval and Flaubert – that women are demure – all while also clearly remarking upon the social conditions that are symptomatic of contemporary Cairo. As he remarks on the proliferation of the veil, the Colombian traveller notes cheekily that if he wishes for the sensuality of the Orient, he should return to Medellín, evoked when he looks at A and C, his two wives. He repurposes Nerval's trope of Cairo as the Oriental veiled woman in his travelogue on 'les femmes du Caire'. In the same comic vein with which he brings along two wives to the Orient under the assumption that he would fit into Oriental society, he discovers that the contemporary Orient is no Orient from the exotic *Thousand and One Nights*, full of sensual Oriental women and black-eyed *houris* (nymphs in paradise). The humour and naivety of the Colombian traveller are part and parcel of his Orientalist parody.

Parodying Orientalist imagery in nineteenth-century French travel literature, the narrator parades stereotypes modelled on Flaubert's dreams and encounter with the Orient. In a letter to his mother on 14 December 1849 at the outset of a one-year journey, Flaubert, who grows his beard, writes, 'Mi barba crece como una sabana de América' (14) ('My beard grows like the savannah in the Americas'). Like Flaubert, the narrator lets his beard grow to conform to the stereotype of the Orientalists. In the end, Flaubert rereads his Orient, in his letter to his mother, quoted from the Italian edition, *Viaggio in Oriente*, of *Notes de voyage* in *Oriente empieza en El Cairo*:

> Le escribe Flaubert a su madre: 'Me preguntas si el Oriente está a la altura de lo que imaginaba. A la altura, sí, y además supera en amplitud mis suposiciones. He encontrado dibujado nítidamente lo que para mí era nebuloso. Los hechos han tomado el sitio de los presentimientos, de tal manera que a menudo es como si volviera a encontrarme con viejos sueños olvidados.' (41)

> (Flaubert writes to his mother: 'You ask me whether the Orient is up to what I imagined it to be. Yes, it is; and more than that, it extends far beyond the narrow idea I had of it. I have found, clearly delineated, everything that was hazy in my mind. Facts have taken the place of suppositions – so excellently so that it is often as though I were suddenly coming upon old forgotten dreams.') (75)[34]

Unlike the intertextual allusion to Nerval noted above, the narrator quotes from Flaubert but superimposes his own Orient, filtered through multiple Orients. Cairo of the twenty-first century pales in comparison to the exotic Orient the narrator expects. His Orient is more discursive than real, drawn from Orientalist sources. The Orient of nineteenth-century Orientalism is in a state of decay, which endures over time. Abad's Orient seems to be no different from Flaubert's. Nonetheless, *Oriente empieza en El Cairo* differentiates between the narrator's imaginary Orient and twenty-first-century Cairo. For him, Cairo seems exhausted and monochromatic, clothed in a veil of dust, and furthest from the image of the exotic Orient he had entertained, though that is also clearly evocative of the travelogues of Flaubert and Nerval that accompany him on his trip and which he interweaves in his travelogue. Abad marshals Orientalist tropes taken from primarily French but also British and American Orientalisms to draw attention to and dispel the Colombian traveller's elusive Orient and the reality that he flees from (Colombia) to Cairo. His Orient is no confirmation of European Orientalism. Rather, it is a parody in that a Colombian traveller who has no colonial relationship to the Orient is ironically Orientalist but also 'Third World'. He emulates the Orientalists in an homage and an inversion, and instead draws links between Medellín and Cairo.

In the middle of a tour of Coptic Cairo and the Jewish synagogue, the narrator wonders about Latin Americans amid such a rich cultural heritage and shares three competing myths of origin that circulate in his family about the surname 'Abad'. The most pious and credible version is that the Abads are old, pure Christians whose ancestor, a soldier or scribe of the king, arrived from Palencia. Another, more likely, version is that they are descendants of a baptised Morisco, not Abad, but Abd, a slave, slave of anything (Allah or faith or the Prophet): 'un morisco bautizado, no Abad sino Abd, es decir esclavo, esclavo de algo (de Alá o de la fe o del profeta)' (55). He notes: 'Abd es un compuesto de muchísimos apellidos árabes' (56) ('Abd is a composite of many Arab names'). The third, and most likely, version he recalls in the synagogue is that he is descended from a rabbi whose name was abbreviated to Abad, Abadi or Abati. In short, he extols the virtues of a chameleon: to be mixed ('mestizo') (56) in Colombia, Spanish in Spain, Muslim in Egypt, Jewish in the synagogues, and Coptic in the churches.

The Colombian traveller's Orient is literary, and he frequently notes the contrast between his bookish Orient and contemporary Cairo. He quotes from Nerval, Flaubert and Twain to emulate and undo the myths of the Orient. Orientalist literature is uniform, he remarks, Orientalists borrowing from one another, from Nerval to Twain, Thackeray and Flaubert. He also reads Arabic literature: *The Thousand and One Nights* and Egyptian Nobel laureate Naguib Mahfouz's novels. He tours the environs of Cairo, the labyrinths of the Orient, and notes 'El Callejón de los Milagros' (The Alley of Miracles), an allusion to Mahfouz's *Zuqāq al-midaqq* (*Midaq Alley*) in Spanish.[35] Likewise, he compares the erratic Fatimid Caliph al-

Ḥākim bi-Amr Allāh to 'el prototipo más antiguo de todas las novelas latinoamericanas de dictadores, desde el Patriarca hasta el Chivo' (109) ('the oldest prototype of all the Latin American dictator novels, from the Patriarch to the Goat'). The 'Patriarch' and the 'Goat' are allusions to García Márquez's *El otoño del patriarca* (*The Autumn of the Patriarch*, 1975), a novel of an imaginary dictator of a Caribbean country who blends the attributes of a number of real Latin American dictators, and Peruvian Mario Vargas Llosa's *La fiesta del Chivo* (*The Feast of the Goat*, 2000), a novel about the assassination of the Dominican dictator Rafael Trujillo. He draws on Borges's erudition and well-known dialogue with the Islamic world. The narrator notes the cafés of Cairo where storytellers would recount tales from *The Thousand and One Nights*, the feats of the Prophet, the misdeeds and conquests of the sultans, the massacre of the Mamluks, and the stories of the thugs and heroes of the neighbourhood, so famously recounted by Mahfouz in his novels.

While he encounters the Orient, the narrator draws from a host of writers. Edith Wharton's *In Morocco*, in which she recounts her trip at the turn of the twentieth century, and her description of Sufi dance is mirrored in the whirling dervishes in Cairo. Mark Twain travelled to Egypt in the nineteenth century and wrote about his trip.[36] Constantin-François de Chasseboeuf Volney, a philosopher, historian, traveller and French Orientalist, wrote *Voyage en Syrie et en Égypte* (*Travels through Syria and Egypt, in the Years 1783, 1784, and 1785*). Kipling visited Egypt in 1929 and wrote about the trip. Thackeray visited Egypt in the nineteenth century and wrote about his trip in *From Cornhill to Grand Cairo* (1845). Andrés Holguín, a Colombian poet, translator, diplomat and critic from Medellín, travelled to Egypt and wrote *Notas egipcias*. Antonius Gonzales, a Spanish Franciscan, wrote about Egypt in *Le Voyage en Egypte du Père Antonius Gonzales, 1665–1666* (Father Antonius Gonzales's Journey to Egypt, 1665–1666).

In the West, images of the Orient are intermingled with a fascination with Scheherazade, and, for the narrator, they originate in dreams. He concedes: 'Toda la sensualidad de Oriente reside en nuestra imaginación, en nuestro imaginario' (95) ('All the sensuality of the Orient rests in our imagination, in our imaginary'). For him, the Orient conjured in books does not exist. The narrator concludes that 'Egipto no es Egipto' (128) ('Egypt is not Egypt'), or what is known as Egypt has nothing to do with the Orient, sought and dreamed of by the West since the Napoleonic invasion of 1798 and Champollion's 1822 deciphering of the Rosetta Stone. It has nothing to do with ancient Egypt nor with the Egyptomania that held the West in thrall for centuries, nor is Egypt the Orient invented by Richard Burton's 1885 translation of *The Thousand and One Nights* or largely invented by the West.

The narrator-traveller is no tourist, but is careful to have direct contact with Egyptian culture. Unlike Latin American writers who never travelled to the Orient and read about its customs, he frequents local cafés (*qahwas*) and muses on the curiosities of Cairo. His aperçus are also sprinkled with criticisms of the phenomenon of fundamentalism and comparisons with his country's violence. When he notes the misadventures of the tourist or traveller in Cairo, he writes, unlike what happens in his country, in Cairo they do not kill one other (143). He acknowledges his fellow Egyptians in Third Worldism ('tercermundismo') and the tragic events of Colombia's history: 'La pobreza de El Cairo es igual a la nuestra, aunque en El Cairo es más digna y conserva' (191) ('Cairo's poverty is like ours, though in Cairo it is more dignified'). The comparison falls short with 'nuestra Violencia' (191) ('our violence'): 'Los atracos y los asesinatos, el pan nuestro de cada día en nuestra tercermundista Colombia, son la excepción y el escándalo en El Cairo' (192) ('Armed robbery and murders, our daily bread in our Third World Colombia, are the exception and scandal in Cairo').

Though the narrator dispels myths of the 'Orient' in Cairo, he remarks upon the features of contemporary Egypt at the turn of the millennium. For example, he notes the censorship of Syrian writer Ḥaydar Ḥaydar's well-known novel *Walīma li-aʿshāb al-baḥr* (A Banquet for Seaweed, 1983). From April to May 2000, the controversy of Ḥaydar's novel erupted on the literary scene in Egypt when a review published in the weekly newspaper *al-Shaʿb* accused Ḥaydar and the novel of blasphemy (Mehrez 2008: 18–19).[37] Subsequently, the novel was banned by the conservative Islamic institution al-Azhar. The narrator further comments on the observations of renowned Egyptian novelist Ibrahīm Aṣlān, the editor of the series that reissued *Walīma li-a'shāb al-baḥr* under the auspices of the Ministry of Culture, on the fraught cultural climate and the practice of self-censorship to elude the state's restrictions on the freedom of assembly, organisation, expression and publication (176), on the one hand, and religious fundamentalism, on the other. Mahfouz was attacked by a fundamentalist and a number of his novels are banned by al-Azhar, the narrator notes. 'Ser escribe en el Egipto de hoy es duro. Poco rentable. Y además peligroso' (175) ('To be a writer in Egypt today is hard. Unprofitable. And also dangerous'), he writes. He expresses his solidarity with fellow writers in the Arab world because 'Incluso en Colombia, un país donde a veces te matan por lo que escribes' (177) ('Even in Colombia, a country where you could sometimes be killed for what you write'), Egyptian society seems more favourable to writing. The narrator thus dedicates his travelogue to Egyptian writers: 'Escribas de Egipto, seguramente este libro nunca será traducido al árabe, pero desde este idioma que ha sido salpicado por la bella lengua que ustedes hablan y escriben, les mando una frase de admiración y solidaridad' (177) ('Egyptian writers, surely this book will never be translated into Arabic, but in this language, sprinkled with the beautiful language that you speak and write, I send you a note of admiration and solidarity'). Indeed, *Oriente empieza en El Cairo* was translated into Arabic (*Al-Sharq yabda' fī al-Qāhira*) in 2018 for the direct interactions it so uniquely traces, and thus circulates directly between Latin America and the Arab world, Spanish and Arabic.[38]

While on his tour of Cairo, the narrator notes that the city retains little of the romantic Orient. He notes: 'Hay un Macondo maravilloso de García Márquez, y una triste Aracataca' (68) ('There is the marvellous Macondo of García Márquez and a sad Aracataca'), conjuring Cairo's evocation of a fictional paradise and García Márquez's hometown, a decrepit, magical Orient and an implausible, dusty city. The Orient is an illusion for the narrator, by turns Orientalist and self-deprecatory, critical and sympathetic, humorous and serious. The evidence that evocations of the Orient in Abad's travelogue are parodies of nineteenth-century French travellers such as Nerval and Flaubert is to be found in the narrator's tone; for example, in the humour in his first encounter with the Orient and again in his observations on its elusive sensuality. The narrator discovers Cairo of the twenty-first century to be unexpectedly different, to fall short of his expectations of the Orient, the standards set by Flaubert's notes. Thus, Abad's travelogue-novel is a parody that is bent on exposing the fallacies of the idea of the Orient through his wry humour and irony in reworking Orientalist tropes drawn from French and British Orientalism.

In the introduction to the Arabic translation of *El olvido que seremos*, Abad notes that *Oriente empieza en El Cairo* evokes the magic and disorientation that possessed him upon his contact with the Orient – frequently the Other for Latin America – on his trip, and, in the end, the solidarity he felt (2014e: 4). He had already expressed his solidarity in *Oriente empieza en El Cairo*, a fictional travelogue that de-exoticises Cairo at the turn of the millennium with touches of humour and hyperbole. It is both an affectionate parody and an intentional exoticisation of the Orient. His travelogue on social, cultural and religious practices and literary and political history mirrors a modern decrepit Orient along with the Colombian traveller's Third World solidarity. Abad's solidarity is avowed in the travelogue itself (and again in the introduction to the Arabic translation of *El olvido que seremos* years later). In the end, he also notes 'Los antioqueños temenos sangre de comerciantes levantinos' (199) ('Antioquians have the blood of Levantine traders'), in a comment on a history of migration from the Levant to Colombia but also solidarity that he expressed with Egyptian writers. With his trip, he cultivated an interest in Egypt to which he would return and to which *El olvido que seremos* and *Oriente empieza en El Cairo* have travelled in Arabic.

Transcontinental Literature

Both *Crónica de una muerte anunciada* and *Oriente empieza en El Cairo* offer examples of semi-peripheral engagement and create links in the global South. While García Márquez's novels integrate Arabs in Latin America and an ambivalent Orientalism is implicit, Abad parodies European journeys to the Orient. García Márquez traces a longstanding Arab presence in Latin America and is familiar with a multi-ethnic Caribbean coast. By contrast, Abad travels to Egypt and offers an example of new Latin American cultural encounters in the twenty-first century. Both examine cultural encounters and contribute to Arab and Latin American literary ties. Reading the two works together is helpful for a better understanding of networks in the semi-periphery that challenge scholars to rethink frameworks of comparative study.

Garcia Marquez's *Crónica de una muerte anunciada* and Abad's *Oriente empieza en El Cairo* have travelled to the Arab world through translation and circulation in Arabic. While the transcontinental encounters in *Crónica de una muerte anunciada* and *Oriente empieza en El Cairo* focus on migration and travel, they are also linked to circulation and translation. García Márquez's novels are widely translated in the Arab world, and Abad's works have also been translated into Arabic. Moreover, Abad's *Oriente empieza en El Cairo* introduces Spanish readers to Arabic literature and fosters ties more directly than the European-sponsored series Colección Año O. *Crónica de una muerte anunciada* and *Oriente empieza en El Cairo* offer a form of transcontinental literature that circulates directly and explores cultural encounters and also show movement such as migration to Latin America and travel to the Arab world.

I return to the argument that Abad's *Oriente empieza en El Cairo*, which entwines a seemingly derivative Orientalism and solidarity, is centred on 'Third World' alignments. In tropes, sources and ideology, *Oriente empieza en El Cairo* is a parody of Flaubert and Nerval, both an homage and a departure, and expresses Third World solidarity. In this sense, Abad problematises European Orientalism in the twenty-first century through the paradox of Orientalist solidarity.

Both Colombian novelists are masters of form, reinventing Arab Latin American cultural encounters. In *Crónica de una muerte anunciada* and *Oriente empieza en El Cairo*, they expand the constellation of Arab Latin American exchanges and further transcontinental ties. They offer a model of contact between semi-peripheral and peripheral regions through exchanges, circulation, translation and reception. In this model, Latin American literature introduces these Arab Latin American interactions. This model expands world literature to include South-South solidarity and migratory routes. Both novelists offer new paths for South-South connections that expand links between Latin America and the Arab world by highlighting the Arab presence in Latin America and intertwining Orientalism with Third World solidarity respectively. Abad's work is unique in its focus on the Colombian traveller in the 'Orient' and draws attention to other ties such as shared Third World struggles. The next chapter explores further direct contact with the Orient in Central American and Mexican novels set in Morocco.

2

The African Shore: Rodrigo Rey Rosa and Alberto Ruy Sánchez in Morocco

> [A]t an oasis in Northern Africa, memory extended a startling and secret bridge that led to the desert of my childhood in Northern Mexico . . . And that caravan of images that carried me from one desert to another, spanning two continents . . . opened an inner doorway to a strange territory of the imagination, a kind of garden in the desert . . .
>
> Alberto Ruy Sánchez, 'Shadow and Light in the Desert'

In the 1980s, Guatemalan writer Rodrigo Rey Rosa (b. 1958) travelled to Morocco where he attended Paul Bowles's creative writing workshop. *La orilla africana* (*The African Shore*, 1999), his novel set in Tangier, intertwines African, European and Latin American shores. In 1975, Mexican writer Alberto Ruy Sánchez undertook a trip to Morocco, which recalled the Sonoran Desert in northern Mexico, and published a series of novels inspired by the ancient Moroccan city of Mogador. Rey Rosa's and Ruy Sánchez's Morocco-set novels explore the relationship of Mexico and Central America to North Africa through Latin American Orientalism and transatlantic travel to the Arab world.

Latin American writers such as Domingo Sarmiento, Rubén Darío, Enrique Gómez Carrillo, Roberto Arlt and Severo Sarduy travelled to North Africa in the twentieth century and published travelogues, chronicles, essays and novels.[1] Cuban writer Severo Sarduy published a brief essay on Tangier, 'Tanger', in *Tel Quel* in 1971, which appeared in his novel *El Cristo de la rue Jacob* (*Christ on the Rue Jacob*, 1992).[2] Both novels are located in a tradition of Latin American Orientalist literature, with Rey Rosa's novel focused on cultural encounters between Latin Americans and Moroccans and a unique relationship to Tangier, while Ruy Sánchez's novel, inspired by and set in Essaouira, concentrates on Moroccan characters. Like Héctor Abad Faciolince who wrote *Oriente empieza en El Cairo* as part of Año O, a collection of travel literature in 2000, Rey Rosa wrote *El tren a Travancore (Cartas Indias)* (*The Train to Travancore*, 2002), an epistolary picaresque travelogue commissioned for the series about his trip to Chennai.[3]

Latin American travel literature on North Africa shows a longstanding interest in the Orient and explores forms of transcontinental contact. One of the earliest and most famous Latin American Orientalist travelogues is the Argentine statesman and writer Domingo Faustino Sarmiento's *Viajes por Europa, África y América 1845–1847* where he writes about his travels to Tangier. Nicaraguan poet Rubén Darío travelled to Morocco and produced an Orientalist travelogue.[4] At the turn of the twentieth century, Guatemalan Enrique Gómez Carrillo (1873–1927) composed a chronicle, *La sonrisa de la esfinge: sensaciones de Egipto* (The Smile of the Sphinx: Sensations of Egypt, 1913), on his travels in Egypt. Argentine Roberto Arlt, dispatched to Morocco in the mid-1930s, wrote a travelogue on colonial North Africa, which examines his journeys from Tangier to Cairo, and a Morocco-themed play *África* (1938).[5] Gorica Majstorovic describes Arlt as a 'reluctant Orientalist' who departed from the Orientalism of Sarmiento and Darío, though he frequently wrote Oriental stories – most of which are set in Morocco – for an Argentine newspaper (2015: 204, 206). His travels to Morocco are recounted in his travelogues *Aguafuertes españolas* (Spanish Etchings) and *Aguafuertes gallegas* (Galician Etchings) (Majstorovic 2006: 109).

In the mid-twentieth century, Latin American literature on the Orient and the Arab world flourished with the short stories of Jorge Luis Borges. Thereafter, Latin American literature increasingly reworked the tropes and conventions of Hispanic Orientalism and exoticism. Like Darío, Arlt and Sarduy, Rey Rosa settled in Tangier, where he composed and set his novel *La orilla africana*, and Ruy Sánchez travelled to Morocco. Like Abad (examined in Chapter 1), they share classic Orientalism's conceptions of the Orient but draw parallels between Latin America and Morocco. Ruy

Sánchez creates connections between Mexico and Morocco in the mythical Mogador of his quintet, comprising *Los nombres del aire* (*Mogador: The Names of the Air*, 1987), *En los labios del agua* (*On the Lips of Water*, 1996), *Los jardines secretos de Mogador: Voces de tierra* (*The Secret Gardens of Mogador: Voices of the Earth*, 2001), *Nueve veces el asombro: Nueve veces nueve cosas que dicen de Mogador* (*Poetics of Wonder: Passage to Mogador*, 2005) and *La mano del fuego* (The Fire's Hand, 2007).

This chapter examines the relationship between Latin America and North Africa vis-à-vis Iberian colonialism through an analysis of novels by Rodrigo Rey Rosa and Alberto Ruy Sánchez. Rey Rosa's and Ruy Sánchez's novels, which are set in Morocco, serve as unique examples of a relationship between Latin America and North Africa. Although the novels may be traced to a long history of Latin American Orientalism in the nineteenth century, I argue that they recover a parallel relationship between Morocco and Latin America vis-à-vis Iberian colonisation. Rey Rosa's frequent travels to Tangier and Ruy Sánchez's longstanding interest in Essaouira renew relationships to Morocco in Central American and Mexican literature based on a colonial history and the Arab heritage of Spain. While Rey Rosa explores Central America's 'African shore', Ruy Sánchez extends a 'bridge of sand' ('un puente de arena') from the Sonoran Desert in northern Mexico to the Sahara in North Africa and thus rethinks links between the cultures of Mexico and Morocco.

Latin America and North Africa

The novels of Rey Rosa and Ruy Sánchez offer unique relationships to Morocco in the late twentieth century. Mary Louise Pratt's 'contact zones' in *Imperial Eyes* may be adopted to study the novels by Rey Rosa and Ruy Sánchez where cultural contact is largely different from imperial encounters in 'social spaces where disparate cultures meet, clash, and grapple with each other, often in highly asymmetrical relations of domination and subordination – such as colonialism and slavery' (2008: 7). However, Rey Rosa's and Ruy Sánchez's Morocco-set novels shape ties between Latin American and North African cultures through a relationship to Iberian colonisation rather than relations of cultural superiority and colonial domination. Ali Behdad's 'belated Orientalism' focuses on a late-nineteenth-century Orientalism based on desire and nostalgia as practices that enabled and perpetuated colonial power. On the other hand, Rey Rosa's and Ruy Sánchez's novels portray an Orient of exoticism, excess, violence, sensuality and desire through cultural difference and kinship.

Rey Rosa's and Ruy Sánchez's novels are framed by a relationship between Morocco and Latin America vis-à-vis Spain. On the one hand is the parallel relationship to Iberian colonisation, with settler colonialism in Latin America and Portuguese rule and Spanish control of Morocco. However, settler colonialism in Latin America differs from the colonial history of the Arab world. Latin American countries gained independence in the early nineteenth century (López-Calvo and Birns 2020: 237). Decolonisation in the Arab world, by contrast, began in the mid-twentieth century. At the same time, there are connections between Morocco and Latin America through the Arab presence in the Iberian Peninsula whose legacy extended to Latin America with the Spanish conquest.

In Rey Rosa's *La orilla africana*, relations between the Latin American traveller and the Moroccan Other are characterised by cultural mistranslation, violence and mutual distrust. *La orilla africana* abounds with Orientalist stereotypes of exoticism, debauchery and violence. While Ruy Sánchez draws attention to an Arab Iberian heritage in his treatment of Moroccan culture in his Mexican novels, he reworks an Orient of feminine desire and sensuality to different ends. Rey Rosa and Ruy Sánchez represent the Orient through Africa, as another shore for Central America, and an ancient Moroccan city that connects Latin America to North Africa, respectively. In the preface to *Tres novelas exóticas* (Three Exotic Novels), Rey Rosa notes the exoticism of his own novels that helps us to situate his novel and his relation to North Africa: 'Las novelas escritas por guatemaltecos son, por definición, exóticas. Las novelas guatemaltecas ambientadas en la selva del Petén, en África del Norte o en el sur de la India pueden no tener el encanto de lo extraño, pero deben llamarse, en rigor, exóticas' (2016b: 9) ('Novels written by Guatemalans are, by definition, exotic. Guatemalan novels set in the Peten jungle, in North Africa or in the south of India may not have the charm of the strange, but you would expect them to be called exotic') (my translation).

Rey Rosa comments on the exoticisation of Central America and the Orient, which they share in common. In a similar vein, Ruy Sánchez has remarked on a horizontal Orientalism in his own relation, as a Mexican writer from the global South, to Morocco in his novels. In what follows, I examine Rey Rosa's and Ruy Sánchez's Moroccan novels against a history of settler colonialism in Latin America and the Iberian colonisation of Morocco.

'Two Exotic Novels'

Rey Rosa is Guatemala's premier writer, whose novels have been translated into English by American author Paul Bowles (1910–99). Born in Guatemala City, Rey Rosa resided occasionally in Tangier where Bowles had settled.[6] In 1980, he enrolled in Bowles's creative writing workshop in Tangier and spent a year in Morocco.[7] Though Rey Rosa is one of the better-known Central American writers in English, his connections to North Africa are understudied.[8] Rey Rosa's travels from Guatemala to Morocco and India explore direct connections among Central America, North Africa and Asia. His novels are infused with the Argentine experimentalism of Borges in Central America,[9] along with Guatemala's violence, which are transposed to Morocco.

Rey Rosa reworks contact between Latin America and the Arab world through Third World encounters and his evocation of Tangier in his novels. *La orilla africana* crosses the Atlantic and the Strait of Gibraltar, creating routes between Latin America, North Africa and Spain. Alexandra Ortiz Wallner has noted the reworking of Central American literature through the presence of the Arab world or the Orient in the Latin American tradition. *La orilla africana* interconnects Spanish American literature with the Arab world or the Orient, more broadly, in the Spanish American literary tradition (Ortiz Wallner 2012: 247). In *La orilla africana*, Rey Rosa recreates cultural and transnational encounters that cross borders between Latin America, Spain and North Africa.

La orilla africana is unique among Rey Rosa's novels for its focus on contact between Latin America and North Africa. Tangier was home to Rey Rosa from 1982 to 1992 and where he spent summers until 2001 (Goldman 2013: 74). The setting of Morocco, Rey Rosa writes, reworks and departs from Bowles's Tangier: 'by 1998 Morocco had become quite different, at least externally, from the Morocco that Bowles had written about, or in a way invented. I guess I looked at Morocco, especially Tangier, as a territory that was his. . . . It's important to understand that I wrote this little novel in a state of happiness mixed with nostalgia' and as a 'double farewell' to Bowles and Morocco.[10] Some of Rey Rosa's novels return to Morocco: *La orilla africana*, his novel fully set in Tangier and penned in the Hotel Atlas (Gray 2013: 144); *El cojo bueno* (*The Good Cripple*, 1996, translated into English in 2004), set in Guatemala and Morocco; and *Severina* (2011), set in Guatemala City, featuring a Moroccan bookseller and a thief who steals *The Thousand and One Nights* and an anthology of Berber tales from a bookstore. Though *La orilla africana* is set in Tangier, Rey Rosa has maintained in interviews that where he writes does not matter to him (Gray 2007: 161). He notes his recreation of Tangier in *La orilla africana*:

> I dared to write the book when I realized that the Tangier that Bowles had written about – or better yet, created – had changed so much that it was no longer the same city. . . . When I started writing the novella, I could sense that I would never live in Morocco again. The book became a sort of farewell. But I never thought of Tangier as a home. I've never been at peace at home – but in Tangier I often was. (Goldman 2013: 74)

La orilla africana brings into focus contact between Guatemala and Morocco, or Latin America, Africa and Europe, where tensions, difference and the legacy of colonialism abound. Rey Rosa recounts:

> It was winter and the heating in the Atlas never worked properly, so that when I was invited to spend the rest of my stay in a big 19th-century European house with large gardens in Monte Viejo, and with views of the cliffs that span both pillars of Hercules and the city of Tarifa set into the Spanish coast, I counted myself the luckiest Guatemalan in all Africa. (Gray 2013: 144)

His commentary captures the confluence of European, Arab and African cultures in which a Guatemalan found himself, creating further Latin American ties to Africa.

La orilla africana tells the double story of a Colombian tourist, stranded in Tangier when he loses his passport, and an adolescent Moroccan shepherd, Hamsa, who wishes to migrate to Spain, seemingly separate but interconnected through an enigmatic owl. Hamsa is recruited by his uncle Jalid who lives in Spain to watch the coast at night for smugglers and thus wishes to wear an amulet made from an owl's eyes to fight off sleep. The Colombian tourist, unnamed for most of the novel, prolongs his holiday in Tangier, where he buys kif, purchases an injured owl from the market, and courts a young French archaeology student, Julie Bachelier. The owl is stolen by Hamsa from the Frenchwoman Madame Choiseul's house where Hamsa's grandparents work as domestic servants and the Colombian tourist is a guest. When the Colombian accepts the Moroccan guide Rashid's proposition to cash betting cards in Mellila for a commission and, with a new passport, crosses the Strait of Gibraltar into Spain, he purchases a ticket to flee to Malaga. He is accosted by a Moroccan, a doppelgänger, who has followed him to Spain, demands his passport and ticket, and declares that his name is Ángel Tejedor (literally, 'weaver', and, as it happens, the Colombian's own name). By the novel's end, the owl is cured, accidentally set free when Julie visits Hamsa in Tangier to bring him news of his uncle's arrest, and takes flight.

Rey Rosa brings together Guatemala (Colombia in the novel) and Morocco and thus explores parallels between Latin America and North Africa in *La orilla africana.* Drawing comparisons between Colombia and Morocco, he writes with an awareness of the polarity between Morocco's arid landscape and Guatemala's 'tropical exuberance' (Goldman 2013: 75). Though Rey Rosa has travelled to New York, Morocco and India, Guatemala pervades his novels.[11] Guatemala casts a long shadow on Morocco, which seethes with violence among Moroccans, Colombians and Europeans in *La orilla africana.* Violence is a central theme in Rey Rosa's novels.[12] *El cojo bueno*, a novel in which a Guatemalan is abducted for ransom, his foot amputated and sent to his father, which Rey Rosa began at the Hotel Atlas in Tangier,[13] was inspired by reports of violence in Guatemala. Rey Rosa captures the violence that radiates from the border between Africa and Europe – the Strait of Gibraltar in which Africans perish as they cross into Europe. A restrained violence – or what he calls 'interior violence'[14] – seeps into the novel, most clearly in Hamsa's final proposition to Julie in exchange for the owl he has stolen and the encounter between the Colombian tourist and his assailant in Spain. Throughout *La orilla africana*, juxtapositions and comparisons between drugs, crime and violence in Morocco and Colombia abound: the Colombian concedes to a Moroccan cab driver that Colombia is 'Más o menos como aquí' (107) ('More or less like here' (88)) or 'Horrible, entonces' (107) ('Horrible, in other words' (88)).[15] Other parallels are drawn between the curtailment of freedom in Chile and Morocco, for example, when Madame Choiseul's dinner guests, a Moroccan and a Frenchwoman, discuss 'del estado del país, de las posibilidades de cambios, del destino de Pinochet y del parecido y las diferencias entre éste y el Sultán' (94) ('the situation of Morocco, the possibilities for change, the fate of Pinochet, and the similarities and differences between Pinochet and the Sultan' (76)).

Implicit in *La orilla africana* is the parallel relationship between Latin America and Morocco vis-à-vis Iberian colonisation. When the Colombian passes through the medina, street names become bearers of a common Iberian past in Morocco: 'Bajó por una calle antes llamada Velázquez y ahora con nombre árabe' (43) ('Turning down a street formerly called Velázquez but that now had an Arab name' (31)). Aware of a legacy of Spanish colonialism, the Colombian, who on occasion is mistaken for a European, and is often taken for an Arab, passes through Tangier.

Tangier revives conceptions of the East in Orientalist literature. In *La orilla africana*, Tangier is characterised by corruption, smuggling, prostitution, repression and shanty towns. The topography and culture of Tangier mirror its cultural syncretism and colonial history: the city is home to Europeans, Muslims, provincial Moroccans, Africans (who come there to cross the Strait of Gibraltar) and the Colombian. Rey Rosa has observed that Tangerines are 'polyglots',[16] whose languages recall an ethnically and culturally mixed heritage. Moreover, the city sets the stage for further encounters and tensions among Europeans, Moroccans and Colombians. Scenes evoke common stereotypes of poverty in the Maghreb: 'mientras varios niños pordioseros revoloteaban entre ellos, y besaban sus manos o las mangas o faldas de sus camisas' (75) ('Several begging children circled among the tourists, kissing their hands, their sleeves and the folds of their shirts' (58)). In one of her faxes, the Colombian's wife reports what his uncle thinks of Tangier: 'Dice que todo el mundo sabe que es una de las capitales de la perdición' (131) ('He says everyone knows it's one of the sin capitals of the world' (111)). Tangier, a labyrinthine Mediterranean city, looks 'Asian' (43), replete with European stores and American food chains. It is not only the locus of Arab, Portuguese, French and Spanish influences (Ortiz Wallner 2012: 246), but also where the Latin American traveller is distanced from the Moroccan Other.

La orilla africana captures Moroccan-Colombian interactions, drawing us into how Colombians and Moroccans read (or misread) each other. While Rey Rosa offers the Colombian tourist's conceptions of Morocco and Moroccans, he also offers Moroccans' perceptions of foreigners. For Hamsa, foreigners are the Other, a perspective rooted in the encounter between the Islamic world and Europe. The way that Hamsa sees the Colombian tourist at Madame Choiseul's house highlights resemblance and difference between the Colombian and Moroccans: 'Ahora un hombre, que podia ser un magrebí pero que, a juzgar por la ropa y el andar, debía de ser un europeo' (27) ('Now a man, who could have been Moroccan but who, judging by his clothes and way of walking, must have been European' (17)). Likewise, a local cab driver mistakes the Colombian for a Moroccan, Tunisian or Egyptian. Though he may pass for a local, his status of foreigner likens him to the colonial European. The guide Rashid holds stereotypes of the tourist and exploits him, conflating Colombians with Europeans. This is confirmed by the 'tourist-traveller' ('el turista-viajero'), who recalls the travellers to the Orient and moves seamlessly between the European residences in Monte Viejo, Sidi Mesmudi, and the environs of Tangier and the Arab medina. Attracted to Tangier, drawn to sensuality and drugs but distant from the culture, the Colombian tourist maintains the pose of foreigner or cosmopolitan in an exotic city. When he is stranded in Tangier, his thoughts of a Moroccan future in which he would learn Arabic, become a Muslim and 'Compraría una esposa bereber' (81) ('buy a Berber wife' (64)) betray a commodification and exoticisation of the Orient. On one occasion, when Madame Choiseul notes that he has a 'cara de marroquí' (89) ('Morrocan face' (72)), the Colombian admits that he would not like to be a Moroccan, nor does he like being Colombian.

Julie observes that 'habría sido mejor nacer europeo' (90) ('it would be better to have been born European' (72)), with a colonial acknowledgement of superiority to both Moroccans and Colombians.

The Colombian's contact with Moroccans is characterised by distance and otherness: 'Frente a él, las cabezas marroquíes pasaban por la plaza y parecían multiplicarse. . . . Ojos que recordaban otros ojos, pero en caras diferentes' (49) ('In front of him, Moroccan heads passed by, then seemed to multiply. . . . Eyes that reminded him of other eyes, but in different faces' (34–5)). The Colombian does not attempt to read the Other, but notes the multitudes in passing, with 'heads' and 'eyes' a synecdoche for Moroccans. His contact with Hamsa is cursory, and he shows no understanding of the young Moroccan shepherd. All cultural encounters converge on the moment in which the Colombian tourist, whose anonymity has hitherto been preserved, encounters Rashid's partner who has followed him to Spain. The encounter epitomises mutual distrust, an 'elemental struggle' and the instinct 'que el otro neceitaba matarlo para convertirse efectivamente en él' (145) ('that he [his assailant] had to kill him if he was going to become him [the Colombian]' (125)). The encounter uncovers the name of the Colombian and sets the Moroccan as his 'other' (García 2009: 31) and double.

Ottmar Ette notes the triangulation of Colombia-Morocco-France in the novel and its implications for literature in general:

> Africa, Europe, and America, or accordingly, Morocco, France, and Colombia, are so interwoven with one another that the transcontinental and transnational dimension in Moroccan Tangier creates a translocal microcosm, so to speak, upon which is superimposed, in a concentrated form, the long history of Spanish and Portuguese, English and French colonialism. (2016: 47)

As Ette observes, Rey Rosa is 'intimately familiar' with the locales of *La orilla africana*, the transnational Central American novel, and the cultural translation in the 'insular world of Tangier' (2016: 47–8). The cultural encounters in Tangier and the Central American novel further enmesh cultures and languages, creating a transcontinental literature and literary ties between Latin America and North Africa.

La orilla africana centres on the enigma and exchange of an owl

– mystical, magical, but also sinister – that characterises these Colombian-Moroccan cultural encounters. Paul Bowles described Rey Rosa in his creative writing workshop as 'a Guatemalan, who wrote in Spanish' and invented 'situations which were generally sinister' (Gray 2013: 140). The owl brings together the characters and intersects the plotlines through interactions that converge on its possession. It stands for a complex system of exchange, sale, purchase and resale where the forms of transfer are subject to cultural mistranslation.[17] It also offers a set of cultural referents – superstition, bad luck, magic and ancient knowledge. Purchased by the Colombian and stolen by the Moroccan, a curiosity for the tourist and talismanic for Hamsa, the owl sees both. The owl splits and brings Ángel and Hamsa together. In the section 'Los ojos de la lechuza' ('The Owl's Eyes'), the owl inspects the Colombian with curiosity. In the end, the novel refocuses attention on the talismanic owl, 'coveted by both sides – Christian and Muslim' and 'through whose eyes and ears we sometimes see and hear the world, both sides of it', the translator Jeffrey Gray notes (2013: 143), echoing the eyes the Colombian blindly passes in Tangier. Only the enigmatic owl sees both sides in the novel – Colombian and Moroccan – and is sought by both, though they misread each other. Hamsa and the Colombian rarely come into contact in *La orilla africana* and their plotlines are almost separate. The novel ends with the owl's flight over the cliff overlooking the Strait of Gibraltar, 'between cultures and continents', and beyond African and European shores (Gray 2013: 146).

'La orilla africana' refers to 'the African side' of the Strait of Gibraltar rather than the European shore, or Spain (Gray 2013: 142). The novel's special emphasis is thus on Africa in Latin American-North African encounters. As Ortiz Wallner has noted, *La orilla africana* enfolds not only the European shore of Africa but also the border of the Islamic world and thus can be interpreted as another shore for Central America (2012: 254). Ortiz Wallner, describing Rey Rosa as 'the most universal and cosmopolitan of contemporary Guatemalan writers', notes that 'the presence of diverse settings serves to relativize borders, be these national, regional, or continental' (2013: 137). *La orilla africana* circumvents national, cultural and continental borders and renews contact among European, African and Latin American cultures in Central American literature.

More recently, Rey Rosa has extended the routes from Guatemala to Tangier further in *Fábula asiática* (2016; translated into English as *Chaos, A Fable* in 2019). Rey Rosa returned to Tangier in 2015 and produced a new novel set in Morocco. *Fábula asiática* is steeped in the violence of 1980s Guatemala and the twenty-first century more broadly. In *Fábula asiática*, a Mexican writer, Rubiorosa (whose name echoes 'Rey Rosa'), attends a book fair in Tangier where he looks for an old Moroccan acquaintance, Mohammed Zhrouni. The Mexican is drawn into the adventures of his Moroccan friend's son, Abdelkrim, that take him from Tangier to Istanbul, which creates further routes between Latin America and the Middle East.[18] The Mexican knows well the 'laberíntica medina' (13) ('labyrinthine medina' (3)).[19] Paul Bowles and Moroccan writer Mohammed Mrabet make an appearance in the novel.

Fábula asiática, clearly a post-9/11 fable that takes us to Tangier and Istanbul, is rife with stereotypes of Jihadists in the Middle East and the Syrian Civil War. The novel spins from Abu Ghraib to Guantanamo, from Syria and Iraq to a Central American jail. Like *La orilla africana*, *Fábula asiática* is sprinkled with unobtrusive Moroccan Darija, Spanish and French in a simulacrum of intertwined cultures. When the Mexican is smuggled from Tangier to Istanbul, Rey Rosa invites us to read Istanbul thus in an echo of *La orilla africana*: 'Estaban en la orilla asiática' (183) ('He was standing now on the Asian shore' (179)). In a hall-of-mirrors, Borges recites from 'The Aleph': 'la cadencia, el acento porteño. Era un fragmento (sin duda deformado) de "El Aleph"' (192) ('the cadence and the Buenos Aires accent – a fragment (albeit distorted) of "The Aleph"' (189)). Borges recites: '"Vi en un gabinete de Alkmaar un globo terráqueo entre dos espejos que lo multiplicaban . . ."' (192) ('"I saw in a study of Alkmaar a globe of the world placed between two mirrors that multiplied it endlessly . . ."' (189)). The event transports us to the cellar in Borges's 'El Aleph', which holds the totality of the world. The Aleph in Borges's story, 'el lugar donde están . . . todos los lugares del orbe, vistos desde todos los ángulos' (338) ('the place where . . . all the places of the world, seen from every angle, coexist' (281)), is mirrored in *Fábula asiática*, where events in the Americas, Africa and Asia coexist.[20] Like the Aleph, *Fábula asiática* mirrors the totality of the world. Erasing borders between

Latin America, Africa and Asia, the novel is oriented towards Central America's Asian shore.

'Another Mexico'

Alberto Ruy Sánchez (b. 1951) – Mexican novelist, critic, editor and founder of the premier Latin American arts magazine *Artes de México* – sets his novels in Morocco and mirrors Arab culture in his *Quinteto de Mogador* (Mogador quintet). When he undertook a trip to Morocco in 1975, he discovered Mogador, the ancient name of Essaouira on the Atlantic coast of Morocco, which inspired his quintet. His novel *En los labios del agua* features a Mexican of Arab origin – a heritage that Ruy Sánchez reworks in his novels. By his account, he was enamoured of the Arab world and read the novels of Paul Bowles (1997: 63). At a Moroccan oasis, in a library of ancient manuscripts, following Morocco's Green March toward the Western Sahara and occupation of the Atlantic coast when tensions mounted with Algeria over the Algerian-Moroccan border, he fervently wished to read Arabic's 'whirling calligraphy' (1997: 64).

In 'The Nine Gifts that Morocco Gave Me', Ruy Sánchez observes that Mogador, a Moroccan port on the Atlantic coast and an entrance to the Sahara Desert, is characterised by a mixed culture – Jewish, Muslim, Berber and Arab (2006: 261). The colonial history of the city of Mogador includes a period of Portuguese rule in the sixteenth century and Essaouira is the pre-colonial name that was reclaimed in 1953. Mogador, an emblem of cultural syncretism for Ruy Sánchez, focuses attention on the Iberian colonisation of Morocco in his novels. Like Tangier in *La orilla africana*, Mogador in Ruy Sánchez's novels, a port that links South and North Africa with Europe (Ruy Sánchez 2006: 261), is central to his themes and connects Morocco to Mexico. Mogador highlights a parallel relationship, with Spanish settler colonialism in Mexico and the Portuguese colonisation of Morocco. Attracted to Morocco, Ruy Sánchez writes:

> But why does a Mexican feel compelled to write about Morocco? . . . What Morocco gave me is much more than an interesting location for my stories, as some people tend to believe. And certainly not a northern fascination for the exotic south, described by Edward Said as Orientalism.

> I come from another south, and that changes everything, allowing me to develop the theory of a possible south-south relationship which I ironically term 'Horizontal Orientalism.' (2006: 261–2)

His 'horizontal Orientalism' rests on understanding, rather than alterity and colonial conquest, as a writer from another South. In *The Mexican Mahjar*, Camila Pastor examines the Arab Orient in Mexico 'since the Spanish-Amerindian colonial encounter in 1525', with 'Spanish conquerors' descriptions of Tenochtitlan, Mexico's Aztec capital, as bristling with mosques' and Spaniards' descriptions of 'Yucatán marriage habits as Moorish' (2017: 213). She argues that conceptions of the Arab Orient in Mexico 'are in dialogue with but not merely derivative of Euro-American production on the Orient' (2017: 213). Ruy Sánchez's 'horizontal Orientalism' shows a relationship of affinity that is nonetheless expressed through the Orientalised treatment of an Arab woman in his novel.

On his trip to Essaouira, Ruy Sánchez encountered a culture that was different yet so familiar that Morocco appeared to be 'another Mexico' (2006: 262). Moroccans, too, felt the same when they arrived in Mexico, a sentiment which he attributes to a shared legacy: 'Our legacy derives from five centuries of mixing Indian and Spanish blood, but we must not overlook the Arabic heritage running through our veins, introduced by the Spaniards' (2006: 262). In 'The Nine Gifts that Morocco Gave Me', Ruy Sánchez traces a common legacy to the Arab presence in the Iberian Peninsula and suggests that Mexicans are descended from Berbers in North Africa and Moorish ancestry through contact with Spain, a heritage that can be found in his Mexican *mestizaje* (2006: 264). Arabic in the Spanish language and Arab culture travelled to the Americas through language, *mestizaje* and craftsmanship (pottery and textiles), and, for him, Morocco and Mexico are descended from Andalusian Spain (2006: 266). His discovery of Morocco through 'the walled city of Essaouira-Mogador' (2006: 268) uncovered parallels with Mexico, that Morocco and Mexico share a common cultural heritage through Spain.[21] In rethinking links between Mexico and Morocco, he draws upon the history of the *convivencia* and the Spanish conquest of the Americas. Not only does Ruy

Sánchez draw parallels between the Spanish conquest of Latin America and Morocco's Iberian colonial history, but he also traces his Moorish and Mexican *mestizaje*.

Mexico and Morocco are intimately intertwined in Ruy Sánchez's evocation of Arab characters in a Moroccan setting. He traces this interconnection to the cultural and historical proximity of Mexico and Morocco, connected by al-Andalus. In 'Writing on the Body's Frontiers', he notes: 'In Morocco, I discovered a cultural territory that borders on my own; an alternate Mexico separated by many seas' (2000: 68). For him, Mexico and Morocco are descended from an Arab-Andalusian heritage. He maintains that he expresses no exoticism (2000: 65) in his novels. Like Rey Rosa, implicit in his endeavour is that literature has no borders. Moreover, he focuses on a shared culture beyond Europe and a form of Orientalism 'that is not only clearly horizontal but that flows in two directions' (2000: 69). As he further notes in 'Writing on the Body's Frontiers', 'If the word Maghreb means "west," and Morocco thus constitutes the Far West of the East, then Mexico is also the Far West of its own continent' (2000: 69). He suggests that Mexicans are descended from Arab Andalusian immigrants to America instead of Spanish and indigenous Mexicans, a relationship that underpins the Arab Latin American ties in his novels.

The novels of Ruy Sánchez are immersed in Arab-Islamic culture, which is reworked in Latin American literature, as well as the connections among Andalusian literature, Moorish culture and the landscape of Mexico and Morocco. Intimate ties are framed in the notion of 'horizontal Orientalism' that he has adopted to explain the South-South relationship of Mexico to Morocco and which also recalls Kushigian's attention to Hispanic Orientalism's dialogue with the Orient.

Los nombres del aire focuses on a young Moroccan woman's desire in the ancient walled city of Mogador.[22] The novel opens with Fatma at her window, protected by a lattice-work screen, gazing at the sea. Her grandmother Aisha, versed in the art of reading cards, interprets the signs of Fatma's desire and reads her fate. Fatma, enigmatic and secluded in Mogador, is possessed by desire. Her melancholy and solitude grow and she seems absent so that when the inhabitants of Mogador speak of her, 'no decían "allá está", sino "allá parece que está"' (41) ('they wouldn't say "there she is", but rather, "it seems as if she's there"' (30)).[23] Rumours of Fatma's affliction begin to circulate in Mogador. A young scholar who frequents the local school of the Koran becomes besotted by her as he passes by her house. When he is met by indifference, he seeks out a forbidden book, Ibn Hazm's *The Ring of the Dove*, a treatise on love and lovers, and peruses the chapter on the signs of love. Subsequently, he composes poetry, languishes in a public plaza, writes heretical books, and is executed. Desired by a scholar, a fishmonger and a fisherman, Fatma repulses her suitors and desires Kadiya, the woman she chances upon in the public bath who was abducted from her nomad tribe and sold to the owner of a floating brothel. Thereafter, Kadiya eludes her and an elder unspools her tale in the plaza. Ironically, Fatma is unaware that the woman in the story is Kadiya whom she has known in the bathhouse.

The cover of *Mogador: The Names of the Air* describes the Arab Latin American interactions in the novel through a 'fusion of Latin American magical realism with Arabic geometric and mystical imagery'. Evocations of Fatma's budding sensuality intimately capture her desire in a manner that evokes the cultural milieu of Essaouira and the literary aesthetics of Latin American literature. *Los nombres del aire* abounds with Orientalist evocations of an Arab woman's desire. López Baralt reads the opening scene of Fatma in a manner that recalls nineteenth-century French Orientalism. Framed in a wooden lattice window, Fatma appears to be the subject of an Orientalist painting (López Baralt 1988: 59). Her appearance is evocative of odalisques who languish in an enclosed harem in French Orientalist painter Eugène Delacroix's painting *Femmes d'Alger dans leur appartement* (Women of Algiers in their Apartment). At the same time, the novel extends beyond the Orientalised woman towards an interconnected Mexican and Moroccan heritage.

Mogador, the colonial name of Essaouira, evokes the Portuguese colonisation of Morocco. However, Morocco's Iberian history is eclipsed by the emphasis on Orientalist evocations of Arab-Islamic culture. Morocco uncovers the shared heritage Ruy Sánchez proclaims,[24] though he is of no Moroccan origin. Arab-Islamic origins can be traced to the *convivencia* and Spanish conquest of the Americas. Among the conquistadors in the

Americas from the Iberian Peninsula were Moriscos and *conversos* who fled Spain and came with Columbus to the New World (Lahrech 1998). Ruy Sánchez invokes an Andalusian heritage in Latin America. For Ruy Sánchez, Mexico inherited the ethnic and cultural mixing that characterised al-Andalus. He recovers Mexico in Mogador, and Morocco offers him an understanding of Mexican culture and his *mestizaje* (2006: 272). Like Tangier in Rey Rosa's *La orilla africana*, Mogador connects both sides of the Atlantic. Ruy Sánchez evokes Mogador, the port, and public bath (*hammam*) in the novel. The walled city-port of Mogador is described as a labyrinth of markets and bathhouses:

> la calle principal, La Vía o calle Del Caracol, que dando giros lleva de las murallas que rodean toda la isla a la plaza central, donde están los baños públicos y los tres templos de las religions que conviven en ese Puerto. La ciudad, para la gente de Mogador, era imagen del mundo: un mapa de la vida tanto externa como spiritual de los hombres. (17–18)

> ([T]he principal street, The Way or Street of the Snail, which leads by twists and turns from the walls that surround the island to the central plaza, home to the public baths and to the three temples of the three religions that cohabit the port city. To the people of Mogador, the city was an image of the world: a map of the external, as well as the spiritual, life of men.) (14)

Evocations of Mogador capture a *convivencia*, or coexistence, of the three religions that harkens back to the Iberian Peninsula rather than colonial history.

Ruy Sánchez interpolates medieval Arabic literature by the Córdoban littérateur, jurist and theologian Ibn Hazm (Ibn Ḥazm) and Sufi mystic Ibn Arabi (Ibn ʿArabī) into his evocations of Mogador and Fatma's desire. Ruy Sánchez's discovery of classical Arabic literature is central to the themes of *Los nombres del aire*. The novel was inspired by Ibn Hazm's *Ṭawq al-ḥamāma fī al-ulfa wa al-ullāf* (*The Ring of the Dove: A Treatise on the Art and Practice of Arab Love*). Ibn Hazm's love treatise is central to Ruy Sánchez's exploration of the signs of love and intensity of desire (Lahrech 1998). The young scholar of the Qur'an, 'sarraceno de corazón'

(30) ('a Saracen at heart' (18)), besotted by Fatma, looks through the Qur'an for signs to interpret her behaviour. One day he enters the library and opens the case of 'forbidden books':

> Ya había oído hablar del tratado sobre el amor y los amantes de Ibn Hazm, y cuando lo tuvo en las manos fue directamente hacia el capítulo sobre *Las señas del amor hechas con los ojos*. 'Los ojos hacen a menudo las veces de mensajeros y con ellos se da a entender lo que se quiere. Si los otros cuatro sentidos son puertas que conducen al corazón y son ventanas hacia el alma, la vista es entre todos el más sutil y el de más eficaces resultados. Con la mirada se aleja y se atrae, se promete y se amenaza, se reprende y se da aliento, se ordena y se veda.' (30)

> (He had already heard mention of the treatise on love and lovers by Ibn Hazm, and holding it in his hands, he went straight to the chapter on *The signs of love made with the eyes*. 'The eyes often play the role of messengers and thus convey what is desired. If the other four senses are doors that lead to the heart and windows that open onto the soul, sight is, of all the senses, the most subtle and offers the most effective results. The gaze repels and attracts, promises and threatens, reprimands and offers encouragement, commands and forbids.') (18–19)

The young scholar senses that Ibn Hazm's treatise holds the key to Fatma's gestures. In *Ṭawq al-ḥamāma*, Ibn Hazm observes the signs of love of which the first is the gaze: he parses the variety of the signs of love, remarking upon the lover's brooding gaze, his affectation of disinterest, his rapt attention, his desire to be in the beloved's company, the confusion and excitement upon the beloved's sudden appearance, or agitation on beholding someone who resembles his beloved or on hearing his beloved's name. Instead, the narrator comments on the signs of Fatma's desire, and notes that they could have formed a poetic inventory of the signs of love interpreted by Ibn Hazm. The scholar, while reading the forbidden books, 'descubría una tradición muy arraigada en la literatura arabigoandaluza, la tradición del *adab*: del tratado que es a la vez una narración y un poema, generalmente vividos, en gran parte, por el autor' (32) ('would discover a deeply-rooted tradition in Arabic-Andalusian literature, the tradition of . . .

adab [literature], the treatise that is at once a narrative and a poem, usually based in large part on the personal experience of the author' (20–1)). Ruy Sánchez, and the narrator, presumably Mexican and conversant with Moroccan culture, draw upon an Arabic tradition of *adab*, literature and prose encompassing comportment and eloquence. In a similar vein, Ruy Sánchez draws upon the Sufi mystic Ibn Arabi in 'the nine fundamental steps' Fatma takes to master the silence of the nine senses and thus open herself to the world.

The evocation of love and desire in magical and ancient Mogador, exotic and hermetically sealed, creates an exoticism that characterises Orientalist literature, especially through the male and foreign gaze directed at Moroccan women and Fatma in particular, not only within the prohibited domestic space of women but also within the intimate quarters of the public baths. Ruy Sánchez recreates Mogador, 'the imaginary city of desire', in his novels. The narrator (foreign male) intimately describes the ritual of the *hammam* and women's sexual initiation, dreams and desires when he could not have been admitted into the sacred, enclosed quarters. His exoticisation of the Arab woman omits the male gaze of the European colonial so common in European Orientalist literature. Like Delacroix, he passes through and represents the sacred space of Arab women. In 'Writing on the Body's Frontiers', Ruy Sánchez notes that he employs the complex geometry of Morocco's architecture to create a structure that evokes desire: 'With their marvelous architecture of the initiation into desire, the Arabic public baths, the *Hammam*, become a symbol for Fatma's own initiation in *Los nombres del aire*' (2000: 71). The narrator violates the sanctity of the public bath frequented by the women of Mogador and Fatma where she encounters Kadiya, a mysterious woman: 'Lo que afuera es ilícito, dentro del hammam es tan inconsistente como una fruta cuya cascara se diluye en el aire' (49) ('What is illicit outside is, inside the Hammam, as unsubstantial as a fruit whose peel dissolves in the air' (38)). He enters 'las salas prohibidas del hammam' (68) ('the forbidden rooms of the Hammam' (56)) to describe women's desires. In the section 'Los nombres' ('The Names'), the narrator evokes the forbidden and interrupted desires of the inhabitants of Mogador: the secluded and sensual Fatma who encounters Kadiya in the public baths; Amjrus, the corpulent auctioneer in the fish market who desires Fatma; Mohammed, a fisherman who courts Fatma and attempts to interpret her gestures and melancholic gaze; Kadiya, a woman of 'nocturnal transactions' (89) who, desired by Fatma, eludes her. There are no Mexican-Moroccan encounters in the novel. Rather, the Mexican novel centres on a Moroccan woman and Morocco. Clearly, Ruy Sánchez's evocations of an Arab woman's desire and illicit love, the private quarters of the public bath, and a garden in the desert are in keeping with a tradition of Orientalism. Mogador is a fictional space of sensuality and exoticism. Mexican and Arab motifs – the magical and the mystical – are interwoven in the novel, creating an interconnection between Mexico and Morocco vis-à-vis Spain. An Iberian colonial history and common Arab heritage are highlighted by the ancient name of Mogador.

'Another Shore'

Together, Rey Rosa's *La orilla africana* and Ruy Sánchez's *Los nombres del aire* refocus on Morocco: Rey Rosa is aware that all his novels, set in Guatemala and Morocco, are exotic; Ruy Sánchez approaches Morocco through a shared Arab heritage. Both novels further contact and exchange between Latin America and North Africa through the connections that are unique to the novels of Rey Rosa and Ruy Sánchez. In *La orilla africana*, centre and periphery converge in the owl which circles beyond Africa and Europe (García 2009: 42). In *Los nombres del aire*, Ruy Sánchez's Orientalist evocation of Fatma's desire and sensuality exoticises Morocco and Moroccan women. While the violence of Rey Rosa's novels permeates encounters between cultures in *La orilla africana*, desire pervades Ruy Sánchez's evocation of Morocco.

Unlike Rey Rosa who highlights violence and exoticism through tensions and mistranslations in cultural encounters, Ruy Sánchez reworks the Orient from a shared heritage between Mexico and Morocco. Rey Rosa and Ruy Sánchez portray new itineraries of Central American and Mexican authors who travelled to Morocco and recreated relations between Latin America and North Africa. Rey Rosa looks beyond the dichotomies structuring his novel. On the other hand, Ruy Sánchez's understanding of Orientalism, exoticisation of Arab women and Morocco, and his knowledge of Arabic literature, the ancient manuscripts he wished to learn Arabic to read, intertwine Moroccan and Mexican cultures. Both focus attention on South-South connections and horizontal Orientalism in novels that are concerned with intercultural, albeit Orientalist, contact.

Rey Rosa's and Ruy Sánchez's novels focus on direct exchanges and a parallel relationship between Morocco and Latin America vis-à-vis Iberian colonisation. Whereas Latin America's and Morocco's parallel relationship to Spain is central in *La orilla Africana*, the Portuguese colonisation of Mogador is obscured by the novel's exoticisation of an Arab woman. Ruy Sánchez's novel shows the differences between a Colombian or Argentine writer of European descent and a Mexican writer of *mestizo* and *mulatto* origins. His *mestizaje* raises the relationship between Latin America, the Occident and whiteness that Rey Rosa also raises in his novel. The relationship of Latin America and Morocco to Iberian colonisation is central to a further understanding of the connections he makes between Mexicans and Moroccans. While Tangier and Mogador are exoticised, the novels purport to extend beyond exoticism and explore a South-South relationship. Rey Rosa calls attention to connections between Latin America and North Africa vis-à-vis Spain, and Ruy Sánchez recovers cultural relations between Mexico and Morocco that he attributes to an Iberian-Arab heritage. Direct contact between Latin America and the Arab world in Arabic will be discussed in the next chapter.

3

Children of Scheherazade: Gabriel García Márquez in Arabic

I wrote like a blind man.

Elias Khoury, 'Elias Khoury, the Art of Fiction'

Comparative studies of twentieth-century Latin American and Arabic literatures have long been dominated by attention to the reception of *The Thousand and One Nights* in Latin America and its influences on Latin American writers such as Jorge Luis Borges and Gabriel García Márquez. However, there are other connections between the two literatures: a long history of migration from the Levant to Latin America; the presence of the Orient in Latin American literature; and the translation, reception and influence of Latin American literature in the Arab world. One influence of Latin American literature in the Arab world can be found in adaptations of magical realism, a style popularised by the novels of the Latin American Boom in the 1960s. Comparative work on Latin American and Arabic literatures offers a rich area of exploration and new frameworks, especially ones that extend beyond conventional literary comparisons.[1] These new comparisons turn the focus from the more common attention to examinations of colonial relations in world literature, which have commonly focused on literatures of the East and the West rather than comparative frameworks for literatures of the global South.

Egyptian novelist Naguib Mahfouz (1911–2006) read *Cien años de soledad* by Colombian writer Gabriel García Márquez (1927–2014) before the publication of his novel *Layālī alf layla*.[2] In *Najīb Maḥfūẓ yatadhakkar* (Naguib Mahfouz Remembers), Mahfouz notes in a conversation with the

Egyptian writer Gamal al-Ghitani (Jamāl al-Ghīṭānī) that he read García Márquez's *Cien años de soledad* in 1980 – two years before the appearance of *Layālī alf layla*: 'This year I read *Cien años de soledad* by García Márquez. If you had not loaned it to me, I would not have read it . . . and note that García Márquez is from Colombia – Latin America' (al-Ghitani 1987: 92).[3] In addition to confirming his reading of *Cien años de soledad* (which he would not have read if a member of the younger generation of Egyptian writers had not brought the novel to his attention), he alludes to García Márquez's national origin and continent, which implicitly expresses a fellowship with García Márquez as a Colombian writer from the global South. Furthermore, his allusion suggests that his appreciation of and identification with García Márquez rest on shared concerns and global networks. This explains the relationship to García Márquez, which is central to Mahfouz's reworking of magical realism and his creation of an antecedent of the genre in Arabic literature.

Looking at two pairs of novels, this chapter will explore relationships to García Márquez in Arabic. A comparative reading of two sets of novels of the second half of the twentieth century, García Márquez's *Cien años de soledad* (*One Hundred Years of Solitude*, 1967) and Mahfouz's *Layālī alf layla* (*Arabian Nights and Days*, 1982), and Lebanese novelist Elias Khoury's *Majma' al-asrār* (*The Assembly of Secrets*, 1994) and García Márquez's *Crónica de una muerte anunciada*, illustrates connections between Latin American and Arabic literatures. Mahfouz's *Layālī alf layla*, a novel that offers a modern Arab adaptation of *The Thousand and One Nights*, reworks the style of magical realism popularised by García Márquez in his masterwork *Cien años de soledad*. Examining Mahfouz's inspiration by García Márquez's magical realism reveals a connection between two world literatures that reflects the importance of other, non-Western literatures to Arab writers. A reading of Mahfouz's novel along with García Márquez's *Cien años de soledad* and Khoury's reworking of *Crónica de una muerte anunciada* shows ways in which literary connections extend beyond common frameworks of comparison and draws deeper connections between two world literatures. I will focus on how the novels of Mahfouz and Khoury show the relationship to García Márquez and *Majma' al-asrār*'s critique of the Orientalism of *Crónica de una muerte anunciada* within post-Mahfouz Arabic novels and the Lebanese Civil War novel. In this chapter, I focus on a dialogue with García Márquez in Arabic that may not be discernible to the non-arabophone reader.

One Hundred Years in One Thousand and One Nights and Days

A comparison of *Layālī alf layla* and *Cien años de soledad* and the use of magical realism in Mahfouz's novel, as well as an examination of his departure from social realism, explore ways in which *Layālī alf layla* revises our assumptions about magical realism and that genre's relationship to politics. The ways in which *Layālī alf layla* reworks that genre's standard conventions and engages with Mikhail Bakhtin's carnivalesque offer important readings that illuminate the importance and implications of magical realism for Mahfouz. In what follows, I read Mahfouz's political context against García Márquez's chronicle, concentrating on García Márquez's mythologising of Latin American history and Mahfouz's allegory, and examining ways in which *Layālī alf layla* draws on the style of *Cien años de soledad* to reflect the world of *The Thousand and One Nights*, a path of revolution, and the need for political reform.

The novels of Naguib Mahfouz achieved the status of world literature with his reception of the Nobel Prize in 1988. In 1982 his novel *Layālī alf layla* represented a departure from the social realism characteristic of the rest of his career and his more experimental novels in the late 1950s and 1960s – *Awlād ḥāratinā* (*Children of the Alley*, 1959), his post-1967 postmodern short story collections, and later novels in the 1970s such as *Malḥamat al-ḥārafīsh* (*The Epic of the Harafish*, 1977). Among his experimental novels, *Layālī alf layla* is the novel in which he experimented with the style of magical realism that is evocative of García Márquez's *Cien años de soledad* at the same time that he revisited a medieval Arabic tradition. Edward Said has noted that Mahfouz's novels narrated 'the phases of Egyptian nationalism in the *Cairo Trilogy*, culminating in the 1952 Revolution, and did so critically and yet intimately as a participant in the remaking of Egyptian society', and his post-1967 works concerned the history of Egypt after the 1967 War (2000: 318). With the changes in Egyptian history, Mahfouz rethought the Arabic novel, and departed from European realism, moving toward more experimental literature after he had exhausted the historical, realist and modernist fiction which spans Egyptian history, not only by returning to a classical Arabic tradition but also by adapting a major global trend that developed in Latin America.

The two important writers and Nobel laureates, García Márquez and Mahfouz, produced some of the most enduring works of world literature. García Márquez is arguably the chronicler of Latin America who expressed local Latin American culture and history and deeply influenced the development of the genre of magical realism. On the other hand, following the publication of *Zuqāq al-midaqq* (*Midaq Alley*, 1947) and *al-Thulāthiyya* (*Cairo Trilogy*, 1956–57), Mahfouz dominated the Egyptian cultural scene and, after being awarded the Nobel Prize, became the most widely known Arab writer outside the Arab world. Further, the novels of García Márquez and Mahfouz are both revolutionary in style and present fictional realities in which revolutions are central: for example, García Márquez explores local insurrections and labour strikes in *Cien años de soledad* and Mahfouz, who explored the topos of revolution in his novels, depicts revolts in the alley in *Layālī alf layla*. Both align themselves with the dispossessed in the novels: García Márquez presents the exploited workers of Macondo and Mahfouz privileges the voices of the disempowered in a medieval Arab world.

Another reason for comparing two of the most important writers of the twentieth century in world literature has to do with the central role of *The Thousand and One Nights* in the two novels: García Márquez has expressed his inspiration by the collection, to which I will return, and Mahfouz reworks *The Thousand and One Nights* and is inspired by magical realism, and returns to *The Thousand and One Nights* by way of *Cien años de soledad*. Though Mahfouz revisits a medieval Arabic tradition in his adaptation of *The Thousand and One Nights*, he engages with García Márquez and a style that is strongly connected with twentieth-century Latin American literature. So far, readings of Mahfouz's novel have not considered the scope and implications of the relationship of Mahfouz to García Márquez, especially with regard to magical realism, or fully explored the reception of Latin American literature in the Arab world, where, as Said notes in 'After Mahfouz', Arabic translations of major novels by Carlos Fuentes, García Márquez and Miguel Angel Asturias appeared during the 1970s (2000: 322).

Compared to García Márquez's *Cien años de soledad*, which has been interpreted as a mythical reading of Latin America – a perspective that Gerald Martin cautions against (1987: 113) – Mahfouz's *Layālī alf layla* offers an allegory of Egyptian politics in the 1970s.[4] While García Márquez's novel has been interpreted as an expression of Latin American popular history, Mahfouz's novel, which centres on a famous fictional ruler and ends with popular rule, can be read as his critical reflections on political authority. Mahfouz adapts *The Thousand and One Nights*, which clearly inspired García Márquez's novel and magical realism, and creates an allegory of a political regime in 1970s Egypt. *Layālī alf layla* narrates an Egyptian reality through the world of *The Thousand and One Nights*, while the chronicle of Macondo offers an expansive history. Against this expansive history of García Márquez's mythical Macondo is Mahfouz's allegorical medieval alley. Therefore, García Márquez's novel mythologises or chronicles Latin American history, while Mahfouz's novel allegorises national history – and, as I argue, the difference between 'chronicle' and 'allegory' is important to understanding the concerns and contexts of the two authors, especially Mahfouz's adaptation of magical realism in his novel.

In the prologue to his novel *El reino de este mundo* (*The Kingdom of this World*, 1949), Cuban writer Alejo Carpentier introduces the term 'magical realism'. In 1943, he writes, 'I was fortunate enough to visit the kingdom of Henri Christophe' where he 'came in daily contact' with what he calls '*lo real maravilloso*' ('*the marvelous real*') (2017: xiii, xvii). Carpentier recounts that he encountered a marvellous reality in Haiti:

> After feeling the all-too-real enchantment of the land of Haiti, finding signs of magic by the sides of the red roads of the central plain, and hearing the drums of Petro and Rada, I was driven to compare this recently experienced marvelous reality with the tiresome attempts to evoke the marvelous that characterized certain European literature of the last thirty years. (2017: xiii–xiv)

Carpentier contrasts Latin America's marvellous reality to European Surrealism and traces the origins of magical realism to Latin America's landscape, indigenous and Afro-Caribbean cultures, and racial mixing (*mestizaje*): 'America *mestiza*, as José Martí called it' (1995: 89). He defines a Latin American form of magical realism whose distinct aim is to present a reality that is not governed by European logic.

Though 'magical realism' is a term that has typically defined a Latin American style characterised by the synthesis of the magical and the real, where the fantastic is commonplace and mundane, there is much criticism on the political implications of the genre. For example, Martin argues against a reading of the novel through magical realism because it collapses 'many different political perspectives, into one single, usually escapist, concept' (1987: 107). Other readings suggest the contribution of magical realism to the examination of political themes in contemporary world literature. In her observations on magical realism in *The Decline and Fall of the Lettered City*, Jean Franco draws attention to the reality against which the genre developed in Latin America in a way that suggests it restores the political contexts of novels. As a style that recuperates indigenous New World cultures, it also draws on a history of conquest and colonialism (Franco 2002: 9). Likewise, Lois Parkinson Zamora observes that magical realism has provided explicitly 'political literature' that highlights local abuses through allegory: 'The effectiveness of magical realist political dissent depends upon its . . . allegorizing of the human condition' (1995: 504). She affirms the political role of Latin American literature whose writers invent fantastic strategies for 'political purposes' (1995: 543). The use of magical realism highlights historical events in literature, which levels criticism at political regimes and challenges state-sponsored narratives. Focusing on the implications of magical realism, Wendy B. Faris further contends that the style provides the means to challenge 'repressive political regimes' (2004: 139–44), a feature that is especially central to Mahfouz's novel.

The politics of magical realism has much to do with its roots in Latin America, which has long established it as a style of the global South. A number of readings draw attention to magical realism's enlistment of indigenous cultures that set it in opposition to the rational West. Franco observes that magical realism was deployed in the service of 'Latin American specificity (but dependent on the clichéd cartography that separates "rational" Europe from the nonrational rest)' and describes it in terms of a style that was increasingly identified with Latin America (2002: 9, 160). As she observes that García Márquez draws on the popular culture of indigenous Colombian populations, she revisits the opposition between 'rational' Europe and 'the nonrational rest'. Magical realism with its valorisation of local cultures and the history of American discovery becomes a form of resistance to European influence: 'The lure of "magical realism" was that it reenchanted the world by drawing into literature popular beliefs and practices as a form of dissent from post-Enlightenment rationalism' (Franco 2002: 159). In the 1960s, she argues, magical realism, or drawing on indigenous forms, was redefined as a 'form of reenchantment, as a challenge to European cultural hegemony' (2002: 166). Because it brought into focus Latin American originality, creativity and energy, magical realism promised to liberate literature from the framework of European realism (2002: 159–60). As such, it was a celebration of Latin American cultures and a return to the history of discovery that illustrated the difference between European rationalism and the cultures of the New World. In his reading of magical realism in film, Fredric Jameson observes that magical realism is 'a kind of narrative raw material derived essentially from peasant society, drawing in sophisticated ways on the world of village or even tribal myth' (1986: 302). His observation focuses on the rediscovery of indigenous culture to explain magical realism's synthesis of the magical and the real in a way that equates magic to the rediscovery of indigenous cultures.

Criticism of magical realism has drawn a clear relationship between the style and parts of the world that have been subjected to colonialism, suggesting that magical realism appeared against a history of colonialism as postcolonial discourse (Cooper 1998: 15). Stephen Slemon specifically draws a connection between magical realism and postcolonial writing, by which he reads magical realist literature as a form of postcolonial discourse, engaged with colonial history and a legacy of 'fragmentation', and notes the prevalence of magical realism in marginal cultures, which suggests that the style incorporates a sort of 'resistance toward the imperial center' (1995: 422). Similarly, Faris contends that magical realism is concerned with examining the politics of postindependence nation-states. Focusing on the political contexts in which literature is produced, Faris locates magical realism in both the metropolitan 'first' world and the postcolonial 'third' world, exploring the ways in which the style helps to define 'other' traditions against the 'centre'. Examining realism, Faris argues that the style's challenges to the dominance of 'Western realism', associated with colonialism, enabled literatures of the formerly colonised world to appear (2004: 133). Magical realism, then, invigorated the traditions of the formerly colonised and created new literatures by drawing on indigenous cultures, which had not been influenced by European colonialism. As a style that has flourished in postcolonial cultures, it also appears to challenge and revitalise European realism. As Faris argues, 'Magical realism creates a new decolonized space for narrative, one not already occupied by the assumptions and techniques of European realism' (2004: 135). It liberates authors from discourses linked to imperialism and offers a discourse of 'plurality, of disagreement' in literature produced 'in reaction to specific repressive regimes' (2004: 144, 141). It further produces frameworks that not only read the style against European realism, or in a framework focused on European rationalism and New World re-enchantment, but also examine the connections among literatures of the global South in terms of rethinking magical realism.

There is a connection between magical realism and Bakhtin's carnivalesque that will become clearer with regard to Mahfouz's novel in a reading that is enabled by Mahfouz's adaptation of *The Thousand and One Nights*. Importantly, the irreverence of carnival provides a mode of resistance to political authority. In his observations on Dostoevsky, Bakhtin describes carnival as 'a second life outside officialdom' (1984: 5–6). Scenes of carnival and celebration are prevalent in García Márquez's novel, which poses questions about the political implications of the carnivalesque and magical realism. Carnival in *Cien años de soledad* pervades Macondo with the arrival of Melquiades and the gypsies, which is itself an introduction of modernity and the process of decline. While the carnivalesque opens García Márquez's magical realism to humour and parody, it also introduces irony and critique of excess, power and solitude. In Mahfouz's novel, however, the carnivalesque appears in scenes where the ruler's authority is challenged, rather than as the onset of decline, suggesting that it belongs to a process of change.

Magical realism is a shared style between the two authors that is reworked to different ends. As Martin observes, *Cien años de soledad* offers a reading of the myths of Latin American history in addition to being 'a metaphor for the history of the continent since Independence' (1987: 97). Clearly, the novel engages the indigenous cultures that preceded modernity and capitalism. Furthermore, if we consider *Cien años de soledad*, it evokes a sort of nostalgia as it rethinks Latin American history in the present (Wood 1998: 103), but *Layālī alf layla* is deeply critical of the present and looks toward the future. Magical realism enabled Mahfouz to create an unstable reality instead of what Edward Said has described as twentieth-century Egypt's 'fundamentally settled and integrated society throughout all the turbulence of the country's wars, revolutions, and social upheavals' (2000: 319). In *Layālī alf layla*, events in an unnamed medieval Arab city appear to be modelled on the pattern of political life in contemporary Egypt. Through the novel, Mahfouz creates an antecedent of magical realism in the Arab world whereby literature draws on local cultures and challenges the narratives of nation-states. This represents a departure from European realism, which has a number of implications for Mahfouz's novel. First, Mahfouz's reworking of an ancient Arabic tradition enabled him to publish an allegory without fear of censorship or political repression. Second, Mahfouz had exhausted the form of European realism in his pre-1960s novels and replenished his late-twentieth-century novels with a New World genre. Third, Mahfouz had discovered a growing genre of world literature that he revised with a focus on the politics of the Arab world, producing his own adaptation of magical realism.

Before examining how *Layālī alf layla* complicates the assumptions of magical realism and the carnivalesque, I will contextualise the novel in the broader history of Egypt in the 1970s when it was written. Though Mahfouz wrote *Layālī alf layla* in 1979 (Ghazoul 1996: 137), the novel appeared in 1982 in post-Sadat Egypt. The context of the novel's publication is important because it provides an understanding of the allegory at an important historical moment concerned with the change of regimes in Egypt. Indeed, Samia Mehrez has noted Mahfouz's vexed relationship with political authority – in particular, the tensions between the 'political commitment' of the writer and his 'disengagement from politics' or between the writer and the bureaucrat (1994: 18). Importantly, she has drawn attention to Mahfouz's 'increasing caution, not so much in what he writes as in how and when he circulates what he has written' (1994: 19). Publishing the novel in post-Sadat Egypt and experimenting with magical realism, then, enabled him to produce a novel with political themes that were clear to his Arab readers. Though the novel was allegorical, it was still published when he could level criticism at Anwar Sadat's rule after a change of regime. In this adaptation of *The Thousand and One Nights*, Arab readers drew many parallels between the magical reality of the novel and the political context of 1970s Egypt, which became associated with economic inequity as a result of Sadat's Open Door (*Infitāḥ*) policies, the rise of Islamic fundamentalism, and growing unemployment. It was a context in which unrest and discontent were prevalent: the 1972 student movement; the famous Bread Riots in 1977; opposition to the Egyptian-Israeli peace treaty in 1979; and the arrest of nearly 1,500 intellectuals in September 1981. *Layālī alf layla* evokes this historical context through disturbances in the medieval quarter in Mahfouz's novel, which reflects corruption, political oppression and the rise of religious fundamentalism. Through events in the alley, it becomes clear that magical realism enabled Mahfouz to recapitulate the political context of the 1970s and weave it in the extended frame story of *The Thousand and One Nights*.

Layālī alf layla is a commentary on politics which offers important insights into political reality that further appear to motivate Mahfouz's turn to magical realism rather than social realism. In an interview in a special issue of the Arabic quarterly journal *Fuṣūl: Journal of Literary Criticism* devoted to *The Thousand and One Nights*, Mahfouz describes his appropriation of *The Thousand and One Nights* in his novel as both political realism (*al-wāqi'iyya al-siyāsiyya*) and metaphysical or Sufi reflections (*al-ta'ammulāt al-mitafīzīqiyya/al-ṣufiyya*) (1994: 380). He describes his style in terms that do not refer to magical realism but rather to his own literary culture, context and philosophical background, though in an earlier conversation he had commented on his reading of *Cien años de soledad*. His admission about the 'political realism' of his novel is important in considering its political themes together with his status outside the Arab world as a writer who addressed universal themes, which complicates assumptions about his adaptation of magical realism. While Mahfouz's novels pertain to the history and context of Egypt and the Arab world, they are also valued for expressing global themes. At a lecture during the Naguib Mahfouz centennial celebrations at the American University in Cairo on 18 October 2011, the Swedish Academy member Sturé Allen emphasised the universal value of Mahfouz's novels. Clearly, Mahfouz poses themes related to humanity and Egypt's context in *Layālī alf layla*, yet, as I argue, there is ample evidence to support a reading of magical realism in the novel as an allegory for politics. Mahfouz's adaptation of *The Thousand and One Nights* and magical realism reflect the political reality on which he comments, as he focuses on Shahriyar's abuses and universalises them to present the important themes of popular rule and social justice at the end of one regime and the start of another, examining cycles of corruption in a genre that is more powerful than social realism in that context, where *Layālī alf layla* also duplicates the infinity of *The Thousand and One Nights*.

The sequencing of history is central to both *Cien años de soledad* and *Layālī alf layla* and to the distinction between 'chronicle' and 'allegory', which has to do with the radically different historical contexts within which the two novels were produced. *Cien años de soledad* chronicles one hundred years in the history of the New World mythical town of Maçondo, from its settlement by the Buendías to its decline through urbanisation, modernity and neo-colonialism. On the other hand, *Layālī alf layla* creates a modern political order in a medieval world, one that centres on tyranny, corruption and injustice in such a way that the alley's disruptions allegorise the growing unpopularity of a political regime in modern Egypt. To explain the importance of the chronicler, Franco alludes to the Latin American novel of the 1960s, which sets the author against the figure of 'the chronicler/storyteller, whose skills derive from orally transmitted culture', and further observes:

> The chronicler or storyteller belongs to what is most archaic in the culture, evoking a time when power was exercised through speech. As the unofficial historian of a predominantly oral/aural culture, the storyteller and singer of tales derive authority from knowledge of tradition, from

> inventive skills deployed with ritualistic forms, and also from the close coordination between the individual memory of the storyteller and the collective memory of the listeners. (1999: 147–8)

The effect of the chronicle in *Cien años de soledad* appears most clearly in Melquiades's manuscript, which offers a parody of the chronicles of the Renaissance and the history of the Spanish conquistadors as well as a reflection of the discovery of a paradise in the New World. In contrast, Mahfouz adapts *The Thousand and One Nights* (returning to classical Arabic literature) and rethinks Latin American magical realism to present a particular world in which Shahriyar stands for an Arab ruler, and magical events in the alley represent injustice and corruption during his rule. The effect Mahfouz produces is a parody of 1970s Egypt with allusions to historical events in the novel – where groups such as the 'Shiites' and the 'Kharijites' represent the Muslim Brotherhood and the communists in contemporary Egypt – which creates a complicit relationship with the reader (Ghazoul 1996: 139). While the founding of a Latin American town unknown to Western culture provides the reader with a chronicle in *Cien años de soledad*, the old alley in *Layālī alf layla* provides an allegory of a political regime. The effect produced in the two novels is that of a chronicle of a mythical history and an allegory of political authority – the discovery and paradise of the New World against the decay and exhaustion of the Old World.

Experimenting with magical realism and *The Thousand and One Nights*, Mahfouz Arabises magical realism in a way that provides an example of that style in Arabic literature, reflecting a relationship to Latin American literature, yet constantly calls attention to its own Arab traditions and contexts through *The Thousand and One Nights* characters and allusions to Arab regimes. Mahfouz draws on both Latin American literature and *The Thousand and One Nights*, but contextualises events in the Arab world. By contextualising *Layālī alf layla* in a medieval political world, Mahfouz highlights local abuses in ways that not only level criticism at a particular regime but also look toward political change in Egypt.

Children of Scheherazade

In his memoir *Vivir para contarla* (*Living to Tell the Tale*, 2002), García Márquez alludes to the influence of *The Thousand and One Nights* on the narrative voice in *Cien años de soledad*:

> Hasta que me atreví a pensar que los prodigios que contaba Scherezada sucedían de veras en la vida cotidiana de su tiempo, y dejaron de suceder por la incredulidad y la cobardía realista de las generaciones siguientes. Por lo mismo, me parecía imposible que alguien de nuestros tiempos volviera a creer que se podia volar sobre ciudades y montañas a bordo de una estera, o que un esclavo de Cartagena de Indias viviera castigado doscientos años dentro de una botella, a menos que el autor del cuento fuera capaz de hacerlo creer a sus lectores. (265)

> (I even dared to think that the marvels recounted by Scheherazade really happened in the daily life of her time, and stopped happening because of the incredulity and realistic cowardice of subsequent generations. By the same token, it seemed impossible that anyone from our time would ever believe again that you could fly over cities and mountains on a carpet, or that a slave from Cartagena de Indias would live for two hundred years in a bottle as a punishment, unless the author of the story could make his readers believe it.) (219–20)[5]

Examining magical realists such as García Márquez, Faris observes:

> These children of Scheherazade have a powerful precursor to overcome. In the case of the Latin American fiction to which the label of magical realism has most frequently been applied, that precursor is European realism – a tradition that dominated Latin American letters until mid-century and remains strong in modern and contemporary fiction. (1995: 165)

As she notes examples of magical realist literature written 'in reaction to totalitarian regimes', she further observes:

> These texts, which are receptive in particular ways to more than one point of view, to realistic and magical ways of seeing, and which open

> the door to other worlds, respond to a desire for narrative freedom from realism, and from a univocal narrative stance; they implicitly correspond textually in a new way to a critique of totalitarian discourses of all kinds. Scheherazade's story is relevant again here, for even though she narrated for her own life, she had the eventual welfare of her state on her shoulders as well, and her efforts liberated her country from the tyranny of King Shahriyar's rule. (Faris 1995: 180)

Faris's observations interestingly bring us to *The Thousand and One Nights*, which Mahfouz takes up in his novel to overcome the powerful influence of European realism for which he is known, and relate to the authors' projects by which they resist injustice with magic.

The reference García Márquez makes to Scheherazade in his memoir demonstrates the intertwined affiliations of influence: the influence of *The Thousand and One Nights* on García Márquez's novel and echoes of *Cien años de soledad* in that of Mahfouz, or the use that each author made of a naturalised tradition in order to write back to local abuses. In García Márquez's inventions, Mahfouz recognises his own world, the world of *The Thousand and One Nights*, which can be read as a Spanish book in the universe of *Cien años de soledad* as much as it is an Arab one. Mahfouz's inventions are simultaneously a return to form for the Arab novelist in his use of *The Thousand and One Nights* and an adaptation of a relevant global trend or the Arabisation of magical realism. García Márquez accumulates marvellous details in the chronicle of Macondo to capture that reality where the magical is mundane, such as the gypsies' flying carpets and magical lamps, but the style also demonstrates a return to indigenous cultures.

Importantly, Mahfouz's novel illustrates the ways in which magical realism enables 'the fusion, or coexistence, of possible worlds' that would be otherwise irreconcilable (Zamora and Faris 1995: 6). Magical realism creates an effect in which the novel offers a world of political excess, where supernatural forces disrupt the alley and coexist with the more 'real' events. As Ferial Ghazoul has noted, Mahfouz reinvents magical realism by infusing the magical with the 'familiar' (1996: 139). In his novel, Mahfouz interwines magical realism and the supernatural in premodern literature and blurs the relationship between the real, the magical and the supernatural in the alley. Mahfouz draws on a classical Arabic work to imagine a medieval city that replicates a reality where corruption and injustice are prevalent. Through magical realism, the novel poses the problems of justice, the competence of rulers, and citizenship (Hafez 1994: 41). While García Márquez recounts marvellous events as mundane, Mahfouz recreates a reality drawn from routine political events.

Set in Shahriyar's sultanate after one thousand and one nights, *Layālī alf layla* tells the story of a medieval Arab city at the end of Shahrazad's narration and after the supposed reform of Shahriyar. *Layālī alf layla* opens with the end of Shahrazad's narration in *The Thousand and One Nights*. Mahfouz ushers in a new frame story in which Shahriyar pardons Shahrazad after one thousand and one nights, but a mood of distrust settles over the sultanate. The sultanate seethes with crime, violence, corruption and repression. An omniscient narrator assumes the role of storyteller in the novel, with an extended frame tale and episodic plot that refashions tales of *The Thousand and One Nights*. Sindbad the porter and sailor returns and offers counsel to the sultan. The novel ends with the abdication of Shahriyar and popular rule by Maʻrouf the cobbler, crowned governor of the quarter, and his subjects.

In the very first scene of the novel, Shahriyar's allusion to Shahrazad's stories as 'white magic', which 'open up worlds that invite reflection' (2) ('ḥikāyātuha al-siḥr al-ḥalāl tafattaḥat 'an 'awālim tad'ū li-l-ta'ammul' (8)), highlights the connections between storytelling and reform, since Shahrazad had 'found stories to divert the sultan from shedding blood' (6; 12).[6] The opening depicts both a ruler who appears to have changed his ways and reflects on justice, wisdom and existence and, on the other hand, an exhausted storyteller who invokes self-sacrifice and bloodshed when she learns that Shahriyar has pardoned her: 'Whenever he approaches me I breathe the smell of blood' (4) ('kullama iqtaraba minnī tanashaqtū rā'iḥata al-damm' (10)). Though the novel begins with the end of Shahrazad's narration, a strategy she uses to extend her life, and Shahriyar's pardon, Shahriyar's history and corruption unsettle the quarter. In particular, allusions to 'blood' and Shahrazad's 'white magic' ('al-siḥr al-ḥalāl') – literally 'legal magic' – of storytelling remind us of the injustice of Shahriyar's rule.

The world of *Layālī alf layla* adds to *The Thousand and One Nights*. The supernatural forces that intrude on the alley amplify local abuses as they disrupt politics and affirm the characters' desires, anxieties and insecurities. Eventually, characters come to realise that they live in an 'age of genies' (48) ('zaman al-'afārīt' (66)). In the first scene in which magic appears in the novel, a jinni's appearance inaugurates the disruption of the political order, producing a series of murders, arrests, interrogations, confessions and executions. These events highlight the importance of individual responsibility in the alley, especially in the absence of a just ruler. In another story, the chief of police Gamasa al-Bulti miraculously morphs into the Ethiopian Abdullah the porter, who becomes known as Abdullah of the Land. As Gamasa al-Bulti morphs into Abdullah the porter, Abdullah the madman (*al-majnūn*) and Abdullah the sane (*al-'āqil*), we note that the interrogations, arrests and forced confessions are real and modelled on familiar events in 1970s Egypt.

The appearance of supernatural forces, which represent godlessness (*kufr*) and evil (*sharr*), sparks an epidemic of evil in the alley. One demon appears in the quarter as a seductive woman, Anees al-Galees, who causes a general madness that 'engulfed the quarter like a deluge' (134) ('tadaffaqat litaghmur al-ḥayy ka-l-ṭuf ān' (177)). The epidemic and deluge provide echoes of the plague of insomnia and flood in Macondo. In the story, Anees al-Galees seduces the alley's rulers in her palace, and they are led naked to cupboards that she plans to auction for sale in the marketplace to expose them. However, Abdullah the madman appears at the scene and releases them to save the alley. As they stumble awkwardly in the quarter, Abdullah the madman notes that rulers must possess a sense of shame, which makes an important political comment in the context in which the novel was produced: 'Woe to people under a ruler without a sense of shame' (146) ('waylun li-l-nās min ḥākim lā ḥayā' lahu' (191)). Anees al-Galees's seduction exposes the hypocrisy of the alley's rulers in a story that comments on the state of the alley and the ideal ruler, and appears to make far-reaching political statements about rulers that were especially telling at the end of Anwar Sadat's rule and the start of Hosni Mubarak's.

As Mahfouz recreates a medieval world, he comments on a contemporary political order. With rampant corruption and injustice, disruptions in the alley mirror the sultan's lawlessness and provoke questions related to accountability, freedom, injustice and the problem of evil. Events in the alley turn attention to the precedent of the sultan whose injustice creates the conditions for corruption and impunity. Magical realism in the novel creates the disorder in Mahfouz's world, which furnishes an analogue to a reality of political unrest. Ironically, Mahfouz creates a magical world, pervaded by political realism, to offer a commentary on rule and reform. There are many references in the novel to the saving of the quarter (*khalāṣ al-ḥayy*) – which are significant especially with the general frustration and disaffection with Sadat's rule in the late 1970s – that suggest he is commenting on the ideal form of government.

García Márquez's Macondo and Mahfouz's Ḥāra

García Márquez's Macondo and Mahfouz's alley (*ḥāra*) are central to the way in which both authors envision social justice in the novels. García Márquez's Macondo, a paradise (*paraíso*), 'going back to before original sin' ('anterior al pecado original'), dreamed and founded by José Arcadio Buendía, can be read in opposition to Mahfouz's alley, an inferno of political repression and corruption (11; 21).[7] The chronicler of Macondo, Gene H. Bell-Villada observes, 'an engaged voice from the Macondo "tribe" itself' (2010: 116), reports magical events in a fictive coastal Colombian town. On the other hand, the scribe of the alley in *Layālī alf layla* – also a storyteller in the tradition of *The Thousand and One Nights* – evokes the voice of the narrator in the prologue of his allegorical novel *Awlād ḥāratinā* (*Children of the Alley*), who documents 'the life of our alley' ('ḥikāyāt ḥāratinā'), by writing 'the petitions and complaints of the oppressed and needy', and represents the condition of 'the alley's beggars' ('al-mutasawilīn fī ḥāratinā') (3–5; 7–8).[8] The historical context accounts for the differences between the two novels: García Márquez is a New World author, while Mahfouz is steeped in the traditions of the Old World, which explains the distinction between chronicle and allegory discussed in this section, with a focus on the banana company massacre in *Cien años de soledad* and the carnivalesque in the popular tribunal in *Layālī alf layla*.

In *Layālī alf layla* the metaphorical crowning and uncrowning of a ruler and popular rule provide examples of Bakhtin's carnivalesque, which Mahfouz weaves into magical realism to create the effect of a collapsing and reformed political order.

García Márquez depends on the chronicler's voice to document the history of armed uprisings and revolutions in Latin America from European conquest to the Thousand Days' War between Liberals and Conservatives in the nineteenth century and the Ciénaga railway workers' strike in Colombia in 1928. Colonel Buendía's thirty-two defeated uprisings and the banana workers' strike represent revolutionary action in the novel. In a famous chapter in *Cien años de soledad*, José Arcadio Segundo survives a massacre of three thousand demonstrators who strike against the United Fruit Company. Focusing on the death of three thousand strikers, which is officially denied by the Colombian government, demystifies the event, offering it as history (Martin 1987: 108). However, García Márquez hyperbolises details of the massacre of the strikers to demonstrate the scope of the tragedy. After the massacre, José Arcadio Segundo's account contradicts the official proclamation that the union leaders have survived. Though the government denies reports of the massacre, José Arcadio Segundo reiterates his eyewitness account of the massacre of 'tres mil cuatrocientos ocho' (464) ('three thousand four hundred and eight' (273)). The banana massacre in the novel offers an example of the reworking of a real historical event through hyperbole in an otherwise mythologised history.[9] Revolutionary change pervades the Buendías' account of the massacre of the banana workers, which Martin reads as a 'proletarian revolution' where the final Buendía is the only survivor and observer of a historical reality suppressed by official proclamations, interpreting the magical reality of the novel as the 'prehistory' before the workers' struggle (1987: 111).

Revolt in *Layālī alf layla* is presented differently: rather than a scene of insurrection in the alley, we observe an event in which the ruler is challenged in a parody of the alley. The parody of events appears to restore order in the alley, which evokes Mahfouz's old Cairene neighbourhood of al-Gamaliyya that has played a central role in his novels since *Zuqāq al-midaqq*. In *Awlād ḥāratinā* the narrator provides 'an underground, unwritten history of the alley' as one of its residents who has witnessed some of its events (Mehrez 2008: 42). Mehrez observes that the *ḥara* (alley) in the historic Islamic neighbourhood, which dominated representations of Cairo and reflected the well-ordered urban infrastructure of the old city, suffered collapse during the Sadat period (1971–81) and had to adjust to the historical and political challenges produced by Sadat's policies (2008: 145–6). In the novel, the medieval alley is one that is in disarray, especially as the political regime sets the stage for further disorder.

The alley furnishes a new setting for the tales of *The Thousand and One Nights* with its own political conditions and laws, offering a medieval parody of modern Egypt. While Macondo is a paradise at the outset of *Cien años de soledad*, Mahfouz's alley is infernal because of Shahriyar's violence. One of his subjects' observation that 'only hypocrites are left in the kingdom' (4; 9) confirms the legacy of the sultan's execution of his wives. The chief of police Gamasa al-Bulti notes, 'What an extraordinary sultanate this is, with its people and its genies!' (32; 44) and, through his meditation as the reformed Abdullah the porter, reveals the essence of the alley as 'the world of outward piety and latent corruption' (54; 72). An 'epidemic of evil' (169) disrupts the alley, where assassinations, robberies, executions, campaigns of arrests and interrogations amplify the abuses of the government and create a reality in which 'he who's too decent goes hungry in this city' (31; 44).

The Café of the Emirs (Café of Princes) affords a spectacle of popular celebration. Ironically a café for characters from a range of social classes, the Café of the Emirs prefigures the carnivalesque world Mahfouz creates and his inversion of the political order in the frame story. Frequented by both notables and the people, the café (*qahwa*) enacts divisions that Mahfouz's novel subsequently subverts, but serves as a contact point for the residents of the alley. It is in the café that the alley's denizens remember the sacrifices of 'the God-fearing who have been martyred for saying the truth in protest against the shedding of blood and the plundering of property' (6–7; 13).

Though the café reinforces the hierarchy of the alley, Mahfouz displaces Shahriyar's rule with the voices of the people and challenges the injustice of the regime. He deploys a full array of carnivalesque devices to recreate the alley in opposition to Shahriyar's palace. As Bakhtin elucidates the world of the carnival:

> The laws, prohibitions, and restrictions that determine the structure and order of ordinary, that is noncarnival, life are suspended during carnival: what is suspended first of all is hierarchical structure and all the forms of terror, reverence, piety, and etiquette connected with it – that is, everything resulting from socio-hierarchical inequality. (1984: 122–3)

In the popular tribunal that some of the alley's residents create to uphold justice, divisions are suspended – albeit on a symbolic level – producing '*free and familiar contact among people*' (Bakhtin 1984: 123, emphasis in original).

The suspension of the rule of law during carnival has broader implications in the extended frame story. During his nocturnal excursions with his vizier and executioner, Shahriyar chances on Ibrahim the water-carrier in the role of the sultan of an imaginary kingdom, where all subjects are equal and governors are elected from among the people. The crowned water-carrier announces that the nocturnal parody of the sultan's rule was inspired by Aladdin's unjust execution and that the people hold a divine tribunal, 'at which justice would take its course after it had been unable to do so in the world' (178; 233), to uncover the plot to frame Aladdin for an insurrection against the sultan and the theft of the jewel of the governor's wife, Qamar al-Zaman. During the tribunal, the 'other sultan' issues a proclamation that expresses the desire for the real sultan's penance: 'I thank God, Who has helped me to repent after I had become immersed in the shedding of innocent blood and in plundering the property of Muslims' (174; 229). He then sentences the perpetrators of the crime to death and dismisses the corrupt governors. In this scene the carnivalesque does not mock the ruler but makes a statement about justice: the impersonator of Shahriyar overturns his sentence in the imaginary kingdom. Though Shahriyar calls the tribunal a 'farce' (176) ('mahzala' (231)), after observing its proceedings he returns to his court and instructs the vizier to relay to him public opinion about the death of Aladdin, and, finally in the real sultanate, passes a decree that is identical to that of 'the sultan Ibrahim the water-carrier' (178; 234). Consequently, the ruler takes counsel from his subjects after observing the proceedings of the popular tribunal, where his subjects not only comment on the affairs of the alley but also challenge and reform the real sultan's laws and decrees. This is a world where law has the power to uphold justice, which has been subverted, and the carnivalesque appears in Mahfouz's Cairo alleyway as popular restoration of the traditional function of law and jurisprudence, which have traditionally been guarantors of justice.

The popular tribunal in the alley assumes importance as a means of 'free familiar contact', as Bakhtin observes in his theory of carnival: 'People who in life are separated by impenetrable hierarchical barriers enter into free familiar contact on the carnival square' (1984: 123). For Bakhtin, the carnivalesque in the novel allows for resistance to authority and political change. Through the carnivalesque, social hierarchies of the alley – solemnities, laws and sentences – are profaned and overturned. The popular tribunal, which summons the voices of the oppressed to enact justice in the alley in Mahfouz's novel, forms new relationships that subvert the all-powerful hierarchical divisions in the real or noncarnival world, and frees the behaviour of Ibrahim the water-carrier from authority. The exchange between Shahriyar (the uncrowned ruler) and the crowned sultan illustrates the carnivalesque dissolution of hierarchical divisions and anticipates the inversion of roles at the end of the novel, where the alley's beggars become men of state. The ceremony of the mock crowning of Ibrahim the water-carrier offers a parody of Shahriyar's rule that fulfils the dream of popular rule and the possibility of challenging the ruler. It also produces a real uncrowning of the sultan and democratisation of the alley.

The novel concludes with popular rule in the alley as it was envisioned in the mock tribunal, a form of revolutionary action against injustice. Importantly, while García Márquez's novel appears to erase 'proletarian history' (Martin 1987: 108), Mahfouz inaugurates popular rule, and though Macondo is obliterated by a whirlwind at the end of *Cien años de soledad*, the carnivalesque in *Layālī alf layla* produces a reordered world and anticipates a more democratic alley.

In Power and Solitude

Modern Arab interpretations of *The Thousand and One Nights* have focused on the political nuances of the medieval narrative and examined its frame story to re-evaluate the situation in the Arab world (Ghazoul 1996: 135). In shifting the focus from Shahrazad the storyteller to Shahriyar the tyrant and from the ruler to the residents of the alley in his novel, Mahfouz envisions both an old and a new political order. Mahfouz revises *The Thousand and One Nights* to portray the abuse of power in a world where, as Zamora and Faris aptly note, 'politics collide with fantasy' (1995: 1) and rulers with demons.

In *Layālī alf layla*, magic is presented as a logical consequence of injustice, which reflects the connection between magical realism and political dissent. In the opening of the novel, Shahrazad explains the unease that spreads through the city with the distrust of the ruler. With Shahrazad's storytelling, Shahriyar is still 'unreliable' and must demonstrate that he has changed from 'severity' to 'wisdom' (*al-ḥikma*) to be fully reformed. It is suggested that the change of Shahriyar from a despot to a just ruler is more miraculous than the appearance of supernatural forces in the quarter. Though Shahrazad's narration ends the cycle of violence, Shahriyar is further reformed by means of lived experience rather than storytelling. In his nocturnal tours of the city, Shahriyar experiences a reality that replicates Shahrazad's tales and, in his capacity as ruler, learns through the confessions of his subjects of the involvement of supernatural forces in the alley's assassinations. At first Shahriyar attempts to reform himself by following the methods of 'the kings of old [who] were cured at night by wandering round and investigating the circumstances of the people' (55; 74). One night he overhears one of his subjects – Fadil Sanaan, a revolutionary suspected of belonging to the Kharijites in the novel – who comments on the ruler's duty to protect his kingdom: 'It is for the ruler to dispense justice [*al-'adl*] from the beginning so that genies don't intrude on our lives' (64; 86).

Mahfouz offers further commentary on political rule in the novel: the tales of 'The Cap of Invisibility' and 'Ma'rouf the Cobbler' suggest ways of ruling the alley. In the former, the jinni of 'godlessness' furnishes Fadil

Sanaan with the cap of invisibility and instructs him to commit a series of crimes. Fadil Sanaan succumbs to the temptations of the cap of invisibility and, when he confesses to his crimes, he is executed. In contrast, the tale of Ma'rouf the cobbler, who falsely claims ownership of Solomon's ring, ends in popular rule. When Ma'rouf the cobbler claims that he has discovered Solomon's ring and levitates in the Café of the Emirs, reports of his miracle spread in the city, and the sultan summons him to his palace. However, a jinni stages Ma'rouf the cobbler's miracle in the sultan's presence and instructs him to murder the mystic Abdullah al-Balkhi and Abdullah the madman. In the end, Shahriyar appoints Ma'rouf the cobbler governor, creating a new order, reflected in the comic crowning of Ibrahim the water-carrier and the parody of Aladdin's trial. Rather than rule the quarter, the cobbler donates his wealth to the residents of the alley in a world in which Mahfouz envisions a government founded on social justice. Here Mahfouz appears to comment on rulers whose rule is based on tyranny and corruption. When Shahriyar retreats to the green tongue of land at the end of the novel, Ma'rouf the cobbler and Abdullah are left to rule in the city in a new form of popular rule.

Layālī alf layla focuses on the reform of political rule through philosophical reflection during Shahriyar's travels. In *Layālī alf layla* the mystic Abdullah al-Balkhi sets the precedent for the existence that Shahriyar seeks after his abdication. García Márquez's solitude is different from Mahfouz's mysticism, or the metaphysical reflection to which he alluded in his interview about the novel's style. As the popular governor rules the city, Shahriyar withdraws, and his abdication illustrates that 'the sultan . . . must depart once he has lost competence' (218) ('al-sulṭān yajib ann yadhhaba bimā faqada min ahliyya' (285)).

In the apocalyptic ending of *Cien años de soledad*, Macondo is swept away by a biblical hurricane when Aureliano Babilonia decodes Melquiades's manuscript, so that races 'did not have a second opportunity on earth' (422; 494). In contrast, Mahfouz's ending offers a momentary respite from an infernal city. Sindbad's stories of his travels deeply influence Shahriyar, who perceives their verisimilitude to Shahrazad's stories and concludes, 'Traditions are the past and things of the past must become outdated' (214; 280). Mahfouz portrays the change Shahriyar undergoes from a ruler to a mystic but presents the elusiveness of solitude. In the tale 'The Grievers' (or 'weepers') (*al-bakka'ūn*), Mahfouz concludes the frame story of *The Thousand and One Nights*. A solitary Shahriyar arrives at the green tongue of land – the setting of Abdullah the porter's purification and the popular tribunal. Shahriyar enters a paradise through the weepers' rock by the river, which evokes Macondo's paradise, where he is reborn as a beardless young man. He then enters an otherworldly city populated by women, where his marriage to the queen lasts 'a hundred years'. When he opens a forbidden door, he is expelled from paradise and returns to the grievers at the dome-shaped rock and to old age, 'as though he were a vagabond among his own people' (225) ('ka'annahu aḥada ṣa'alīk sha'bihi' (293)). Like Abdullah the porter before him, he retreats to the date palm near the green tongue of land. Rather than an apocalypse, Mahfouz portrays Shahriyar's fall from a temporary paradise, ending his allegory with a mystical experience – the eternal penance of a former ruler – which opposes power to solitude. While García Márquez creates a city of mirrors and dreams in Macondo, and *Cien años de soledad* chronicles the settlement of Macondo to the extinction of the Buendías, Mahfouz creates an underworld in *Layālī alf layla*, circling from Shahriyar's tyranny to popular rule in the alley. Furthermore, while the ending of García Márquez's novel is metafictional with the destruction of Macondo, Mahfouz's ending is mystical; rule in the alley is reformed and Shahriyar's penance is infinite.

After One Hundred Years

A reading of the echoes of *Cien años de soledad* in Mahfouz's *Layālī alf layla* shows the novel in a new light. Mahfouz creates an allegory of revolution through the politicisation and Arabisation of magical realism. While García Márquez invents a magical reality, Mahfouz enacts popular rule in his medieval Arab world. If García Márquez captures Latin America's marvellous reality, Mahfouz anticipates unrest and revolution in the Arab world. In his novel, Mahfouz contests Egypt's political order by focusing on the tyranny of the ruler and injustice in the alley, and both the classical Arabic tradition and the Arabisation of Latin American magical realism allow him to imagine revolution and reform. Magical realism in the novel produces change in the alley. Just as the enduring power of literature can explain the myths of Latin American history, so Mahfouz's novel continues to challenge reality, especially during the 2011 Arab revolutions. García Márquez and Mahfouz have in common the storyteller in the novels (the chronicler of Macondo and the scribe of the alley), defamiliarisation, an archaic style and circular narrative patterns that are linked to themes of power and political struggle.

Though the novel appears to have been inspired by *The Thousand and One Nights*, it very clearly reflects Mahfouz's political context, and opening the novel with Shahriyar's guilt and ending it with his penance seems to suggest the collapse of that reality. Rather than the formation of a magical world and the history of the discovery of the Americas in García Márquez's novel, Mahfouz's novel centres on revolutionary futures in the Arab world. Reading the novel in new frameworks of comparison based on common concerns and forms in Latin American and Arabic literatures offers new critical interpretations of magical realism in world literature to broaden the understanding of the genre, and produces further readings that illustrate the relevance and prescience of Mahfouz's re-envisioning of the alley.

Transcontinental *Crónicas*

Lebanese writer Elias Khoury's (b. 1948) 1994 novel *Majma' al-asrār* (*The Assembly of Secrets*) reworks García Márquez's *Crónica de una muerte anunciada*. Like Mahfouz's novel, *Majma' al-asrār* offers an example of an intertextual relationship to a novel by García Márquez, but one which is more direct. Khoury's novel tells the story of the effects of reports of Santiago Nasar's death in *Crónica de una muerte anunciada* on the extended family in Lebanon and explores the Orientalism of García Márquez's novel. Although *Majma' al-asrār* is a reworking of the central event in *Crónica de una muerte anunciada*, the novel creates a completely different story that is specific to Lebanon.

Khoury is one of the foremost novelists in Arabic literature who has fashioned the Lebanese Civil War novel. He was a member of the leftist PLO and Lebanese National Movement coalition during the Lebanese Civil War (1975–90). His involvement in the Lebanese Civil War and subsequent exile from Christian East Beirut are refracted in his novels, from *al-Wujūh al-bayḍā'* (*White Masks*, 1981) to *al-Jabal al-ṣaghīr* (*Little Mountain*, 1977). Palestine is a recurrent theme in his novels, from his masterwork *Bāb al-shams* (*Gate of the Sun*, 1998) about the 1948 Nakba to his most recent novels, *Awlād al-ghītū – ismī Ādam* (*Children of the Ghetto – My Name Is Adam*, 2016) and *Najmat al-baḥr* (Stella Maris, 2019). In 'After Mahfouz', Edward Said describes Elias Khoury's unconventional, postmodern novels, which offered a new style in modern Arabic literature during the Lebanese Civil War (2000: 323). In an interview, Khoury maintains that he had no model in experimental or postmodern literature but 'wrote like a blind man' (Creswell 2017: 32). In his 'Foreword', Said sets Khoury's *Little Mountain* in 'the context of the Arabic novel, from which, in equal measure, it derives and departs' and parses the 'curious and tragic' relationship of Lebanon to the Arab world that rose to 'literary prominence' by Mahfouz's 1988 Nobel Prize for Literature (1989: ix). When *Little Mountain* appeared, as Khoury has noted, there was 'little Arabic literature in translation' (Creswell 2017: 31). In both Arabic and world literature, Khoury's novels have appeared on the scene that Said has amply described: Mahfouz's novels have been 'emulated' by other Arab novelists, but, at the same time, Arabic literature is 'marginal' to Western readers for whom Carlos Fuentes and García Márquez have gained 'cultural authority' (Said 1989: xiii).[10] Unlike those of Mahfouz, Khoury's novels appeared in a setting that Said has described as 'fractured' and 'decentered', and Khoury is more experimental, or, as Said puts it, 'postmodern' (1989: xiv, xvii).

Khoury's novels, remarkably, draw on a world literary tradition extending from classical Arabic literature and world literature with which Khoury, a novelist and critic, is conversant. In interviews, he has woven ties between Arabic and world literatures (McManus 2017: 395) and has himself linked Arabic and Latin American literatures. He has also acknowledged that 'the new literatures of the world' are no longer produced in Europe but in the Third World (McManus 2017: 396). Like those of Mahfouz, Khoury's novels have entered circuits of translation in world literature. His novels are widely translated into Spanish and Portuguese and thus circulate in Spain and Latin America.

There are several connections that link Khoury's novel to Latin American literature. Khoury, whose novels have circulated as world literature through translation, creates ties between Latin America and the Arab world in *Majma' al-asrār*, a novel that offers an example of the circulation of Latin American literature in the Arab world and a history of Arab migration to Latin America. He mines the history of Arab migration to Colombia underlying *Crónica de una muerte anunciada*, expanding the story of Santiago Nasar's family in a Lebanese Civil War novel. In his 'Foreword' to *Little Mountain*, Said notes that Khoury was 'a publishing-house editor . . . for a decade during which he established an impressive list of Arabic translations of major postmodern Third World classics (Fuentes, Márquez, Asturias)' (1989: xvii) (also noted in 'After Mahfouz' and cited above). In the 1980s, Khoury oversaw the translation of a series of 'Third World literature', which featured novels by Carlos Fuentes and Julio Cortázar, directly from Spanish into Arabic. In an interview, Khoury notes: 'It was with this series, called *The Memory of the Peoples*, that the boom of translation of these literatures into Arabic began' and the translations arose from an interest in the comparison of Arabic and 'other Third World literatures' (McManus 2017: 396). While the series relates to the Third Worldism of the 1960s, he traces his understanding of world literature to a rich classical Arabic heritage extending to *The Thousand and One Nights* (McManus 2017: 397). Besides the translation of African literature into Arabic, the series expanded to Latin American literature, Khoury notes:

> Cortázar, Fuentes, Márquez, Borges, and so on. You can discover how these literatures are related to each other. Especially with Latin American literature, we discovered how much it was a kind of continuation of the *1001 Nights* from Borges on. This isn't just about what was then called magical realism. I think these [authors] knew *1001 Nights* (Borges wrote a lot about it) and knew this tradition very well, and in a way they were continuing it. This discovery was very important for us. (McManus 2017: 397)

He also acknowledges that vertiginous network of circulation in Mahfouz, the effect of *The Thousand and One Nights* on Latin American literature (which in turn was important to Arab writers). Curiously, Elias Khoury has been compared to the Mexican writer Carlos Fuentes.[11] Jeremy Harding also compares him to Argentine novelist Julio Cortázar: 'In some of Khoury's novels there is a faint echo of Cortázar's melancholic playfulness – the two men were friends in Paris – but Khoury's wit is more vivacious' (2006). Khoury differentiates the Lebanese novel from Latin American novels where authors intertwined

> Hispanic and Indian culture . . . with modern culture, and created what we call 'magical realism.' . . . we discovered that what is unreal, the fantastic, is not in the past, but is part of the present. The fantastic is here. Since the fantastic is here, we must find a way of discovering it through a realistic way of writing. Literature, in our situation, must put together two elements: . . . the real and the fantastic . . . at the same moment. (2009a)

The direct link with *Crónica de una muerte anunciada* that he has remarked upon draws him into a network of relationships with Latin American literature. Khoury has noted that on reading García Márquez's *Crónica de una muerte anunciada*: 'Gabriel García Márquez, when he described the death of Santiago Nasar, took me back to the atmosphere of the 1860 civil war' in Lebanon (2006b: 109).

Khoury's *Majma' al-asrār* tells the story of Santiago Nasar's extended family in Lebanon. *Majma' al-asrār* commences with the murder of the store owner Ibrahim Nasar, the son of Yacoub Nasar (the Arabic form of Santiago) and a distant cousin of *Crónica de una muerte anunciada*'s Santiago Nasar, in Beirut in 1976. Norma Abdel Messih, who has a relationship with Ibrahim Nasar and his friend Hanna Salman El-Maleh, discovers the body. Norma alleges that Ibrahim Nasar deflowered her and rumours abound that Hanna Salman has murdered Ibrahim Nasar to avenge Norma's honour. When Ibrahim Nasar was ten, a letter was sent by Santiago Nasar's family, which had migrated to Colombia, to his father Yacoub Nasar in Lebanon. The arrival of the letter, which reported the death of Santiago Nasar in Colombia, disrupted the Lebanese family's plans to immigrate to Latin America. The plot circles back to the mysterious letter sent by the Nasar family from Colombia and preserved in the box of secrets Ibrahim Nasar inherits from his father.

Khoury retraces the migration of the Colombian Nasars who were displaced by the civil war in 1860 in the South Lebanon mountains and fled to Colombia, along with other Lebanese migrants to South America. He relocates the violence of *Crónica de una muerte anunciada* to the village of Ain Kisrin in Lebanon in 1860, where the Abu Amers and Nasars, Druz and Catholics, had hitherto peacefully coexisted, and Beirut in 1976, thus intertwining Colombia's Violencia and the Lebanese civil wars (1840–60 and 1975–90) (Ette 2006: 246).

In *Majma' al-asrār*, Khoury reworks *Crónica de una muerte anunciada* but nonetheless produces a Lebanese novel about Lebanon. Civantos reads Khoury's 'intertwined story' (2018: 175), and *Majma' al-asrār* is an 'intertwined' novel that has a direct relationship to *Crónica de una muerte anunciada* through intertextuality. Moreover, I argue that the novel revises the Orientalism of *Crónica de una muerte anunciada*. Remarkably, Khoury takes a debate that *Crónica de una muerte anunciada* provokes about the novel's Orientalism and explores it in an Arabic novel.

Khoury's novel is part of a literary network that links Latin America to the Arab world. Ette reads *Majma' al-asrār*'s intertextual allusions to Orientalist imagery in *Crónica de una muerte anunciada* in a 'network of relations linking the two novels together' and characterises the intertextuality of Khoury's novel as 'transcontinental' (2006: 242, 244). He remarks upon the nature of transcontinental exchange evoked by the novel: 'Lebanon and Colombia . . . stand in an intimate relation of exchange . . . What happens in one country has repercussions for the other' (2006: 244). Khoury's novel belongs to a set of works in both Spanish and Arabic that make transcontinental connections through intertextual relationships and the circulation of literature. The novel's intertextuality and the migration of *Crónica de una muerte anunciada* to Arabic connect Colombia and Lebanon.

Khoury refocuses attention on the effects of the murder of Santiago Nasar in Colombia on his extended family in Lebanon. Khoury, who admires García Márquez but is critical of the Orientalism of *Crónica de una muerte anunciada*, reworks and 'expands' the novel by focusing on Santiago Nasar's Lebanese family in Lebanon (Civantos 2018: 175). Thus *Majma' al-asrār* critiques the Orientalism of *Crónica de una muerte anunciada* by refocusing on Santiago Nasar's country of origin.

Like *Crónica de una muerte anunciada, Majma' al-asrār* hinges on a mystery, in this case of a collection of secrets tied to the death of Ibrahim Nasar. Reworking the honour killing of Santiago Nasar, *Majma' al-asrār* focuses on the death of Ibrahim Nasar who deflowered Norma Abdel Messih and speculations that Hanna Salman, his friend and Norma's other lover, might have killed him to avenge Norma's honour. Circling around the mystery and the story, the narrator's musings conjure *Crónica de una muerte anunciada*:

> A secret, as the Arabs used to say, is 'one of those things that is concealed' and 'which is hidden,' and 'to "secrete" a thing means "to conceal it and to reveal it," the word having thus two opposite meanings' . . .
>
> The secret is the thing and its opposite, the concealed and the revealed, for it cannot be concealed from some unless it be revealed to others, and it can only be turned into a story when both of those disappear, in which case the secret is no longer a secret but has become a riddle, and riddles are there to be solved.[12]

Aphorisms ('the secret is the thing and its opposite') – and repetition – help the narrator to name things, as in *Cien años de soledad*'s opening where 'El mundo era tan reciente, que muchas cosas carecían de nombre' (9) ('The world was so recent but many things lacked names' (1)), but the world in which Khoury's novel is set is fractured. Furthermore, Khoury has noted, 'the generation of novelists to which I belong was aware of the need to write the present and name things, and structure our novels on the social and political contradictions that swept Lebanon and the Arab East.'[13] In Arabic, the word '*al-mu'lan*' (literally 'announced'; 'revealed' in the translation) invokes the word 'anunciada' in the Spanish title '*Crónica de una muerte anunciada*', translated into Arabic as '*Qiṣṣat mawt mu'lan*'. In *Crónica de una muerte anunciada*, the narrator describes the stranger in town and Angela's suitor, Bayardo San Román, as having 'una manera de hablar que más bien le servía para ocultar que para decir' (34) ('a way of speaking that served him rather to conceal than to reveal' (25)). The secret, withheld from some and known to others ('concealed and revealed') (*al-makhfī wa-l-muʿlan*), becomes the story that the narrator assembles from the love triangle of the murdered store owner Ibrahim Nasar, his mistress Norma Abdel Messih, and his friend and rival the cobbler Hanna Salman.

Repetition appears in *Majmaʿ al-asrār*'s dizzying beginnings, which Said has also noted in *Little Mountain*: 'Style . . . is, first of all, repetition' which 'permits lyricism' (1989: xix). *Majmaʿ al-asrār* begins 'Bada'at al-ḥikāya hakadhā' (13) ('This is how the story began'), and most of the chapters repeat the opening of the frame tale, creating a simulacrum of the circularity of *The Thousand and One Nights* and the mystery of a detective novel like *Crónica de una muerte anunciada*, whose first three chapters also end with a repetition of Santiago Nasar's name. The beginnings of the chapters echo the openings of tales from *The Thousand and One Nights*. Repetition seems also to be a natural effect of civil destruction and disorientation. As Khoury remarks on the structure of his novel *Ka'annaha nā'ima* (*As Though She Were Sleeping*), circling in on itself, 'the structure helps the story open up, like a rose' (Efthimiatou and Khoury 2013). Describing the structure of *Ka'annaha nā'ima*, he notes: 'When you enter the book, you are in a world of mirrors . . . and all the stories are mirrors of other stories', a technique he draws from *The Thousand and One Nights* where 'the ending of one story is the beginning of another' (Efthimiatou and Khoury 2013). Khoury observes that in his novels 'how and when the story (*al-ḥikaya*) begins is the question. In *Alf layla wa layla*, the story has no end . . . it multiplies, spins, re-forms infinitely. This is what Borges taught us as he read that book' (2019b). As he notes, the beginning, or the frame tale, in which the stories are nested, 'turns the stories into mirrors': 'I say that the stories are infinite, which also means that they have no beginning' (2019b). For him, the novel is always in need of a framework and a frame tale, more so amid social and political fracture. He asks: 'But how do we begin when social, literary, and ideological frameworks are unraveling around us?' (2019b). In 'al-Riwāya, al-Riwā'ī wa-l-Ḥarb' ('The Novel, the Novelist, and War'), he proposes that the rise of the Lebanese novel was coeval with the eruption of the civil war and that a new Lebanese novel rose to 'mirror' the Lebanese Civil War in post-1975 Lebanon (2019b).

The family of Ibrahim Nasar's father Yacoub (Arabic for Santiago and an allusion to his Colombian cousin) was preparing to migrate to Colombia, when a letter reporting the murder of Santiago Nasar arrived and frustrated its plans. The narrator intricately interweaves the ties between *Crónica de una muerte anunciada* and *Majmaʿ al-asrār*:

> What is the relationship between a mysterious murder that took place in Colombia and the family that sold the land in Ain Kisrin and was preparing to migrate to South America?
>
> Did the Colombian writer Gabriel García Márquez know when he wrote his novel *Crónica de una muerte anunciada* that he was uncovering the secret of that letter that remained a mystery for a long time, or is Márquez's story unrelated to our subject, connected only through these names which are one and the same? (35)[14]

The letter sent to the extended Lebanese family in Khoury's novel recalls the anonymous note that is pushed under the door in *Crónica de una muerte anunciada* and reveals the precise details of the plot of Santiago Nasar's murder but which is tragically overlooked by the household until the crime is committed. Reworking Santiago Nasar's death in *Crónica de una muerte anunciada* and the murder of the Arab in colonial Algeria in French Algerian author Albert Camus's *L'Étranger* (*The Stranger*, 1942),[15] the narrator concludes that Santiago Nasar is a 'strange immigrant' (*muhājir gharīb*) slaughtered by the Vicario twins. The novel's intertextual relationships to *L'Étranger* disorient the reader, creating the effect of Khoury's interrogation of Camus through García Márquez, the author of another novel about the death of an Arab.

While Khoury talks back to and contests *Crónica de una muerte anunciada*, his novel is embroidered with Camus's *L'Étranger*, a novel that serves to illuminate the themes of the Colombian novel (the Other) he interweaves. By his account, Khoury first read *L'Étranger* in Arabic and later French.[16] In an interview, he observes: 'The book became a part of me' (Creswell 2017: 29). Khoury reworked the themes of *L'Étranger*, which relate to his exile, as Said has noted (again in relation to Mahfouz): 'he is the minority Christian whose fate has become nomadic because it cannot accommodate itself to the Christian exclusionism and xenophobia shared by other minorities in the region' who is 'very much part of the [Arab] culture' (1989: xxi) but equally a stranger. The narrator frequently quotes from an Arabic translation of *Crónica de una muerte anunciada*, specifically descriptions of Santiago Nasar and the account of his murder. He quotes the Arabic translation of the Spanish description of Santiago Nasar in *Crónica de una muerte anunciada*, replacing 'eyelids' (los párpados) with 'eyebrows' (*ḥājibān*):[17] 'he was slim and pale and had his father's Arab eyebrows and curly hair' (37).[18] Likewise, Ibrahim Nasar is described thus by Norma: 'he was slim and pale and had curly hair and thick, bushy eyebrows. Norma did not say that they were Arab eyebrows, because she is an Arab' (37).[19] *Crónica de una muerte anunciada* reproduces a description of 'Arab eyes and curly hair', common features used to designate Arab immigrants or the *turco* in Latin America. The narrator of Khoury's novel draws attention to the description of Santiago Nasar in *Crónica de una muerte anunciada*, where his ethnic origins are Orientalised, but Norma does not remark upon his ethnicity in Lebanon. Is Santiago Nasar murdered because he is an Arab? This is the question raised most pointedly in Khoury's novel. The narrator wonders about the murder so clearly foretold: 'Because [the town] did not believe it, as they maintained? . . . [or] because he was an Arab?' (37). The implication is that Santiago Nasar was murdered because he is an Arab and thus the narrator draws comparisons with Camus's *L'Étranger*. Civantos proposes that *Majma' al-asrār*, 'by emphasizing points of contact between the Arab world and Latin America, is at once a corrective commentary on the forms of Orientalism that linger in *Crónica de una muerte anunciada* and an homage to García Márquez's narrative techniques' (2018: 177–8). Clearly, the narrator of Khoury's novel circles around the Orientalism of *Crónica de una muerte anunciada*, from which he quotes, but interrogates and overwrites García Márquez.

The transcontinental circulation of *Crónica de una muerte anunciada* is central to Khoury's reworking of the novel. *Majma' al-asrār* depends on and reworks the Spanish original in Arabic as it extends and transposes events to Lebanon. *Majma' al-asrār* thus circulates *Crónica de una muerte anunciada*, and Spanish literature more broadly, in Arabic. Moreover, *Majma' al-asrār* illustrates both the cultural encounters that created connections between Latin America and the Arab world such as migration and the literary ties that are furthered by the circulation of Latin American literature in the Arab world.

Khoury extends the central focus of *Majma' al-asrār* to a history rife with civil wars. More than halfway through *Majma' al-asrār*, one of the chapters begins with a variation of the repeated phrase: 'The story began in Ain Kisrin' (*bada'at al-ḥikāya fī 'ayn Kisrīn*) (143). In an interview, Khoury, who wrote his dissertation at the École Pratique des Hautes Études on the Mount Lebanon civil war between the Maronites and the Druze from 1840 to 1860, focuses attention on the history in which *Majma' al-asrār* is set: 'In my novel *Majma' al-asrār*, which hasn't been translated into English, there's an episode about a massacre that happened during the 1860s civil war' (Creswell 2017: 37). He was concerned that there was no record of the war of 1860.[20] He declares: 'I'm not interested in memory . . . I'm interested in the present. But to have a present, you have to know which things to forget and which things to remember . . . when I began writing novels . . . I found that I wanted to write the present – the present of our own civil war' (Creswell 2017: 27–8). His concern, when the civil war erupted, was: 'how did my ancestors read the war that preceded our war, and why was our war, with all its complexities related to the social and class conflicts, the cold war, the Arab-Israeli war – a repetition of the Lebanese civil war in the nineteenth century?' (2019b). In *Majma' al-asrār*, he underscores the circularity of Lebanese history by returning to civil wars in the mid-nineteenth century and 1946–48.

Khoury's novel 'opens up, like a rose'. There is repetition of the opening of the frame tale that takes us to the mysterious letter from Santiago Nasar's family in Colombia. While Ibrahim Nasar's father, Yacoub, prepares to emigrate, like Lebanese immigrants who settled in Colombia and all the family's men who left in waves to South America, a letter arrives from Colombia. The plot circles around this mysterious letter. Read by Ibrahim Nasar's aunt, it announces the murder of Santiago Nasar: 'I understood that Yacoub had died. It said Yacoub; no it said Santiago. We used to call your father Santiago. Everyone wanted to emigrate in those days, and he told people that he was immigrating to Mexico, but in fact he wanted to go to our relatives in Colombia' (182). The narrator conflates Yacoub (the Colombian Santiago Nasar) with Ibrahim's father (the Lebanese Yacoub). On the eve of the Lebanese Civil War, Ibrahim Nasar resolves to immigrate to South America but recalls the massacre of his distant cousin: 'The story of the massacre is mysterious and there is no evidence of it. The only evidence was that letter that announced the death of one of his cousins called Santiago or Yacoub' (185). On the eve of his departure, Ibrahim looks for that mysterious letter in a box of secrets that belonged to his father Yacoub. The letter, sent in *Crónica de una muerte anunciada* and read in *Majma' al-asrār* – so the narrator maintains – is part of a series of events that intertwine the novels, such as the murder of Ibrahim Nasar's ancestor Abdel Jalil, who, like Santiago Nasar, was brutally stabbed with scimitars in Ain Kisrin during the massacre of Christians in 1860 and walked for hours until he fell. His death is evocative of the murder in *Crónica de una muerte anunciada* where, the narrator notes, the Colombian novelist Gabriel García Márquez will describe the murder of Santiago Nasar as though he was describing that of Ibrahim Nasar's ancestor. Through its commentary on *Crónica de una muerte anunciada, Majma' al-asrār* is an 'intertwined novel' whose intertextuality is vertiginous, so that the narrator, in 1976, appears to foreshadow the novel that García Márquez will write in 1981.

Circling around the mysterious death of Ibrahim Nasar in a way that serves rather to conceal than to reveal, the narrator seems guided by his sentiment that he is a stranger. Ibrahim Nasar wanted to know the story of immigrants to South America in the nineteenth century who returned to settle in the villages of Mount Lebanon and would become strangers. Khoury's narrator draws parallels between the death of the Arab, an Algerian in colonial Algeria, in Camus's *L'Étranger*, and an immigrant who is construed as an Other in a Colombian town in García Márquez's *Crónica de una muerte anunciada*. Entwining the Arab immigrant and Algerian, Khoury transposes the Nasars from Colombia to Lebanon during the Lebanese Civil War. Thus, *Majma' al-asrār* circles back to *L'Étranger*, the novel that has haunted Khoury, circles around the event (and beginnings), and alternates between Lebanon's civil wars.

García Márquez in Arabic

As García Márquez travels in Arabic through direct encounters – an adaptation of magical realism and intertextuality – he inspires Arab writers to turn inward and focus on local struggles. García Márquez acknowledges his influence by *The Thousand and One Nights*, a key text for the conception of magical realism, and Mahfouz, whose novel adapts directly the medieval Arabic work, engages with Arabic and Latin American literary traditions. García Márquez and Mahfouz illustrate a network of mutual influences between Latin American and Arabic literatures. *Majma' al-asrār* redresses the Orientalism of *Crónica de una muerte anunciada* and offers a rare encounter with a Latin American novel in Arabic literature. The encounter with Latin American literature produces Arabic novels that are complex, original and local by Arab authors who have nonetheless acquired world literature status.

While both Mahfouz and Khoury look to García Márquez, the novels they produce are markedly different. Mahfouz and Khoury belong to the same literary tradition, but take a different turn in a *Thousand and One Nights* Arabic adaptation and a Lebanese Civil War novel. Mahfouz mastered 'stable' forms, as Said has put it (2000: 323), whereas Khoury's novel disorients, mirroring a fractured present. Both novels help us to understand connections and direct encounters that redress the asymmetry and inequality in the comparative study of two world literatures.

As I have shown through the novels of Mahfouz and Khoury, transcontinental exchanges no longer require the mediation of the North. Khoury circulates Spanish literature in Arabic by reworking *Crónica de una muerte anunciada* and quoting from the Arabic translation. A study of *Majma' al-asrār* and *Crónica de una muerte anunciada* in Arabic and Spanish, respectively, is necessary to draw these connections. Mahfouz's novels are widely translated (there is no English translation of Khoury's novel currently in print, though his other novels are widely available in translation). In his reworking of García Márquez's novel, Khoury – in the words of Said – 'bids Mahfouz' a 'respectful farewell' (1989: xxi) and sets new directions in Arab Latin American relationships. The next chapter will examine further relationships that frame comparisons in tricontinental networks.

4

Che Guevara's Diaries, Miguel Littín's Adventures: Latin American Iconography in Arabic Literature

Guevara was a romantic figure who has become one of the great political icons of the three continents.

Robert Young, *Postcolonialism: An Historical Introduction*

Guevara is dead
Guevara is dead
The latest news on the radio
in the churches
in the mosques
in the alleys
in the streets
and in the cafés and in the bars
Guevara is dead
The chord of chitchat and comments has stretched out.

Ahmad Fuad Negm, 'Jivāra māt' ('Guevara Is Dead')[1]

In *Al-Riḥla*: *Ayyām ṭāliba miṣriyya fī Amrīka* (*The Journey: Memoirs of an Egyptian Woman Student in America*, 1983), Egyptian writer Radwa Ashour (Raḍwa 'Ashūr) (1946–2014) recalls the 1973 massacre of 5,000 detainees in the Chilean national stadium after Pinochet's military coup against the democratically elected socialist president Salvador Allende. In the 1970s, Ashour was in her mid-twenties, a young PhD student of African American literature at the W. E. B. Du Bois Department of Afro-American Studies at the University of Massachusetts at Amherst. When the widow of Allende recounted the details of the massacre in a small church at Yale University, Radwa was in the audience: 'I cheered along with the crowd for a government of national unity and "*el pueblo unido jamás sera vencido* / the people united will never be defeated"' (90–1; 110, emphasis in original).[2] In *Al-Riḥla*, she buys two records by singer-guitarist Victor Jara and her Puerto Rican friend translates the lyrics. One of the records features on the cover the famous poem about the 5,000 prisoners in Santiago stadium that he wrote before they cut off his hands and killed him. Although Ashour writes about her study abroad (1973–75) in her memoir, the 1970s are framed within African, Arab and Latin American solidarity in the waning days of pan-Africanism and Third Worldism.[3] Ashour's memoir retains the ethos of the 1960s and links Arab, African and Latin American struggles.[4]

Arab writers drew on Latin American literature and political iconography on many occasions, reviving links at historically remote moments. They did so within the frame of two important encounters: on the one hand, Latin American literature had a wide circulation in the Arab world; on the other hand, a generation of leftist Arab writers engaged with Third World movements. Latin American literature mirrored shared political struggles against colonialism and neo-imperialism. Another attraction for Arab writers was a tropical, exotic literature that fostered transnational solidarity. The translation and circulation of Latin American Boom novels in the Arab world had far-reaching effects such as adaptations of the style of magical realism, intertextual relationships and reworkings of well-known novels. Gabriel García Márquez, for instance, is a beloved author whose novels *Cien años de soledad* and *El amor en los tiempos del cólera* (*Love in the Time of Cholera*, 1985) have been translated into Arabic and have circulated widely in the Arab world.[5]

This chapter will focus on an Egyptian novel and memoir that interweave Latin American iconography and literature and examine the central role of transnational solidarity and Third World movements in the Cold War: Sonallah Ibrahim's *Warda* (2000) and Mohamed Makhzangi's *Laḥaẓāt gharaq jazīrat al-ḥūt* (*Memories of a Meltdown: An Egyptian between Moscow and Chernobyl*, 1998), a memoir-cum-travelogue modelled on García Márquez's literary reportage in *Relato de un náufrago* (*The Story of a Shipwrecked Sailor*, 1970) and *La aventura de Miguel Littín:*

clandestino en Chile (*Clandestine in Chile: The Adventures of Miguel Littín*, 1986). I examine how political iconography in *Warda* and the adaptation of García Márquez's reportage in Makhzangi's memoir cement Arab and Latin American ties of the mid-twentieth century. Examining the circulation of Latin American iconography and literature in the Arab world in the 1960s–1980s through the legacy of transnational solidarity, I argue that Arab leftist writers engage Third World solidarity long after this period. *Warda* and *Laḥaẓāt gharaq jazīrat al-ḥūt* typify exchanges between the Arab world and Latin America in Arabic literature. In a way, therefore, they are examples of relationships that may be traced to broader political landscapes and need to be read in light of the 1960s to apprehend Ibrahim's and Makhzangi's motivations and imperatives.

Latin American Iconography

In the late twentieth century, encounters with Latin America in Arabic literature were embedded in decolonisation movements and the Cold War.[6] Connections between Latin American and Arabic literatures redirected the historical ties between the Arab world and Latin America to the cultural sphere. In many ways, Arab writers revived the links noted above in Ashour's memoir. As I will show, these ties can be traced to two moments: anti-colonial and anti-imperial struggles in the 1960s and the translation of Latin American literature into Arabic from the 1970s.

Jeremy Prestholdt examines the iconography of Ernesto 'Che' Guevara within the Left in the 1960s and 1970s through transnational solidarity. The iconography of Che as a symbol of 'utopian dreams of revolution' was employed by leftist movements; 'Che was both a theorist of revolution and a young, idealist rebel' (Prestholdt 2012: 510–11). He was seen as 'an idealist who acted on his principles' (2012: 512). The photograph of Che Guevara, taken in 1960 by the Cuban photographer Alberto 'Korda' Díaz Gutiérrez and named *Guerrillero Heroico* (*Heroic Guerrilla*), printed in 1967 (2012: 513), was the romantic image of Che that circulated after his death: Guevara wearing a star beret (2012: 511). The image in Ashour's memoir in the home of Michael Thelwell, the department chair at the University of Massachusetts at Amherst, where she had enrolled on the advice of Shirley Graham Du Bois, the writer and widow of African American writer W. E. B. Du Bois, is evocative of the icon: 'Hanging on one wall was a giant black-and-white photograph of Che Guevara riding a horse in the jungle, his face glowing like the star on his black beret' (2018: 8–9). Jessica Stites Mor notes that 'OSPAAAL's poster art, which iconographically connected the ideological struggles of Latin American revolution with those of Vietnam, Palestine, the Congo, Yemen, and elsewhere, suggested the ability of individual causes to be considered from within a comparative frame and as interconnected on a trans-regional level' (2019: 59). Between 1968 and 1974 OSPAAAL '[a]rtists depicted African and Middle Eastern liberation struggles with strong visual references to Cuban and Latin American revolutionary iconography' (2019: 58).

Leftist Arab writers engaged with Latin American iconography and literature in the late twentieth century. The Egyptian colloquial poet Ahmad Fuad Negm (Aḥmad Fuād Nigm) composed a popular elegy on the death of the iconic Guevara and other Arab writers variously engaged with Guevara's iconography and death. For example, Palestinian poet and playwright Muin Bseiso (Mu'īn Bsīsū) wrote *Ma'sāt Jivāra* (Guevara's Tragedy, 1969).[7]

In half a century, Latin American literature had a wide circulation in the Arab world. The circulation of Latin American literature began in the 1970s at the time that Ashour was in America and aware of US policy in Latin America, Vietnam and Palestine. The translation and circulation of Spanish American literature in the Arab world was central to cultural exchange. Richard Jacquemond has noted the history of literary translation that led to the circulation of world literatures in Arabic: 'The 1950s and 1960s were the golden age of literary translation in Egypt, promoted and encouraged by the state within the framework of national or bilateral undertakings, such as the *mashru' al-alf kitab*, or Thousand Book Project' (2008: 119). Moreover, canonical literature was translated from hitherto neglected languages, such as *Don Quixote* in 1957–58 (Jacquemond 2008: 119). From the 1970s, there was a steady output of translations of Latin American literature into Arabic that promoted South-South exchange and the circulation of Latin American literature in the Arab world. From 1979 to 2005, translation from Spanish in the UNESCO *Index translationum* accounted for 9 per cent of translations in Egypt (Jacquemond 2009: 13). Since 1995, the National Translation Project, initiated by the Egyptian Higher Council for Culture, has included translation from Spanish (Baker and Hanna 2009: 337). Translations of Latin American literature into Arabic were also issued by Lebanese, Syrian and Moroccan publishers.[8]

A canon of Arabic translations of Latin American literature includes Jorge Luis Borges, Gabriel García Márquez and Jorge Amado. García Márquez has been the most widely read author in Arabic translation in the last twenty years (Jacquemond 2014: 14). There are abundant translations of his novels into Arabic. Arab writers drew on Latin American literature to address urgent and local struggles, as we will see, to make sense of the present; for example, Ibrahim turned to a failed revolution in Oman and Makhzangi to his socialist dreams that drew him to the Soviet Union.

Ibrahim and Makhzangi, who both belong to the generation of the 1960s, are drawn to Latin American culture in *Warda* and *Laḥaẓāt gharaq jazīrat al-ḥūt*. Both were prominent in the new avant-garde in the Arab world. In many ways, the two writers share a literary background and leftist ideology. Both travelled to the Soviet Union to study: Ibrahim had a grant to study filmmaking at the All-Russian State Institute of Cinematography in Moscow (1971–74),[9] and Makhzangi travelled to Kiev on a fellowship to study psychiatry. Both were leftist writers attracted to the Soviet Union; both were imprisoned – Ibrahim in 1959–64 and Makhzangi in the 1970s when he was active in the student movement. Both writers set works abroad: Ibrahim based his novel *al-Jalīd* (*Ice*, 2011) on his study in Moscow, and Makhzangi wrote *Laḥaẓāt gharaq jazīrat al-ḥūt* about his study in the Soviet Union. While Ibrahim is an iconoclast known for his experimental novels and the pioneer of an austere style, Makhzangi is a short story writer who experimented with genre in his short stories and memoir. Both sought to rework Latin American sources, iconography and genres in a documentary novel and a memoir. Ibrahim is known for his methodical research of his novels, while Makhzangi experiments with condensed forms that frame real events.

I draw a link between Ibrahim and Makhzangi through the interweaving of Che Guevara's diaries in *Warda* and García Márquez's reportage in *Laḥaẓāt gharaq jazīrat al-ḥūt*. Moreover, the writers typify the twin strands of Arab Latin American encounters in Arabic literature: the circulation and reception of Latin American literature in the Arab world and Arab engagement with Third Worldist left-wing movements. *Warda* returns to the heady 1960s (from which Ibrahim was far removed in 2000) and adopts the form of the diaries of the revolutionary icon Che Guevara; *Laḥaẓāt gharaq jazīrat al-ḥūt* ruminates on Makhzangi's Soviet study abroad, when he was attracted to a socialist utopia but then became aware of the decline of the Soviet Union, and adopts the genre of García Márquez's literary reportage.

'Guevara Is in Cairo'

Sonallah Ibrahim (b. 1937), a pre-eminent Egyptian writer and pioneer of the 'generation of the sixties' (*jīl al-sitīnāt*) in Egypt, has contributed to avant-garde Arabic literature and drawn many connections among other cultures in novels such as *Amrīkānlī* (2003), *al-Jalīd* (2011) and *Birlīn 69* (Berlin 69, 2014). Venerated in Arab culture for his iconoclasm and asceticism, he was often at odds with the establishment for his political activities. He was imprisoned from 1959 to 1964 for his activity in the Communist Party and released in a general amnesty. By his own account, he avidly read Russian, American and Latin American literature in prison, to which he attributes his cultural formation.[10] His novels are characterised by an archival or documentary style and a tone that is characteristically 'Marxist and anti-capitalist' (Starkey 2016: x).

The historical landscape in which Ibrahim sets *Warda* is telling of the novel's intersection of left-wing movements in the 1960s–70s Third World. Ibrahim revives the age of Third World revolutions in the novel, most of which is set in Oman. *Warda* transposes Latin American political iconography to the Dhofar revolution (1965–76) in Oman and Yemen. By framing events in the novel in a wider context of events in Egypt, Palestine, Vietnam and Cuba, Ibrahim creates ties between the Dhofar revolution and decolonisation in the Third World. He draws on Che Guevara's diaries in the notebooks of an Arab woman revolutionary in Oman from the mid-1960s to the mid-1970s. *Warda* followed Ibrahim's *Dhāt* (*Zaat*, 1992), a novel centred on a woman in 1970s Egypt and critical of consumerism and American imperialism, and *Sharaf* (Honour, 1997), a novel about a young Egyptian, Sharaf (Arabic for 'honour'), sentenced to prison in a capitalist Egypt, and his cellmate Dr Ramzi, an old militant Nasserist, and Sharaf's struggle to retain his 'honour' in prison. In a sense, *Warda* is an inversion of *Dhāt*, countering the iconoclasm of his 1992 postmodern novel of the 1970s culture of post-Open Door (*Infitāḥ*) consumerism with the revolutionary tide of the 1960s.

The plot is elaborately structured between Egypt and Oman. In 1992, an Egyptian narrator named Rushdy undertakes a trip to Muscat, the homeland of Warda (Arabic for, literally, 'flower' and 'rose') – the *nom de guerre* of a young Omani woman revolutionary and former Cairo University student whom he met in the late 1950s and with whom he was enamoured. The narrator, a left-wing revolutionary, was arrested and imprisoned in Cairo in the 1950s. Warda, originally named Shahla, and her brother Yaarib, leftist university friends of Rushdy, moved to Beirut then Oman where Warda became a guerrilla in the Dhofar revolution. Warda's notebooks are furtively sent to Rushdy when he arrives in Muscat. Her diaries recount the story of her involvement in the Dhofar Liberation Front from 1965 to 1975. The narrator arrives in the Dhofar province of Salalah where he has an amorous relationship with Warda's daughter, Waad (Arabic for 'promise'), who is in her uncle's custody. Warda, who wanted to preserve her notebooks, recorded that they be passed on to Rushdy and her daughter furnishes him with the remainder of her journals. There he discovers that Warda, who fled with the guerrillas to the Empty Quarter after the Dhofar Liberation Front lost control of Western Dhofar, then pregnant, was abandoned with a fellow guerrilla and lover, Dahmish, by her brother Yaarib and Bedouin guides in the desert in 1975. In the end, the narrator, frustrated, is forced to return to Egypt, and on his departure from Oman he encounters Yaarib, who had ironically started working with the government.

Warda retraces the ties created during decolonisation and the Cold War in Africa, Asia and Latin America. Set in post-1952 Revolution Egypt and Oman during the Dhofar revolution – spanning the 1955 Bandung Conference to the 1966 Tricontinental in Havana – *Warda* draws on the revolutionary ferment of the 1960s in the Third World. *Warda*, curiously set in the Arabian Peninsula, offers an assessment of thirty years of the

Arab world through a study of the Omani Dhofar revolutionaries and captures the revolutionary ferment of 1950s and 1960s Egypt. The novel offers a complex examination of the Dhofar revolution against Sultan Sa'id bin Taimur and the British and the revolutionary tide in the Third World more broadly.[11]

The structure of *Warda* is intricate. The novel is composed of a frame tale, Rushdy's 1992 diary of his trip to Muscat, and the enframed notebooks of Warda. Rushdy's trip is intimately intertwined with the 1960s Dhofar revolution. Ibrahim favours that *Warda* be read as a novel, though the style is documentary; in the epigraph, he declares: 'Some of the characters and events in the following pages are real. And others are fictional. For this reason, they are better read as a . . . novel!' (6).[12] Warda's diaries chronicle events in the Arab world from 1960 to 1975. The novel is documentary, full of excerpts from newspapers and parts of speeches by Gamal Abdel Nasser and Fidel Castro.[13] *Warda* alternates between the narrator in Cairo, Muscat and Salalah in 1992–93 and Warda's notebooks, which are set in Beirut, 1960–65, Dhofar, 1965–75, and Rub' al-Khalī (the Empty Quarter), 1975. Almost half of the novel is taken up by Warda's journal. The novel interchanges narrators: Rushdy and another first-person narrator, Warda, of the diary.

Warda commences in Cairo in September 1992, returns to Cairo in 1957–59, then Muscat in 1992 in a pattern that almost symmetrically alternates between Rushdy in 1992 and Warda in the 1960s. The second set of Warda's notebooks takes place in the Dhofar mountains in 1965–68. The frame tale recounts the adventures of a young revolutionary (Rushdy) during the 1956 Tripartite Aggression when Britain, France and Israel attacked Egypt over the nationalisation of the Suez Canal. Rushdy encounters Arab students who were political refugees from Yemen, Morocco, Palestine, Sudan and Oman in the Cairo University dorms. Yaarib is a fellow Marxist student in Cairo. When the armed struggle began in Oman in the spring of 1957, Egypt was preparing for the first democratic elections since the revolution and Algeria was in the midst of the War of Independence. In the 1950s there was a tension between nationalism and communism, which led to a split between communists and nationalists. In 1959, Rushdy – like Ibrahim – was arrested because of his involvement in the Egyptian Communist Party. The narrator notes: 'Finally, at the midnight hour on the first day of the new year 1959, pretty much everyone [Egyptian communists] – including me – was arrested and sent off to prison' (49; 65).[14] That was the last he saw of Yaarib and his sister.

Warda, and Warda's notebooks in particular, evoke the revolutionary fervour of the 1950s to 1970s and Tricontinentalism. Her diary is inspired by those of Che Guevara – 'a symbol of rebellion and revolution' in the words of Ibrahim.[15] Warda's notebooks span Third World revolutionary movements and central events in Egypt, Palestine, Algeria, Iraq, Yemen, Cuba, the Congo, China and Vietnam, with coverage of Patrice Lumumba's assassination, Che Guevara, the Cuban Revolution, the Algerian revolutionary Djamila Bouhired, Fidel Castro, Gamal Abdel Nasser's support of the revolution in Yemen, Salvador Allende's election, the coup in Chile, and the death of Allende. Warda blossoms into the modern revolutionary woman during the anti-colonial struggles of Africa, Asia and Latin America.

Che Guevara's diary is a source of inspiration for Warda during the Dhofar revolution. In a training camp in Dhofar Warda quotes from Che Guevara's diaries in Arabic on revolutionary ideals, guerrilla warfare and heroic behaviour. Furthermore, she participates in the revolutionary education of young men and women in a training centre – 'Camp Revolution' – and draws upon a sampling of Arabic translations of the writings of Guevara and Castro. She reads Jorge Amado's *Ocavaleiro de esperanca* or *Vida de Luís Carlos Prestes* (*The Knight of Hope* or *The Life of Luís Carlos Prestes*, 1942), a biography of the well-known Brazilian revolutionary. Che Guevara's diaries are quoted in Arabic and embedded in Warda's notebooks, creating the effect of a seamless translation from the original.[16] In her notebooks, Warda comments on his trip to Egypt in the entry for March 1965:

> Guevara is in Cairo. I wish I was there to meet him. I read an interview he did with a group of Egyptian intellectuals. He talked about the Cuban experience of uniting the five major revolutionary organizations, headed up by the group led by Castro, who had put in place a leadership that was from those petits bourgeois with revolutionary ties. (82; 102)

In 1959, Che Guevara travelled to Egypt on a tour of the Bandung countries in solidarity with the anti-colonial aspirations of the Non-Aligned Movement. The Tricontinental Conference of Solidarity of the Peoples of Africa, Asia, and Latin America, held in Havana in 1966, ushered in an era of Third World transnational solidarity in the common commitment to anti-imperialism that extended the non-alignment of the 1955 Bandung Conference to Latin America. Che Guevara made a second trip to Egypt from February to March 1965 that Warda follows in Muscat and notes among other news items in her diary. Amid her documentation of developments in Egypt and the Third World, she notes with suspicion on 10 April 1965: 'Something's going on with Guevara . . . The international press is talking about his disappearance . . . Could the CIA have assassinated him?' (84; 104) and dreams that she is with Guevara in the mountains.

In the last entry in her 1960–65 notebook, on 12 April 1965, she announces her plans to travel to Dhofar to begin the armed struggle. As she prepares to leave, she announces her adoption of the code-name 'Warda'. Ironically, Warda's name echoes an event and a news item on Sultan Qaboos, who came to power in a coup in 1970, in Rushdy's reports on 1992 Muscat: the Sultan 'would be given this namesake flower' (6). Now a leader of the Dhofar Liberation Front, she recounts in her second set of notebooks her activity in the mountains where she would read Che Guevara's 1961 *Guerrilla Warfare* in Arabic translation, muse on his revolutionary ideals, and wonder how to turn Bedouins into guerrillas. She transposes Che Guevara's diaries to Dhofar in an effort to adapt guerrilla warfare to Omani culture and offers an Arab woman's interpretation of Latin American armed struggle. In June 1965, she observes, and her commentary on the events she documents in her notebooks intertwines, developments in Cuba, Bolivia, Vietnam and Egypt: 'The newspapers are full of competing conjectures about the fate of Guevara and news of American defeats in Vietnam. Shortages roil Egypt: notebooks, cigarettes, matches, fruit' (107; 132). The documentary style of her journal offers a dizzying array of events that are seemingly disconnected but through which the disappearance of Che Guevara becomes interconnected with US imperialism and the socio-economic conditions in Egypt. In her December 1965 entry, she writes about the Tricontinental Conference, attended by delegates from the Congo, Syria, the Palestine Liberation Organization, Cuba and Chile, and the disappearance of Mehdi Ben Barka, the Moroccan revolutionary and chair of the organising council for the Tricontinental Congress. While in camp in the Dhofar mountains, where she sets out to establish a revolutionary regimen for the locals, on 12 April 1967, she notes the arrival of Guevara's open letter to the Organization of Solidarity of the Peoples of Africa, Asia, and Latin America: 'A Treatise on the State of Global Revolution'. She comments on Tricontinentalism while involved in an armed struggle in Oman with shared revolutionary aspirations and with an eye on Egypt. Che Guevara was executed by the Bolivian military on 9 October 1967. On 21 October 1967, she reports: 'His voice breaking in sorrow, Castro announced that Guevara has been killed by Bolivian army forces' (132; 158). The death of Che Guevara is emblematic of a transnational solidarity in the novel. In 1968, commenting on the May 1968 events in France against capitalism, consumerism and imperialism that began as protests by students at the Sorbonne and culminated in general strikes, she observes: 'The uprising of French students proves that revolution is on the march. Guevara's words are inspiring young people in the West' (138; 164). When Yaarib abandons her and Dahmish in the desert in 1975, she goes back to writing in her journal and remarks to her fellow guerrilla lover: 'I said that Guevara was keen to record his daily activity up until the last day of his life. That's the only way we know exactly what happened to him, who broke away from him, and who murdered him' (323; 368).

Ibrahim makes use of the genre of guerrilla literature in *Warda*, a novel that depends on Che Guevara's diary and a woman guerrilla's notebooks. Guerrilla literature is based on personal experience of armed conflict. Inserting Che Guevara's diary into the novel shows the transnational travels of guerrilla literature and the manual *El Quaderno Verno de Che* in Arabic. A lettered elite produced autobiographies and memoirs about revolutionary insurrections in Guatemala, El Salvador and Nicaragua, such as *La revolución perdida* (The Lost Revolution, 2003), by Nicaraguan poet, priest and militant Ernesto Cardenal (Esch 2020: 468), about the Sandinista Revolution (1970s–80s) in Nicaragua.[17] State-funded guerrilla literature circulated in Central America in the 1980s.

In the late twentieth century, insurgency by women appeared in Central America. The masculinity of the guerrilla in armed conflict is prominent.[18] However, *Warda* focuses on the image of the Arab woman revolutionary with a rifle, which is drawn from iconic photographs of Omani women with rifles in the armed struggle. Sophie Esch has astutely noted that 'the woman with the rifle is a highly ambiguous and controversial image' (2018: 22–3). She 'breaks gender roles so drastically' (2018: 23), but is subjected to existing patriarchal structures. In *Warda*, Warda takes up arms and follows Guevarian *foquismo* by joining insurgents in the mountains but her story is rife with struggle against patriarchal structures in Arab culture and the Dhofar Liberation Front. Esch has noted that after the Cuban Revolution the rifle was central to the image of *guerrilleros* and *guerrilleras*, like Che Guevara (2018: 25), whose example Warda follows in Ibrahim's novel.

Warda is unique among Ibrahim's novels for focusing on a left-wing, revolutionary woman. Warda is the antithesis of Dhat, whose story ends tragically, in that she emblematises the global revolutionary ferment of the 1960s. To express revolutionary fervour Ibrahim sets his novel in Third World revolutions and the Tricontinentalism of the 1960s. *Warda* thus epitomises Third World leftist movements and tricontinental solidarities that were obscured in 2000.

In *Warda*, Ibrahim reworks the iconography of Che Guevara in the notebooks of an Arab revolutionary in Oman to recapture the political mood of the 1950s and 1960s. He draws on central events and Guevara's *Guerrilla Warfare*, which was popular and circulated widely in Arabic. Though *Warda* purports to tell the story of the Dhofar revolution in Oman, Warda's diaries interconnect Third World left-wing movements and focus on developments in Egypt. The tone of the notebooks is that of Rushdy and the resemblance of events to that of Ibrahim's biography imparts the sense that they offer a documentary history of Third World revolutionary movements and his own.

Ibrahim is emblematic of the leftist internationalist Arab writer who situates his novels in broader historical and political landscapes. Ibrahim's 2020 *1970*, a novel about the last year in the life of Egyptian president Gamal Abdel Nasser, returns to the political iconography of the historical moment that has concerned him, and the attention to Che Guevara is resumed in his novel.[19] *1970* further resumes the interplay of the documentary and the fictional – the novel is interwoven with newspaper clippings from 1970 – but tellingly returns to the iconography of *Warda*. In *1970*, he recounts that Egyptian soldiers hung pictures of Che Guevara alongside pictures of Nasser in the trenches in the War of Attrition (1969–70) on the west bank of the Canal. Though there is no historical record of the practice, the iconography of Che Guevara persists in a novel that returns to the Egypt of 1970.

Sindbad the Shipwrecked Sailor

More than a decade later, the Egyptian short story writer Mohamed Makhzangi (b. 1950) adopted the form of García Márquez's *La aventura de Miguel Littín* and *Relato de un náufrago* in his memoir *Laḥaẓāt gharaq jazīrat al-ḥūt*, experimenting with literary reportage. Makhzangi blends the realism of journalism with fiction to capture the 1986 nuclear explosion of the Chernobyl plant in the Ukraine. In his memoir, Makhzangi reworks Arab and Latin American encounters through his adaptation of the form of *La aventura de Miguel Littín*.

Laḥaẓāt gharaq jazīrat al-ḥūt is divided into two narratives, 'The Four Seasons of Chernobyl' and 'Moscow Queues'. Makhzangi's 1986 'The Four Seasons of Chernobyl' tells the story of an Egyptian physician who travels to Kiev to study psychiatry. In 1986, Makhzangi travelled to the Soviet Union on a Soviet fellowship for which he had been nominated by the Afro-Asian Solidarity Organization in Cairo. Four months after the physician's arrival, Chernobyl's nuclear reactor erupts, releasing radiation into the serene Soviet spring. Afterwards, the narrator learns of a nuclear explosion through news reports and swirling rumours. Ignoring precautionary measures, the narrator strolls in Kiev in the midst of the radiation. In 'Moscow Queues', Makhzangi returns in 1990, a year and a half later, and, observing long queues in front of shops, a 'McDonalds' that has sprung up in Moscow, and lines of protestors with pamphlets, is unsettled by the changes in the Soviet Union.

Makhzangi's memoir describes moments he collected in the post-Chernobyl seasons. Like García Márquez who remarks upon the process of crafting the adventure of Miguel Littín's clandestine return to Chile to shoot a film under the Pinochet dictatorship into a visceral story, Makhzangi notes that he sought the essence of the story and 'its structural harmony': 'These are thus anti-memoirs [*lā mudhakkirāt*]: moments I collected while traveling through the fearful depths of an irradiated season' (22; 32).[20] In the preface, he describes his memoir as a 'kind of investigative literary reportage' and compares his style to García Márquez's reportage in *Relato de un náufrago* or *La aventura de Miguel Littín*. He further parses the form he has adopted to recount his encounter with the Soviet Union, which he compares to a sinking island on the back of a whale:

> This is reportage, a record distilled through the filter of literature; quotidian moments, very general, that intimately inscribe the very particular, the literary ... A form used by prominent authors under the urgent pressure of events that will simply not wait for the pure fermentation process of the creative spirit (Garcia Marquez, for example, in *The Story of a Shipwrecked Sailor* or *Clandestine in Chile: The Adventures of Miguel Littín*). This form has acquired a narrative sensibility through the efforts of writers who are essentially novelists. In the present case, it is transfigured because the writer is at heart a short story writer. Here, we glimpse the narrative rhythm of each moment and scene. The thread that stretches across these moments and images, stringing them together, is the thread of the queues before which the writer stands, reading and reflecting rather in the manner of an intimate conversation. Thus one shakes off the suspect nature of journalism and penetrates – by means of sensibility, form, and style – the realm of art; a small part of the project begun by the writer. (83–4)[21]

Relato de un náufrago and *La aventura de Miguel Littín* are two works with political overtones. *Relato de un náufrago* is a story crafted from a series of long interviews with a Colombian sailor, who was shipwrecked and spent ten days on a raft at sea, that exposes the duplicity of the government by revealing that the ship that sank was carrying heavy contraband and the official story alleged that the cause of the shipwreck was a storm to cover up the catastrophe. *La aventura de Miguel Littín* is a taut memoir of the famous Chilean filmmaker's adventure in his home country under Pinochet's dictatorship.

García Márquez's *La aventura de Miguel Littín: clandestino en Chile* tells the story of Littín's secret return to Chile to shoot a documentary film about the Pinochet military dictatorship, twelve years after the coup of 11 September 1973.[22] García Márquez parses the form:

> Por el método de la investigación y el carácter del material, *La aventura de Miguel Littín clandestino en Chile* es un reportaje. Pero es más: la reconstitución emocional de una aventura cuya finalidad última era, sin duda, mucho más entrañable y conmovedora que el propósito original y bien logrado de hacer una película burlando los riesgos del poder military. (1986a: 7)

> (In its nature and its method of disclosure, this is a piece of reporting. Yet it is something more: the emotional reconstruction of an adventure, the finality of which was unquestionably much more visceral and moving than the original – and effectively realized – intention of making a film that made fun of the dangers of military power.) (1986b: xxx)

García Márquez employs a form that preserves the tone and immediacy of Littín's visceral adventure in Chile.

Like García Márquez, whose journalism was intimately intertwined with his fiction, Makhzangi crafted a form of investigative literary reportage from both real events and his own encounter with the Soviet Union. Structured as vignettes, framed by 'The Four Seasons of Chernobyl', about the collapse of the famous reactor in 1986, and 'Moscow Queues', composed on his return to Moscow in 1990, *Laḥaẓāt gharaq jazīrat al-ḥūt* draws from the '*uqsūsa*' (very short story or vignette).[23] Makhzangi looks at the common strands of the two works now published together:

> I consider them to be a kind of investigative literary reportage; stories that celebrate the reality of lived moments. But these selfsame moments were selected and realized in the spirit of Art, and not of journalism. This is why I describe them as literary reportage. As journalism, they contain the kernels of real events and situations, and as story, they are products of craftsmanship and sorrow. (3–4; 7–8)

The sorrow is that of one who observes the collapse of the island of his dreams: 'I don't deny, even now, that the former Soviet Union – or more precisely, my hopes and illusions regarding the former Soviet Union – was part of a momentous personal dream' (4; 8). A 'romantic revolutionary' (*rūmānsī thawrī*) (5; 10), an habitué of the authorities' lists of communists and the prison-rosters, he dreamed of a 'socialist utopia' (*al-madīna al-fāḍila aw al-ishtirākiyya*) (6; 11). Attracted to 'a society ruled by social justice and collective solidarities', which seemed to him '(and still does) a beautiful and noble humanistic dream', he observes: 'my choice was already made for the East over the West' (6–7; 11). His choice was rooted in the legacy of the Cold War in Egypt, where a generation of leftist writers leaned towards the Soviet Union.

Makhzangi crafts a visceral memoir of his encounter with the Soviet Union. The memoir recounts the dissipation of his socialist dreams and captures the horror of the nuclear explosion and his impressions in the post-Chernobyl seasons where he became aware of his mortality.

'Enraptured', he arrives in Moscow in early 1986 and describes the 'first magical days' (6; 11–12) in a foreign country and thereafter his confusion. Four months later, when the Chernobyl plant exploded while he was in Kiev, he observed rampant bribery, cronyism, corruption and negligence. He almost suffered 'an emotional collapse' but pressed on with his dream (7; 12). The characteristics that he notes in spite of the 'Soviet ugliness' hold a note of his dreams – cultural opportunities, warmth and unity among Russians, the country's natural beauty, and the study of psychiatric medicine. Chernobyl is a moment of the collapse of 'the magnificent edifice that was the Soviet Union' (7; 13). His 'perfidious dream' is shipwrecked: the collapse of the Soviet Union and the lies were bitter for a dreamer from the South who had set his hopes on 'that happy legend in the Northeast' (8–9; 14–15). His utopian dream is condensed in the story from *The Thousand and One Nights* of Sindbad the sailor (*Sindbād al-baḥarī*) who discovers that the beautiful island on which he has been shipwrecked is a sleeping whale that starts to shudder and sinks into the ocean. The story of the tenuous island is evoked in the Arabic title: '*Laḥaẓāt gharaq jazīrat al-ḥūt*' (literally 'moments of the descent of the island of the whale').

While *Laḥaẓāt gharaq jazīrat al-ḥūt* plumbs the depths of Makhzangi's encounter with the Soviet Union, the form evokes the Arab Latin American ties he so clearly traces. He writes: 'The Soviet Union was just this: the fertile possibility of a fabulous island for humanity [*jazīra insāniyya*], but contingent, tenuously rooted on the back of a huge whale of lies, propaganda, flawed ideology masquerading as truth, and petty rulers attempting to govern a vast and noble country' (9–10; 16). Whereas 'The Four Seasons of Chernobyl' captures 'the black whale's momentous shudder' and the island's earthquake, 'Moscow Queues' shows 'that this island was quickly sinking into the dark sea to whose depths the black whale has plunged' (10; 16). He is shipwrecked on a utopia that was fast sinking in the post-Chernobyl Soviet Union.

The form of *Laḥaẓāt gharaq jazīrat al-ḥūt* echoes that of the memoir of Littín's clandestine adventures and so, too, does Makhzangi's tour of the Soviet countryside in the aftermath of Chernobyl. Makhzangi, a foreigner and exile in Kiev, is painfully exposed to radiation as he strolls through the irradiated Soviet spring. 'The Four Seasons of Chernobyl' heralds the sudden and miraculous eruption of spring in Kiev. References to 'harbingers' and 'the green explosion' abound and Russian words parsed in Arabic impart the ironies: 'There are heralds of spring's eruption, as of this spring's curse. Chernobyl. Molded by the Russian tongue to give shape to a different meaning, thus: churna, "black," and bul, "pain." The black pain' (14; 22). Before the nuclear reactor erupted on 26 April 1986, warnings were ignored or wilfully concealed. His memoir filters '[a] glossy surface [that] covered an ugly reality' (14; 23) of cronyism, bribery and corruption, capturing the drama of Chernobyl in Kiev, when the nuclear reactor erupts, and they are exposed to doses of radiation. While the Kiev spring blossomed, nuclear radiation spread. The Kiev spring blossoms in the shadow of the nuclear disaster, the lush foliage covering the radiation. It is a moment in which his sense of mortality – that he is one among the multitude of the 'Third World, the exhausted South' (21; 31) – is compounded.

In the summer, he returns with a group of foreign students – from Zaire, the Congo, Yemen, Egypt, Cambodia, Bangladesh and Colombia – from the market, laden with baskets of strawberries and buckets of river fish. Aghast, a Ukrainian woman asks if they have overlooked warnings that fruits and fish are likely to be poisoned by radiation. The students joke that they have calculated the average life expectancy in their countries in Africa, Asia and Latin America to be thirty-six. In other words, they would most likely die before the radiation had an effect from 'any number of routine Third World afflictions: disease, famine, floods, drought, prison, civil war' (54; 93). When an onlooker presses them further and notes that radiation causes birth defects, the students exchange jokes that they are unlikely to produce future generations. The dark humour of the narrator and his fellow students from the global South captures the irony that they are likely to suffer a dizzying array of afflictions among them and these precautions are thus superfluous.

Makhzangi begins to collect his observations in a notebook during his wanderings in the city 'shadowed by nuclear disaster' and looks for 'an aesthetic vision with a collapsing reality' (21–2; 31–2) or the essence of the story. He collects moments in the foreigners' dormitory and excursions in the city. His exile weighs upon him and 'explodes' (37; 60) in the spring. On impulse, he boards bus number 30. On his excursions, he collects moments of the exodus of children and foreigners from Kiev: a pregnant woman whose offspring could be a sign of life or the effects of radiation; a dog lying in a mangled radioactive heap in the street; fellow students in the Kiev dorms; and his fellow Egyptian student in the dorm whose son in Egypt is nursed from irradiated powdered milk imported from Europe. He tours the Soviet countryside, collecting scenes of the train station where children are shepherded on to trains to evacuate the city, a sanatorium where children with tuberculosis are quarantined, and the Chernobyl spring, where the harbingers of radiation are concealed.

Makhzangi's evocations of snow in the winter of Chernobyl capture the essence of his terror and encounter with death. In winter, a 'sublime whiteness' (72; 129) of snow covers irradiated dust and the verdure (and the sinking island of his utopian dreams). Snow falls early and covers 'the coffin' (a layer of earth that covers the Chernobyl reactor), creating a general anxiety that the snowfalls and alluvial mud will overflow and release the radiation beneath the snow. It is 'a desolate winter' in which the narrator treads 'carefully' and 'fearfully' on the snow. He passes through a graveyard where he discovers no Chernobyl grave, no inscription that preserves the memory of the explosion, simply the word 'Pochemu' (why) (80; 144) that echoes his bewilderment amid the nuclear horror.

Strolling through the streets of Moscow, Makhzangi puzzles out Russian words and contemplates the refraction of echoes, the most forceful 'Obuv' (shoes), repeating the word to make sense of a new 1990 consumerist society that besieges him, making him mistrustful and desolate. In 'Moscow Queues', Makhzangi puzzles over the phenomena of colourful advertisements and long queues rather than the signs of radiation. He pauses at, notably, the forceful 'shoes' (*obuv*) that recur in 'The Four Seasons of Chernobyl' where he remarks upon the 'humanity of shoes' (57; 99). In Kiev, shoes are removed and left outside to prevent the spread of irradiated dust. Shoes take on a variety of contradictory meanings: the shoes of children who disappear to the evacuation camps and foreign students at the dormitory who travel home with the exodus. The shoes he reads at the doorsteps are emblematic of human frailty and elicit a melancholy in the narrator amid the danger of radiation and exodus. In 1990, however, a new consumerist society assails him, with the forceful 'shoes' now echoing in the long queues jostling for consumer products and the flashing shop signs.

In Moscow, he is accosted by the leader of a gang who mistakes him for a Latin American. He feels foreign or 'other' (96; 163) to the gang leader, and the encounter echoes the group of students returning from the market with contaminated strawberries and fish who so clearly evoke the ill-fated 'Third World' or the 'impoverished South' (9; 15), who look to the Soviet Union for a utopian dream in 'The Four Seasons of Chernobyl'. By comparison, 'Moscow Queues' is a farewell to the dream of Moscow he evokes in 'The Four Seasons of Chernobyl'. Rather than the Chernobyl explosion depicted in 'The Four Seasons of Chernobyl', 'Moscow Queues' is rife with his observations of a rising consumerism and anti-Semitism upon his return to the Soviet Union in 1990.

Like García Márquez, Makhzangi adopts 'investigative literary reportage' to collect and capture moments of the Chernobyl spring. But *Laḥaẓāt gharaq jazīrat al-ḥūt* is more than a newspaper story; it is a visceral return to his Moscow years, written in the first person, and crafted from his own words. Makhzangi's memoir traces the collapse of his dreams of Moscow, his terror distilled in moments in the irradiated city. It recounts the Chernobyl explosion in retrospect. An imperiled narrator who recounts the visceral moments of a nuclear explosion, Makhzangi writes his own memoir.

Both García Márquez and Makhzangi employ reportage and set the story in the midst of a catastrophe. *Laḥaẓāt gharaq jazīrat al-ḥūt* captures encounters with the Soviet Union from Chernobyl to the rapid rise of consumerism and the descent of a socialist utopia. The memoir is produced under the urgent pressure of an event that evokes terror and captures Makhzangi's study abroad in the midst of a nuclear disaster in the Soviet Union during the Cold War.

Che Guevara's Diaries, Miguel Littín's Adventures

The adoption of the forms of Che Guevara's diaries and García Márquez's literary reportage shows a much deeper interplay that makes visible Arab Latin American ties. Ibrahim speaks to revolution in the 1960s that concerned him even when he was in Moscow, in the midst of a novel (he was writing *Najmat Aghusṭus* (*August Star*, 1974)), his labours punctuated by outbursts that he should return to Aden (Yemen).[24] For Ibrahim, it is also a compulsion: he had to write a novel about Third World revolution (after *Dhāt* about an anti-heroine in the post-revolutionary 1970s) just as he had to write a novel about Berlin, Moscow, 1967 (*1967*) and Nasser. In returning to the Chernobyl moment, Makhzangi also recounts his own ideological journey. In Makhzangi's memoir, politics is couched in the form, painstakingly reworked in his 'anti-genre'. In *Warda*, the political is layered into the form: Rushdy's diary, Che Guevara's diaries and Warda's journal in the revolutionary ferment of the 1960s. Makhzangi models his own memoir on García Márquez's literary reportage. The diary in *Warda* and literary reportage in *Laḥaẓāt gharaq jazīrat al-ḥūt* are essential forms. For Ibrahim, the iconic image of Che Guevara is central to Warda's diaries; Makhzangi presents a tenuous utopia. Ibrahim returns to a revolution that is eventually defeated; Makhzangi condenses an explosive moment in Soviet history.

Che Guevara, the romantic and revolutionary icon, echoes from *Warda* to *1970*, from Cairo to Oman. Ibrahim and Makhzangi rework Latin American iconography and literature to different ends. They offer examples of the circulation of Latin American culture in the Arab world and contribute to Arab Latin American literary ties. In focusing on political and ideological interconnections, Ibrahim and Makhzangi further cultural exchange in new ways.

Both typify the strands of Latin American political iconography and literary influence in Arabic literature. Ibrahim draws links to Third World liberation struggles and the Tricontinental. Like Ashour, Ibrahim revives historical links, making direct connections between Arab and Latin American left-wing movements. Latin American literary ties are refracted in Makhzangi's *Laḥaẓāt gharaq jazīrat al-ḥūt*. Like Ibrahim, Makhzangi creates ties to Latin American literature through genre. Translation promotes the readability of Arabic literature in a global market and, as a result, literary ties to Latin America become more visible. *Warda* has been translated into French and recently English, and *Laḥaẓāt gharaq jazīrat al-ḥūt* has been translated into English. While they make clear these connections in translation, Ibrahim and Makhzangi open up further directions for translation between Arabic and Spanish. These literary ties extend to the twenty-first century in direct relationships and experimental literature examined in the next chapter.

5

Dreams of Jorge Luis Borges, Nightmares of Carlos Fuentes: Arabic and World Literature

Reality is a sick dream.

Carlos Fuentes, *Terra Nostra*

In *Waḥdaha shajarat al-rummān* (*The Corpse Washer*, 2010), a novel by Iraqi writer Sinan Antoon (Sinān Anṭūn), a sculptor turned corpse-washer who inherits the family trade in Baghdad during the 2003 US invasion and the ensuing sectarian violence reads in the culture pages of the Iraqi daily *al-Jumhūriyya* 'a long article about the *Arabian Nights* and the Arabic literary tradition and how both had influenced Latin American writers' (37; 60).[1] The article cites 'Borges's fascination with the East' and his short story 'Averroes's Search' (37; 60). When Jawad the corpse-washer takes his uncle, an exile who has just returned to Baghdad, to the book market on al-Mutanabbi Street, a bookseller shows him rare editions of poetry collections by Iraqi poets Muḥammad Mahdī al-Jawāhirī and Saadi Yousef (Sa'dī Yūsif), Jurjī Zaydān's novels and Pablo Neruda's memoir. The book market street, named for the Abbasid poet Abu al-Ṭayyib al-Mutannabī, was bombed in 2007, an event that was emblematic of the obliteration of culture in Iraq. *Waḥdaha shajarat al-rummān* harnesses an Arab cultural heritage and Latin American literature to resurrect culture from the violence that plagued Iraq from the Iran-Iraq war to the US occupation.[2]

There are frequent allusions to Latin American literature in Arabic cultural production in the twenty-first century. Iraqi writers such as Jabbar Yussin Hussin, Sinan Antoon and Hassan Blasim have made connections to Latin American literature that draw on a shared cultural archive. Both Hussin and Antoon draw on Borges's 'Averroes's Search', and Blasim reinvents the magical realism of Gabriel García Márquez and Carlos Fuentes. In the case of Blasim, he has been compared to Latin American writers who have crafted a literature from violence and horror.

This chapter will focus on short stories from Iraq to explore Arab writers' direct relationships to Latin American literature and new directions in the twenty-first century. Arab writers experimented with intertextuality and new literary aesthetics in post-2003 Iraq. The short stories we will examine in this chapter are part of post-2003 Iraqi literature of war, occupation and migration by writers such as Alia Mamdouh (Aliya Mamdūḥ), Inaam Kachachi (In'ām Kachāchī), Iqbal al-Qazwini (Iqbāl al-Qazwīnī), Sinan Antoon, Ali Bader (Alī Badr) and Fadhil al-Azzawi (Fāḍil al-'Azzāwī). These writers, many of whom are translated and based in Europe, the US or the Arab world, have helped Arabic literature travel abroad.

Arabic literature of migration has burgeoned in Europe in the twenty-first century. World literature centres have moved to European capitals along with exiles and migrants. Johanna Sellman ties Arab migration to Europe to Arabic cultural production: 'Berlin, Stockholm and Amsterdam have become important centres for Arab cultural production in Europe, displacing the primacy of London and Paris' (2018: 754). Thus, Arab migration has created new world literature routes of circulation and translation. Arabic literature gains visibility in world literature through translation or when Arab writers travel abroad. The effects of transnationalism on comparative models may be seen in the connections that Arab writers foster with Latin American literature. The reworking of genres and forms that travel from Latin America in Arabic literature refocuses attention on interconnections among literatures.

The study of the relationship of Arabic literature to Latin American literature in the twenty-first century offers an example of a model of Arabic literature that travels abroad and is no longer local. These relationships promote new comparative models, helping us to read two world literatures that are rarely examined together. Moretti describes world literature as 'one world literary system (of inter-related literatures); but a system which is different from what Goethe and Marx had hoped for, because it's profoundly unequal' (2000: 56). The examination of direct linkages between Arabic and Latin American literatures allows us to rethink the asymmetry and inequality of world literature.

The circulation of Arabic literature draws attention to connections to Latin American literature and allows us to focus on non-Eurocentric models of comparison and new links between literatures. Hussin and Blasim are two cases in point. The translation of their short story collections has offered ways for them to migrate into world literature and to circulate again in Arabic. The fact that stories by Hussin and Blasim are translated into English, French and Spanish makes such connections visible.

This chapter examines intercultural exchange and international networks that open up new directions in Arabic literature in the twenty-first century by focusing on the relationship of the Iraqi writers Jabbar Yussin Hussin and Hassan Blasim to Argentine writer Jorge Luis Borges and Mexican novelist Carlos Fuentes. In this chapter, I focus on 'Yawm Bwinus Ayris' ('The Day in Buenos Aires', 2000) from the collection *Al-Qāri' al-Baghdādī* (*The Reader of Baghdad*, 2003) by Jabbar Yussin Hussin[3] and 'Kawābīs Kārlus Fwintis' ('The Nightmares of Carlos Fuentes') from the collection *Majnūn sāḥat al-ḥurriyya* (*The Madman of Freedom Square*, 2009) by Hassan Blasim. Both writers migrated to Europe and published story collections that circulate in translation. While there has been scholarship on Hussin's story, direct reworkings of Latin American literature in Arabic have been little noted. Short story collections by Hussin and Blasim experiment with new relationships to Latin America and the Arab world in the twenty-first century. Hussin's and Blasim's stories are shaped by intertextuality and intercultural exchange. Blasim experiments with magical realism, employs the modes of fantasy and horror, and makes connections between Latin America and the Arab world. Both writers offer an Arab Latin American model that may be read as world literature: Hussin reworks Jorge Luis Borges's 'La busca de Averroes' ('Averroes's Search', 1947), a short story that draws on an Andalusian heritage; Blasim makes allusions to Latin American literature and the *Thousand and One Nights* tradition, frequently reworked in Latin American literature, in the midst of the Iraq war and explores the effects of migration. While Hussin evokes the dream of a shared Andalusian heritage and intercultural dialogue, Blasim employs nightmares to evoke the horror and violence of neo-colonialism and migration.

This chapter will begin with a brief survey of Borges's 'La busca de Averroes' insofar as Hussin's story echoes Borges's and will focus on Arab Latin American contact in the two stories. Instead of a comparison between Borges and Hussin, the chapter examines how the focus on Averroes (Ibn Rushd in Hussin's story) and intercultural exchange compares to Blasim's borrowings from Latin American literature. Both rework Latin American literature in Arabic and illustrate particular circuits in which their stories are available in translation and may be read in connection to Latin American literature.

Dreams of Jorge Luis Borges

Jabbar Yussin Hussin (b. 1954), an Iraqi short story writer and journalist, went into exile in France in 1976, returning briefly to Iraq after the US invasion in 2003 (Manguel 2007: 111). Hussin's 'Yawm Bwinus Ayris' was first published in French translation in the francophone journal issued by L'Institut du Monde Arab, *Qantara*, in a special issue dedicated to the Córdoban philosopher Ibn Rushd in 1998. 'Le Jour de Buenos Aires' ('The Day in Buenos Aires') found its way to Hussin's short story collection, published first in French translation, *Le lecteur de Baghdad* (1999), and thereafter in Arabic in *Al-Qāri' al-Baghdādī*, and was subsequently translated into Spanish. Hussin's 'Yawm Bwinus Ayris' offers an Arabic rewriting of Jorge Luis Borges's (1899–1986) 'La busca de Averroes', a story about the Argentine author's interpretation of the Andalusian philosopher.[4] Hussin characterises 'Yawm Bwinus Ayris' as a continuation of Borges's story.[5] I read 'Yawm Bwinus Ayris' through Borges's 'La busca de Averroes' and Hussin's relationship to Latin American literature. The Andalusian philosopher Ibn Rushd, whose effects on the East and the West, influence on Arab-Islamic philosophy, and model of rationalism make him suited to themes of cultural exchange, plays a central role in the Latin American and Arabic stories. 'La busca de Averroes' focuses on mistranslation, while 'Yawm Bwinus Ayris', I argue, reworks the central events and characters of Borges's story to mirror Hussin's exile and intercultural exchange.

Hussin's stories are particularly unique in Arabic literature in general in that they appear to circulate more widely among world circuits – French and Spanish – than in Arabic and offer fantastic treatments of the effects of the Iraq war. Hussin writes in Arabic and French and often publishes his fiction first in French. He has been compared to Borges owing to his epigraphs, erudition, evocation of Babel, and telescoping of time,[6] and his stories resemble Borgesian parables. Hussin's collection *Al-Qāri' al-Baghdādī* synthesises the fantastic and the real in stories about conquest and pillage: wolves who run wild on the banks of the Tigris; Ibn Rushd's dream of Jorge Luis Borges in Buenos Aires; and the Mongol invasion of Baghdad (1258).

Borges's 'La busca de Averroes' evokes Averroes, the twelfth-century Andalusian Muslim philosopher, physician and jurist, composing the eleventh chapter of *Tahāfut al-Tahāfut* (Incoherence of the Incoherence). As he writes the eleventh chapter during the siesta, Averroes is aware of the sounds of the garden, the orchard and 'la querida ciudad de Córdoba' ('the beloved city of Cordova') (286; 180).[7] He puzzles over two Greek words that had interrupted his commentary on Aristotle's *Poetics*: tragedy and comedy: 'Esas dos palabras arcanas pululaban en el texto de la *Poética*; imposible eludirlas' (287) ('Those two arcane words pullulated throughout . . . the *Poetics*; it was impossible to elude them' (181)). But they elude him: he is distracted by children playing in the patio below and looks through the balcony at the scene in which they enact the roles of a muezzin, a minaret and the faithful worshippers. Afterwards, he is invited to dinner with the traveller Abulcasim Al-Ashari, who has returned from Morocco, in the home of the Quranic scholar Farach. Abulcasim recounts his trip to China, where he was taken to a theatre where fifteen or twenty actors performed a story. Ironically, the examples of drama elude Averroes who mistranslates the words in his manuscript: '"Aristú (Aristóteles) denomina tragedia a los panegíricos y comedias a las sátiras y anathemas. Admirables tragedias y comedias abundan en las páginas del Corán y en las mohalacas del santuario"' (293) ('"Aristu (Aristotle) gives the name of tragedy to panegyrics and that of comedy to satires and anathemas. Admirable tragedies and comedies abound in the pages of the Koran and in the *mohalacas* of the sanctuary"' (187)). With the mistranslation, the narrator appears in the story, as Averroes disappears, and declares: 'En la historia anterior quise narrar el proceso de una derrota . . . Recordé a Averroes, que encerrado en el ámbito del Islam, nunca pudo saber el significado de las voces *tragedia* y *comedia*' (293–4) ('In the foregoing story, I tried to narrate the process of a defeat . . . I remembered Averroes who, closed within the orb of Islam, could not know the meaning of the terms *tragedy* and *comedy*' (187, emphasis in original)). In the postscript, the narrator interrupts the story and merges with Averroes as he acknowledges his own defeat: 'Sentí que Averroes, queriendo imaginar lo que es un drama sin haber sospechado lo que es un teatro, no era más absurdo que yo, queriendo imaginar a Averroes, sin otro material que unos adarmes de Renan, de Lane y de Asín Palacios' (294) ('I felt that Averroes, wanting to imagine what a drama is without ever having suspected what a theatre is, was no more absurd than I, wanting to imagine Averroes with no other sources than a few fragments from Renan, Lane and Asín Palacios' (187–8)). Borges likens his evocation of the untranslatability of Averroes to Averroes's mistranslation of theatre.

'La busca de Averroes' belongs to a group of stories in which Borges shows an earnest interest in the Islamic Orient and is unique in its focus on the Muslim philosopher.[8] The ambivalence of Borges's Orientalism vis-à-vis Averroes and Islam in 'La busca de Averroes' is characteristic of his Orient. Ian Almond acknowledges Borges's Orientalism: 'His East is, to a large extent, the East of a host of European travelers and scholars – Sykes, Müller, Burton, and Renan – a mixture of the exotic and the esoteric, the scholarly and the fantastic, the orthodox and the arcane' (2004: 437–8). An ambivalent Orientalism pervades 'La busca de Averroes' in that the narrator declares that Averroes is enclosed in 'the orb of Islam' and therefore can never fully know drama. Christina Civantos notes the story's Orientalist assumptions by observing that Averroes never knows that he is 'enclosed in the orb of Islam' (2017a: 65). Ironically, the narrator can never fully understand the Orient he describes and professes to know. Almond reads the narrator's comments on the limitations of his evocation of Averroes from fragments of Renan, Lane and Asin Palacios as a disavowal of his Orient, an acknowledgement that Orientalism is 'fictitious' and 'illusory' (451). In my view, 'La busca de Averroes' highlights

Averroes's (and the narrator's) defeat and otherness, that no one in the world of Islam can conjecture the meaning of tragedy and comedy, while the narrator never acknowledges his own Orientalism. Civantos concludes that the irony in 'La busca de Averroes' is that the narrator acknowledges the limits of language, but 'he is unaware or uncritical of Orientalist assumptions' (2017a: 71).

Hussin's 'Yawm Bwinus Ayris' inverts Borges's story and centres on Ibn Rushd's encounter with Borges. Borges has appeared in francophone Arab literature, making his appearance an antecedent to Hussin's story, which appeared in French in *Le lecteur de Baghdad.* The Moroccan writer Tahar Ben Jelloun (b. 1944) models a character on the Argentine Jorge Luis Borges in his novel *L'Enfant de sable* (*The Sand Child*, 1985), winner of the 1987 Prix Goncourt. The blind troubadour (*le troubadour aveugle*), who appears in a café in Marrakesh, is 'Habillé d'un costume sombre, grand et mince' (171) ('[t]all and thin, wearing a dark suit' (134)).[9] 'Nous sommes donc à Marrakech, au cœur de Buenos Aires' (174) ('So, we are in Marrakesh, and in the heart of Buenos Aires' (136)), the narrator remarks. The blind troubadour is a well-travelled character who has landed in Marrakesh and has been to the University of al-Azhar in Cairo. Shuttered in a library and holding an old coin, an avid reader of encyclopedias and dictionaries, he is 'ce visiteur venu d'un autre siècle, venu d'un pays lointain et presque inconnu' (185) ('a visitor from another century, from a distant, almost unknown country' (145)).[10] In a café, he tells a story of a woman who 'avait suivi un étranger, un Arabe d'Amérique latine. C'était un commerçant égyptien ou libanais venu acheter des tapis et des bijoux' (186) ('had followed a stranger, an Arab from South America, an Egyptian or a Lebanese merchant who had come to buy carpets and jewelry' (145)) and left with him. 'Versé d'un bidonville argentin dans une médina arabe' (192) ('Thrown from an Argentinian shantytown into an Arab medina' (151)), his character captures his transcontinental travels and the novel's migration between Latin America and North Africa. Critics have examined the import of Ben Jelloun's inclusion of an unnamed character modelled on the Argentine Borges in a novel that tells the story of Ahmed-Zahra, a daughter raised as a man by a patriarchal father who has seven daughters and wishes for a son. The appearance of the character contributes to the fabulism of a novel characterised by the exoticisation of Arab culture and locales. The story of Ahmed-Zahra evokes the magical world of Borges, dovetailing into magic and exoticism (El Younssi 2014: 241) in drawing upon Moroccan folklore and Arab-Muslim culture. Critics have argued that *L'Enfant de sable* draws upon Moroccan folklore, Arab-Muslim culture and Latin American magical realism, and produces self-Orientalisation, in French, in order to gain a wide readership.[11] Hussin's story has an antecedent in Arab francophone literature and draws from the Oriental themes of Borges (who, for Arab writers, is not of the West and has an interest in the Arab world) that attract Arab writers like Ben Jelloun and Antoon.

The epigraph of Hussin's story is drawn from Borges's 'La busca de Averroes'. Hussin quotes from Borges's story: 'With firm, painstaking calligraphy, Averroes added these lines to the manuscript "Destruction of the Destruction": "*Aristotle gives the name 'tragedy' to panegyrics and the name 'comedy' to satires and anathemas. In the Quran and the mu'allaqat of the mosque, there is room for neither tragedy's magic nor for comedy*"' (113; 101, emphasis in original).[12] He quotes a mistranslation into Arabic most likely by Borges's translators, the translator notes, because the assumption that tragedy and comedy exist in the Qur'an in the original is 'blasphemous' (Jarrar 2007: 112). The quote from 'La busca de Averroes' shows Averroes in the process of translating the two enigmatic words: 'There are many admirable tragedies and comedies in the Quran and the mu'allaqat of the mosque.'

Hussin's 'Yawm Bwinus Ayris' reworks Borges's 'La busca de Averroes'. Hussin's story commences with the Córdoban Ibn Rushd (1126–98) who, one afternoon, remembers a woman crossing an alleyway in Marrakesh while he was en route to Sultan Yusef, to whom he was to expound Aristotle.[13] Awakened by a red-headed chambermaid's song in the courtyard, he remembers his siesta's dream of Borges. Ibn Rushd then entertains the trader Abu-al-Qasim al-Ash'ari, who has just returned from China, and Farah, a Quranic scholar. To distract his guests from a rift between them, Ibn Rushd relates part of his siesta's dream of Jorge Luis Borges. In his dream, a blind librarian, Borges, welcomes him into his home. Upon recounting his dream, Ibn Rushd remembers that the passage Borges quotes to him is his own.

Hussin depends on the same characters in Borges's story but brings together Ibn Rushd and Borges. The story commences with Ibn Rushd's dream of the woman in Marrakesh. Though the woman is unveiled, and the image of her face is embedded in his memory, there is no description of her face. The almost-sensual image of the woman passes through his memory on the border between sleep and wakefulness, a daydream or memory of Marrakesh. He is awakened by his chambermaid's song. The red-haired chambermaid, who sings in the courtyard, echoes the red-haired slave girl who is tortured by the dark-haired slave girls in the harem in 'La busca de Averroes', though her plaintive song about Córdoba in 'Yawm Bwinus Ayris' sets the tone of Hussin's story. The gathering with Abu-al-Qasim al-Ash'ari and Farah echoes Borges's story. Like 'La busca de Averroes', the conversation with his guests centres on al-Ash'ari's trip to China.

Ibn Rushd, in al-Andalus, recounts his dream of Buenos Aires:

> 'While you were on your way in, I felt as though I were in a different world. On my way there, I didn't see anything except a river that was wider than Jehoon and greater than Sehoon [rivers in Paradise] cutting through green quarters that were neither Jenan nor Andalusia. Empty spaces, in which there were no people or animals, but it was, God knows, real. I found myself in a strange city, without any voyager's dust.' (116; 106)

Farah declares: 'It was a trip to paradise' (116; 106). Ibn Rushd recounts his dream to his guests:

> 'A blind man who welcomed me into his elevated house . . . told me it was a city in a new world, and he called it "Buenos Aires," or something similar to that, and that he was one of its residents and had heard of Córdoba and Andalusia. As though he's just been there the day before.' (116; 106)

Ibn Rushd's comments invoke Borges's story through the description of Borges, who is familiar with al-Andalus to which he seems to have recently travelled, as he in a sense has in 'La busca de Averroes'. Buenos Aires, the dream's city, appears to be real. Ibn Rushd's dream is 'real' in that his fantastic encounter, in which he travels to another continent and meets a modern author, appears to be plausible. Hussin's story blurs the borders between the real and the magical, the gathering with his guests and the meeting with Borges. Ibn Rushd offers us no description of his host's face (like the woman from Marrakesh):

> 'He told me his name was Borges, and I don't know what this name means, neither in Castilian nor in Arabic. He was a blind man who spoke to me in a Castilian dialect . . . He said he knew me, and spoke my full name. He seemed like a wise man or a poet, like ibn-Ma'ra, memorizing everything he hears, for he spoke with me at length about the ancient texts and stated that reading them was important.' (116; 106–7)

Ibn Rushd compares the Arab Abbasid blind poet Abū al-'Alā al-Ma'arrī to Borges.[14] The moment of Ibn Rushd's discovery that the passage Borges recites is his own mirrors Borges's admission that Averroes's defeat is also his own in 'La busca de Averroes'. Unlike Borges's story where Averroes is distracted by Abulcasim's description of a theatrical performance he is unable to relate to his translation, Ibn Rushd is distracted by his memory and his own passage that he is unable to locate in his dream. Ibn Rushd's encounter with Borges in Buenos Aires in his dream may be read as a metaphor of the unity of thought and the world in spite of temporal and spatial differences.[15]

Ibn Rushd's dream of Borges is central to Hussin's inversion of Borges's 'La busca de Averroes'. Al-Ash'ari's comparison of afternoon dreams to 'chimeras' (*aḍghāth*) (illusory and fantastic), forgotten and incomplete, while Farah likens Averroes's dream to 'a myth told by a blind man' (*khurāfa*) (117; 107), comments on the irrationality of the dream. The narration of the dream itself is deferred in the story: Ibn Rushd does not recount the full dream to his guests and wishes to recount the rest of his dream to al-Ash'ari. Like Borges-the narrator who interrupts the story of Averroes in the midst of the philosopher's (mis)translation in 'La busca de Averroes', the narrator interrupts Ibn Rushd's narration of his dream in Hussin's story. Haunted by the image of the woman from Marrakesh, Ibn Rushd brushes her aside and parses the rest of his dream: 'The image of a red fruit, which he'd never seen in his life, had captivated him. A few pieces of the fruit were placed in a decorated plate on the blind man's table. He smelled its strange scent while the blind man asked him the reason for his exile' (118; 108). Curiously, the Arabic reads 'He thought of Marrakesh' (108) instead of 'Again he thought of the woman from Marrakesh' in the translation (117), and Marrakesh, from which he was exiled to Córdoba by Caliph Sultan al-Mansour, is the focus of the rest of his dream of Borges. In Arabic, the feminine pronoun in 'lākinahu azāḥaha' (108) ('but he brushed her aside', my translation) refers to Marrakesh, and the phrase is followed by the woman's face that he remembers. The image of the red fruit he has never seen is superimposed over the dream of the woman. Like the strange city, the fruit has an unfamiliar aroma and a foreign name.

Ibn Rushd's dream of Borges is centred on exile and intercultural dialogue. Hussin shares with Ibn Rushd the condition of exile. The philosopher's exile 'mirrors' the author's (Berg 2010: 155). Ibn Rushd recounts to Borges his fall from favour and banishment from Marrakesh to Córdoba by Caliph al-Mansour for an error by a stuttering scribe to whom Ibn Rushd dictates his words, and his story echoes Hussin's exile from Iraq. Like Borges's story, where Averroes's defeat mirrors Borges's, Ibn Rushd's exile mirrors Hussin's. Ibn Rushd is aware of the irrationality of dreams: 'In myths and dreams – and this was something that confused him – a person possesses a degree of courage he is unable to possess in reality' (118; 108). The irrational in his dream rests in his courage in explaining the cause of his exile. Thus, Ibn Rushd remembers 'his catastrophe' ('*nakbatuhu*') (109, my translation) – his exile – that conjures the word '*miḥna*' ('ordeal') in the Arabic translation of the title of 'La busca de Averroes' in the epigraph of Hussin's story, 'Miḥnat Ibn Rushd' ('Averroes's Ordeal'), with overtones of the author's own catastrophe, and Marrakesh.[16] Hussin, who most likely read Borges in Arabic or French translation, focuses on Ibn Rushd's 'catastrophe' or 'ordeal'. Ibn Rushd's dream shows the centrality of exile to Hussin's story. Hussin's story reworks the oblique allusion to exile in 'La busca de Averroes' when Averroes, tormented by nostalgia for Córdoba in Marrakesh, recites an apostrophe to an African palm. Whereas Borges's story focuses on mistranslation, Hussin's story centres on exile. In Hussin's story, Ibn Rushd's afternoon dream of Marrakesh evokes his blind host guiding him around a house full of books, both ancient and modern. The anachronistic modern literature (he does not know) in his host's library also connects Borges, Ibn Rushd and Hussin.[17] The dream bridges time, space and culture and interconnects them: Borges and Ibn Rushd, the librarian and the philosopher, Jorge and Jabbar. In the dream, he is captivated by 'the image of red fruit' (117; 108). Curious about 'the taste of the red fruit' (118; 109), whose aroma lingers in his memory, Ibn Rushd plans to ask al-Ash'ari the traveller about the word in 'Castilian', which is retained in Arabic. By the story's end and the dream's completion, he recalls 'the blind man in his dream calling them "*los tomates*"' (118; 109). Hussin recalls 'los tomates' in Egyptian filmmaker Youssef Chahine's film about Ibn Rushd:

> 'Los tomates' winks at Egyptian filmmaker Youssef Chahine's film, *Al-Maṣīr* (Destiny, 1997). In the film, there is a basket laden with tomatoes and other fruits that often appears. I was interested in that scene; tomatoes, which are considered a kind of fruit, not present in the Old World; they were brought to Europe by an Italian and cultivated widely in the sixteenth century. In Italian, the word is 'Pomodoro' – 'pomo d'oro' (golden apple). Tomatoes are originally golden colored and originated in Central America and especially Mexico. Therefore, the word for tomato in Syria, Lebanon, and Palestine resembles the Italian: '*Banadora.*' The idea of tomatoes in Chahine's film intimated for me Ibn Rushd's question about them; in effect, he does not know them and they are present in the blind writer's homeland, Argentina.[18]

'Los tomates' are unfamiliar, an exotic fruit originally from Latin America, but the story ends with the translatability of that which has no equivalent in al-Andalus (and Arabic).

The translator's note of Hussin's 'Yawm Bwinus Ayris' states: 'This story is a response to Borges's 'Averroes' Search', in which Borges writes about that old master's attempts at understanding the meaning of the words comedy and tragedy' (Jarrar 2007: 112). Randa Jarrar observes: 'the translation of the following story – its anecdote about the stuttering scribes, its genesis in another story, which itself is based on history – continues the tradition that Borges began' (2007: 112). It is a tradition of intercultural translation. Civantos has argued that Hussin responds to Borges's Orientalism and the focus on untranslatability in his story through the character of Ibn Rushd, who combines both rationalism and irrationality and 'makes contact with Borges' (2017a: 79). The irrationality is to be found in the dream he has in his siesta that he recounts to his guests (Civantos 2017a: 80). Ibn Rushd's dream underscores dialogue and translatability.

The dream of Borges is emblematic of intercultural dialogue. Ibn Rushd has a conversation with Borges in Buenos Aires, an event by which Hussin invokes a shared heritage of the Arab world, al-Andalus and Latin America and, more specifically, Borges's 'La busca de Averroes', which is also part of Hussin's shared culture and began the tradition in which he writes. While Borges's story is Orientalist, Hussin conjures intercultural translation through the Córdoban Ibn Rushd's dream of Borges.

Hussin translates Borges through Ibn Rushd's encounter with him (instead of Borges who translates Averroes translating Aristotle in 'La busca de Averroes') in his story. In contrast to defeat in Borges's story, Hussin's story offers a simulacrum of dialogue and exchange. Whereas one appears and the other disappears in Borges's story, Borges and Ibn Rushd meet in Hussin's. Hussin transposes Ibn Rushd (like Borges for whom Averroes is a mirror of himself), the exiled philosopher and his nostalgia to Argentina and refracts his own exile. Like the passage that Borges recites, Ibn Rushd's exile that Borges also asks about is his own.

While Borges's 'La busca de Averroes' is a story about mistranslation and defeat, Hussin's 'Yawm Bwinus Ayris' is a story about intercultural contact. Hussin's story is multi-layered: Hussin rewrites Borges's story about Averroes who mistranslates Aristotle. Hussin's story imports Borges's story into Arabic literature, like Borges who introduces Averroes through modern Spanish literature.[19] Furthermore, Hussin appropriates Ibn Rushd. In contrast to Borges's Averroes, 'enclosed in the orb of Islam', Hussin's Ibn Rushd, who travels to Buenos Aires where he meets Borges, is open to other cultures.

The otherness of the Orient is redressed in Hussin's story. The story's tone is different. It does not focus directly on translation; rather, it focuses on Ibn Rushd's dream and encounter with Borges. As an Arab writer who speaks to Borges's story through Ibn Rushd, Hussin contests Borges's Orientalism. Rather than the self-Orientalisation in Ben Jelloun's novel, Hussin's story evokes kinship between Ibn Rushd and Borges, and between Ibn Rushd and Hussin through the condition of exile.

In another story, 'El mensajero de México' ('The Messenger from Mexico', 2006), Hussin explores further Arab Latin American cultural encounters. Hussin's 'Le messager de Mexico' was written in French and translated into Spanish at the behest of his friend, Argentine writer Alberto Manguel. Manguel assembled *Sol Jaguar: Antología de cuentos sobre México* (Sun Tiger: An Anthology of Stories about Mexico, 2010), a collection of world literature centred on Mexico and featuring short stories by Jorge Luis Borges and Julio Cortázar. 'El mensajero de México' was thereafter translated into English ('The Messenger from Mexico') and Arabic ('Rasūl Mexico').

In 'El mensajero de México', the narrator recounts a strange encounter with an Indian he met by chance in the ruins of Tequila and again at the entrance to his lodgings in Guadalajara. In a café the Indian, who seems to have travelled through time and appears to be enigmatic and familiar, approaches him. Afterwards, the Indian reappears frequently in his dreams: in a park, on a balcony and in Baghdad. He reappears at the narrator's lodgings with a parchment (*pergamino*), encoded in hieroglyphics (*jeroglíficos*), from which he reads a history of conquest by white settlers in another language. The Indian unrolls the parchment and tells the narrator that he will be able to read from the coded parchment and will understand in the language he thinks in. Upon the Indian's departure, the narrator unfurls the parchment and begins to read a page that never ends. By the story's end, the narrator has been reading the parchment of misery and has not finished it yet.

In 'El mensajero de México', the Iraqi narrator encounters the Indian, conjured from the ruins of an Aztec city in Mexico. When he encounters him again, the narrator has the impression 'that it had all happened before in a distant dream, a dream in which my whole life could be seen in this square, recounted by this Indian, who had also come from far away' (130).[20] The narrator describes the Indian through both dreams and nightmares: 'I let myself be guided by this stranger who had come from my dreams (*aḥlamī*) perhaps or my nightmares (*kawābīsī*)' (131). The Indian reads 'all that had not yet been written' and the narrator 'again had the feeling that all this had already happened. He was talking about a dream lived long before I had arrived in this city' (132). The narrator reads, in the parchment about ruins, the destruction of the temple of Quetzalcoatl at Teotihuacan. He evokes both the unity of language and the shared fate of Mexico and Iraq in the parchment brimming with the destruction of ancient cultures. Hussin's Mexico-set story recuperates Mexico's indigenous heritage and Iraq's ancient civilisation, which have both been destroyed. The encounter with the Indian recalls Borges's 'El libro de arena' ('The Book of Sand') where a stranger, a Bible peddler, offers the narrator a sacred book that has no beginning and no end. The word 'rasūl' (Arabic for both 'prophet' and 'messenger') refers to the Indian who rises from the ruins and furnishes the Iraqi with the parchment, which encodes his own country's destruction. 'El mensajero de México' is reminiscent of another Borges story and an allegory for Iraq's occupation (evoked by the destruction of a pre-Columbian city and, in a story from his collection *Le lecteur de Baghdad*, the Mongol invasion of Baghdad).

Hussin's story 'Le songe de l'officier américain' ('The Dream of the American Soldier') also appeared in Spanish translation in an anthology.[21] The story makes no allusions to Latin American literature, but belongs to Iraq war literature and recounts a curious encounter and dream that are strangely evocative of 'Yawm Bwinus Ayris'. Like Hussin, the narrator has just returned to Iraq after the US invasion in 2003. The story commences with a dream he had of an American soldier, when he was already in exile in France. In his dream, an American soldier appears among the trees in a garden. A very young narrator stands in a desolate square during the bombing of Baghdad. Years later, the narrator returns to Baghdad and stumbles through the ruins, patrolled by American soldiers. One afternoon, he crosses into the 'Green Zone' in central Baghdad during the occupation of Iraq and returns to his home on the banks of the Tigris. American soldiers lounge on deckchairs on the banks of the river, seemingly on holiday because the war has not started. He sees an American soldier and they greet each other. The encounter uncannily mirrors his dream. The story ends enigmatically when the soldier recounts that he had a dream when he was young: he was in a garden in Baghdad, where women danced, magicians conjured tricks, caravans passed, and a king read the future from an open tome. The American soldier's dream is intermingled with his own.

'Le songe de l'officier américain' ends with the narrator looking at the officer who is peering at him, wondering if he could have been among the faces in his dream. Strangely, both the narrator and the American soldier have a sensation of uncanny familiarity with the other. Each has met the other in his dream before the actual encounter in Baghdad. Thus, the story creates a simulacrum of cultural, spatial and temporal unity in the midst of war and occupation.

One of the few instances in which the Arab Latin American encounter arises from a direct relationship, Hussin's reworking of 'La busca de Averroes' displaces postcolonial adaptations or writing back to the colonial empire, evoking instead a meeting of al-Andalus and Latin America, Old and New World. Like the Palestinian poet Mahmoud Darwish (Maḥmūd Darwīsh) who composes a poem about Pablo Neruda's home, on the Pacific, Hussin takes Ibn Rushd to Borges's home, in Buenos Aires.[22] Ibn Rushd's nostalgia in exile is the author's. In essence, he returns Ibn Rushd to al-Andalus and connects Arab and Latin American cultures.[23]

The Nightmares of Carlos Fuentes

Finland-based Iraqi Hassan Blasim (b. 1973) – short story writer, poet, filmmaker and playwright – gained attention in the West with the publication of his short story collections *Majnūn sāḥat al-ḥurriyya* (*The Madman of Freedom Square*, 2009) and *al-Masīḥ al-'Irāqī* (*The Iraqi Christ*, 2013).[24] In 2000, he illegally crossed the border on foot into Iran, Turkey, Bulgaria, Serbia and Hungary, arriving in Tampere in 2004,[25] and sought asylum in Finland. Blasim's collections have been censored in Arabic and his stories are deemed controversial because they break religious, political and sexual taboos. Blasim's experimentalism attracted Western attention and courted Arab controversy. His collections have travelled from Arabic to English and Arabic again: published online, his short stories appeared first in short story collections in English translation (Ashfeldt 2015a), followed by expurgated editions in Arabic. The subsequent publication of his collections in Arabic invites speculation on the effects of translation on Arabic and world literature.[26] Blasim, who won the English PEN Writers in Translation award twice,[27] and has been described by *The Guardian* as 'perhaps the greatest writer of Arabic fiction alive',[28] has travelled from the Arab world, where his work is widely read online in Arabic, to the West through translation.

Blasim rose to prominence in the Arab world and abroad through his story collections, which offer an example of experimental Arabic literature in the twenty-first century. His story collections synthesise the horrors that Iraq has endured and adopt surrealism as a medium that evokes the violence of post-2003 Iraq. His short story collections are concerned with the effects of borders and migration on refugees (Litvin and Sellman 2016). Moreover, Blasim's story collections refract clandestine migration and the ordeals of migrants and refugees.

Blasim's short story collections mark the rise of a new wave of Iraqi literature that displays the characteristics of horror and fantasy. He employs nightmares, hallucinations, dreams and the supernatural in stories that are surreal, macabre and fantastic: a smuggler abandons a truck of Arab migrants in a Serbian forest in 'Shāḥinat Berlin' ('The Truck to Berlin'); a refugee recounts his hallucination of a wolf in his flat to an author named Hassan Blasim at a bar in Finland; a story about an Iraqi immigrant in Finland who dreams he has turned into a dung beetle echoes Kafka's *The Metamorphosis*; and an Iraqi migrant carries a bag of his mother's bones from Baghdad to Iran, Istanbul and Athens. Set in Baghdad, Helsinki, Berlin, Malmö, Istanbul and Athens, the stories travel the route of clandestine migrants and mirror the effects of illegal migration. Both collections are replete with dismemberment, metamorphosis and cannibalism. Though Blasim's horror is cobbled together from Edgar Allan Poe, Franz Kafka, Ghassan Kanafani (Ghassān Kanafānī) and Carlos Fuentes, his style is uniquely his own. Like Hussin, his surrealism recalls Borges. Unlike the comparisons made in the West, he draws on Arabic sources. For example, 'The Truck to Berlin' in which a smuggler abandons refugees in a truck echoes Palestinian writer Ghassan Kanafani's *Rijāl fī al-shams* (*Men in the Sun*, 1963) where three Palestinian refugees suffocate in a truck on the Iraq-Kuwait border.

Reworking horror, magical realism and *The Thousand and One Nights*, Blasim's fiction is evocative of Jorge Luis Borges, Italo Calvino,

Franz Kafka, Gabriel García Márquez (Litvin and Sellman 2016) and Roberto Bolaño. Surrealism characterises stories that focus on occupation, war and migration. He adopts a form of magical realism resituated in contemporary Iraq. Blasim's stories lend themselves to a comparison with Latin American precursors, though his form of magical realism blends the macabre and the real instead of the 'marvelous real'. As Robin Yassin-Kassab has noted of *The Iraqi Christ*: 'The collection is more generally Bolaño-esque in its visceral exuberance, and also Borgesian in its gnomic complexity. Both Latin American writers share with Blasim a fascination with texts' (2013). Blasim shares with Bolaño an iconoclasm and evocation of nightmare, war and brutality, conjuring the making of literature from terror and the banality of violence.

Blasim dovetails the implausible and the real in unexpected ways. He bemoans the absence of experimental genres such as fantasy and surrealism in Arabic literature in favour of realism. Instead, he intertwines magic and horror, employing magical realism and dark humour in *al-Masīḥ al-'Irāqī*. Acknowledging that the West ties his style to magical realism and Kafka's expressionism, he concedes 'a modicum of magical realism' but insists that he writes in what he calls 'nightmare realism' (*al-wāqi'iyya al-kābūsiyya*).[29] His stories appear surreal, characterised by a unique style Blasim characterises thus: 'They say to me, for example, "Your style is magical realist like Marquez." And I say: "No, I write nightmare realism."'[30] In spite of categorisations of his style in the West, he characterises his style as 'nightmare realism'. The story collections unspool the violence set between Iraq and Europe to which the characters migrate, blurring the borders between fantasy, nightmares and reality.

In 'Alf sikkīn wa sikkīn' ('A Thousand and One Knives') from his collection *al-Masīḥ al-'Irāqī*, the narrator tells the story of his brother-in-law Jaafar, an amputee in a wheelchair, who was wounded in the Kuwait war, and the referee of a local football team under the US occupation. A group made up of the narrator, his wife and Jaafar's sister Souad, Jaafar, and others has mastered a knife trick whereby they make knives disappear and reappear. Tormented by the mystery of the disappearing knives, the narrator learns: 'the knives were just a metaphor [*majāz*] for all the terror, the killing and the brutality in the country. It's a realistic phenomenon [*ẓāhira wāqi'iyya*] that is unfamiliar' (124; 263).[31] The narrator creates a logic for the world of his characters where the disappearing knives are mundane and commonplace instead of an extraordinary phenomenon that appears to be familiar. The title itself, 'Alf sikkīn wa sikkīn', evokes the circularity of *The Thousand and One Nights* and violence in post-2003 Iraq.

'Alf sikkīn wa sikkīn' brings together Iraq's heritage, *The Thousand and One Nights* and a style that flowered most in Latin American literature, magical realism, with the reality of the US occupation of Iraq and sectarian strife. Blasim adapts *The Thousand and One Nights*, a collection frequently reworked in Latin American literature, and magical realism to Iraqi reality. In effect, Blasim reappropriates *The Thousand and One Nights* and transposes Latin American magical realism to Iraq. Blasim notes that the forms of *The Thousand and One Nights* are multifarious, 'from magical realism to science fiction'.[32] As Yassin-Kassab has noted in his review of *The Iraqi Christ*, Arab and Latin American forms are intimately intertwined:

> 'A Thousand and One Knives' owes something to the *Arabian Nights* and the ancient fantastic tradition of Arabic writing, now revived by the pains of Arab modernity, particularly in post-invasion Iraq. But *The Iraqi Christ* also seems to belong with the literature of Latin America, likewise struggling with contesting cultures, political violence and overbearing religion. (2013)

Like Borges, *The Thousand and One Nights*, books and doubles are prevalent in Blasim's stories and, in his case, help to explore a reality of neo-colonialism and sectarianism.

'Kawābīs Kārlus Fwintis' ('The Nightmares of Carlos Fuentes'), from Blasim's collection *Majnūn sāḥat al-ḥurriyya*, tells the story of Salim Abdul Husain, an Iraqi municipality worker who migrates to Holland and adopts the name Carlos Fuentes. When Salim, who sweeps up the rubble of explosions for the municipality in Baghdad, requests asylum in Holland, he changes his name from Salim Abdul Husain to Carlos Fuentes, allegedly out of fear of fanatical Islamist groups, but in fact upon the advice of his cousin who lives in France. His cousin volunteers a Spanish name that he has read in a literary article in a newspaper that would suit him but has no inkling of the Mexican writer. Thereafter Salim becomes Carlos Fuentes in Amsterdam. When he has integrated into Dutch society, he begins to have dreams of Iraq. Dreaming that he is in central Baghdad, Fuentes exterminates the residents of a building to purge himself of his nightmares, but when he storms a flat, he and Salim Abdul Husain face each other. He shoots him, but Salim leaps out of the window. Fuentes's wife, in turn, discovers his body on the pavement in Amsterdam. By the story's end, the Dutch newspapers report that an Iraqi immigrant had committed suicide and his brothers repatriated his corpse to Iraq.

Salim-Carlos Fuentes's death opens and closes the story, his nightmares ensnaring and defeating him. Fuentes embraces his host culture – he learns Dutch, no longer speaks Arabic, shuns Arab and Iraqi immigrants, extols the beauty of Amsterdam, and compares the city's cleanliness, eating habits, women, peacefulness and decent government with his country. He scoffs at immigrants and foreigners who work illegally, pay no taxes, break the law and speak no Dutch. By contrast, he works, pays his taxes, introduces himself as an emigré of Mexican origin, and describes his countrymen as 'uncivilized' and 'backward' (78; 70).[33] Ironically, when he obtains Dutch citizenship, takes a Dutch wife, and has fully assimilated to the culture, he begins to have dreams in which he becomes Iraqi again. In his nightmare, Fuentes shoots Salim, his double, and Salim-Carlos Fuentes's death blurs the borders between the nightmarish and the real. A final note of irony creeps into the story when the narrator observes that Fuentes may have forgiven the Dutch newspapers for the lapse but not his brothers for burying him in Najaf.

In an interview, Blasim has noted: 'For the last fifty years Iraq has been living a nightmare of violence and terror' (Holland 2014). As one reviewer has described *The Iraqi Christ*: 'Blasim's stories are nightmares.'[34] In 'Kawābīs Kārlus Fwintis', Salim-Carlos's dreams (*aḥlām*) evolve into nightmares (*kawābīs*) in which the naturalised Carlos Fuentes is Iraqi again. In his nightmares, he is unable to speak Dutch and reverts to an Iraqi dialect, children in his Iraqi district make fun of his new name, and he plants a car bomb in Amsterdam. 'Kawābīs Kārlus Fwintis' focuses on the effects of sectarian violence and migration on an Iraqi migrant in Europe and blurs the borders between Iraq and Holland in his nightmares. Blasim recreates familiar situations through nightmare realism and dark humour. His form of 'nightmare realism' produces a defamiliarisation of the effects of occupation, sectarianism and migration that captures real and familiar violence.

Though the name seems randomly chosen in the story, the allusion to the Mexican novelist Carlos Fuentes (1928–2012) is by no means accidental. The story begins: 'In Iraq his name was Salim Abdul Husain . . . He died in Holland in 2009 under another name: Carlos Fuentes' (75; 67). Salim's cousin observes that a foreign name would be more suited to Europe: 'It's a hundred times better to be from Senegal or China than it is to have an Arab name in Europe. But you couldn't possibly have a name like Jack or Stephen, I mean a European name. Perhaps you should choose a brown name – a Cuban or Argentine name would suit your complexion' (76; 68). The name, chosen randomly, attracts no attention and helps the Iraqi refugee migrate and integrate into Dutch society. By Blasim's own account, the choice of name is simply a gesture of affection (*'ishārat maḥabba*) out of admiration (*i'jābī al-shakhṣī*) of Carlos Fuentes.[35] Furthermore, he chose the name for dramatic irony because Carlos Fuentes is well-known in the Arab world.[36] Nonetheless, there are a number of oblique comparisons between Fuentes and Blasim, notably, exile: Carlos Fuentes wrote his novel *La muerte de Artemio Cruz* (*The Death of Artemio Cruz*, 1962) in New York.[37] Known for his hallucinatory and magical fiction, frequently interwoven with recurrent themes, Fuentes is an influence on Blasim.

Blasim creates intertextual relationships to Latin American literature and magical realism through the allusion to the famous Mexican author. Khaled Al-Masri observes that Blasim invites 'comparisons between his own characters and those of Fuentes, who exist in another time and on another continent' (2018: 123). As one reviewer of *The Corpse Exhibition* has noted, Blasim's stories draw on the 'dream logic of Carlos Fuentes' and Julio Cortázar, though his originality distinguishes him from 'Latin American fabulism'.[38] Black humour abounds in the matter-of-fact adoption of the Latin American pseudonym and Fuentes's ill-fated assimilation to Dutch society. Nightmare realism blurs the borders between Fuentes's wakefulness and nightmares, Carlos Fuentes and Salim Abdul Husain, the real and the unreal, Amsterdam and Baghdad. The Borgesian double (Salim-Carlos Fuentes) in the nightmare who is none other than the Iraqi immigrant Salim blurs the borders between nightmares and reality, though the story ends with the restoration of the real: his death and repatriation to Iraq. The nightmares and death of Salim-Carlos Fuentes explore the phenomenon of migration and the destruction of Iraq. His death underscores that there is no refuge from a nightmarish reality that has followed Fuentes to Europe.

While 'Kawābīs Kārlus Fwintis' is mostly set in Amsterdam and focuses on the effects of migration rather than the migration itself, the nightmares of migrants and refugees simulate the violence of reality. Haytham Bahoora examines the representation of '"unreal" violence' in Iraqi literature through 'the supernatural, horror, and the monstrous' (2015: 187) in Blasim's stories. In his dreams and nightmares, Salim-Carlos Fuentes is unfettered by legal and geographical borders. Like Borges's stories, Fuentes (the character) searches in books for an antidote to his nightmares, in which he reverts to his roots, and meets his double. Ironically, Salim remains ignorant of the author Carlos Fuentes.

As Blasim has noted in the introduction to *Iraq +100*, an anthology of science fiction from Iraq that he edited, it was not difficult to encourage contemporary Iraqi writers to imagine Iraq a hundred years after the US occupation and to 'reread Iraq's former nightmares' (2016: 7). Blasim's stories evoke the nightmarish and the real, mirroring the 'irreality' of post-2003 Iraq. Blasim adopts nightmare realism to express the trauma of occupation, sectarianism and migration. Whereas violence is mundane in 'Alf sikkīn wa sikkīn', 'Kawābīs Kārlus Fwintis' filters the reality of migration through fantasy and nightmare.

Blasim's stories elaborate a new aesthetics to respond to the reality of neo-colonialism and migration. Blasim employs forms of surrealism that replicate reality and do so in ways that seem to amplify the nightmarish. As Spitta and Parkinson Zamora have noted, 'Even the "magical realists" among them [Latin American writers] use the "magic" to expose the "real"' (2009: 197). In his stories, the surreal creates connections with

Latin America: Blasim uses magic to expose the nightmarish, the horror of what has become mundane.

This chapter has explored direct relationships to Latin American literature in Arabic. 'Yawm Bwinus Ayris' and 'Kawābīs Kārlus Fwintis' centre on dreams and nightmares, Borges's Buenos Aires and Mexico's Carlos Fuentes, respectively. Both appeared in and should be read against a context of exile and migration. Hussin's Ibn Rushd travels to Buenos Aires; Blasim's character takes the name of a famous Mexican author because a Latin American name is better suited to Europe (instead of a Muslim name). Blasim experiments with the Arabic short story and looks to Latin American literature to explore the problem of migration. Both Hussin and Blasim illustrate a sense of kinship with Latin American authors (irrationally in Hussin's story, where Ibn Rushd travels to another continent and meets a modern Argentine author in his dream, and accidentally, and ironically, in Blasim's story, where Salim is ignorant of Carlos Fuentes the author). Hussin's story shows direct contact through intertextuality and the encounter between Ibn Rushd and Borges. In Blasim's story, contact is indirect: Salim takes on the name of Carlos Fuentes; in other words, he impersonates him. While Hussin's story focuses on exile, and appeared in a context in which the author was exiled, Blasim's story centres on the post-2003 ordeals of refugees and migrants. Hussin's story crosses cultural, geographical and temporal borders. On the other hand, Blasim's story intertwines Arab and Latin American characters, who ultimately cannot coexist, resulting in self-destruction. While Hussin's story bridges cultures, Blasim's story unmasks cultural differences. Whereas Hussin employs the fantastic, Blasim experiments with the uncanny, the surreal and the nightmarish.

As the migration of Hussin's and Blasim's stories in world circuits shows, Blasim's story collections have entered world markets and Hussin has deep ties with world literature in French and Spanish. Both are highly visible in translation, helping to make the connections they establish clear: Hussin is especially visible in French and Spanish circuits, and Blasim is well-known in translation. The direct links they establish with Latin American literature help us to draw connections between two important world literatures and advance a rare or infrequent model of comparison.

They show examples of Arabic literature that has been translated into English, French and Spanish and migrates to world literature. They also serve as a model of direct Arab Latin American relationships in experimental literature that captures the realities of the twenty-first century and has been translated into Spanish. Both animate Arabic literature through translation, intertextuality and transcontinentalism.

Epilogue
The Legacy of Transcontinental Ties

In Pablo Neruda's home, on the Pacific
coast, I remembered Yannis Ritsos.

Mahmoud Darwish, 'Fī Bayt Ritsus' ('In Ritsos's Home')

More than a hundred years after Martí's prophetic *crónica* on Egypt, where a bust of Martí adorns al-Ḥurriya Garden in Gezīra Island in Cairo (alongside monuments of Egyptian poets Ahmed Shawqi (Aḥmad Shawqī), 'the Prince of Poets', and Hafez Ibrahim (Ḥāfiẓ Ibrāhīm), 'the Poet of the Nile'), Palestinian poet Mahmoud Darwish (1941–2008) was in the home of Chilean poet Pablo Neruda (1904–73). In 'La revuelta en Egipto', Martí parsed British and French imperial designs exactly right, and to read his *crónica* is to understand how it was prophetic of the British occupation of Egypt in 1882. To read Martí on Egypt and Darwish in Neruda's home is to note a largely overlooked horizontalism in both Martí's *crónica* and Darwish's poem.

In Neruda's home, Darwish turned to Chile, which marked a central event (as far as Arab Latin American routes are concerned) in which an Arab poet had undertaken a trip to Latin America.[1] In 2001, Darwish published a poem he had read in Jordan in 1997. Darwish's poem 'Fī Bayt Ritsus' (literally 'In Ritsos's Home'; 'Like a Mysterious Incident') invokes the Chilean poet. The poem begins: 'In Pablo Neruda's home, on the Pacific / coast, I remembered Yannis Ritsos / at his house' (*Fī dār Bāblū Nirūdā, 'ala shāṭi' / al-Bāsifik, tadhakkartu Yānnis Ritsus / fī baytihi*) (306–7). When Darwish visited Neruda's house in Isla Negra on the Pacific coast of Chile, he remembered his fellow poet Yannis Ritsos (1909–90) who had welcomed him in Athens. Neruda's lavish house on the Pacific reminded him of his fellow poet's ascetic home in Athens. The poem centres on the friendship of Darwish and Ritsos who suffered exile, displacement, imprisonment and poverty. The central event in the poem is Darwish's exchange with Ritsos. To Darwish the speaker's 'What is poetry?' Ritsos's response that 'It is the mysterious incident' (*huwa al-ḥadath al-ghāmiḍ*) (306–7) is telling. The poem encloses two mysterious incidents: first, while Darwish was in Neruda's home, he was overtaken by the memory of his friend, Ritsos, whose death he would go on to read about in the newspaper soon after. Thus, the central theme in Darwish's poem is his friendship with his fellow poet Yannis Ritsos and the mysterious incident is that at the moment he recalled him in Neruda's home – Neruda's home furnishes the occasion for him to remember Ritsos – he was dying. In other words, the poem is an elegy for Ritsos, his 'brother in poem' (*akhī fī al-qaṣīda*) (2007: 306–7). Second, though the poem is dedicated to Ritsos, Darwish's presence in Neruda's home in Chile and the first line intimate a much deeper relationship to Neruda the poet that he would go on to explore further. While the central poet in the poem is Yannis Ritsos (indeed, the Arabic title is 'In Ritsos's Home'), the poem also holds up a troika of poets: Neruda, Ritsos and Darwish.

In 1975, Darwish had published a poem dedicated to Pablo Neruda, 'Dhāhibūn īla al-qaṣīda – īla Bāblū Nīrūda' ('On the way to the poem – to Pablo Neruda'), in the PLO Research Center's journal *Shu'ūn Filasṭiniyya* (*Palestinian Affairs*) of which he was editor. The distribution of the issue was interrupted by the outbreak of the Lebanese Civil War, and the poem was doomed to obscurity.[2] Nonetheless, Darwish would occasionally recite the poem to friends in small gatherings, making it an intimate and prized poem.[3] The poem pays homage to Neruda and turns to him for the source of the form of '*al-qaṣīda*' (the poem).

Further exchanges have burgeoned in the twenty-first century and returned to some of the themes of the 1960s and 1970s. In recent years, direct relationships have arisen from the effects of further waves of migration, political movements, travel and literary translation in literature, art and popular culture. In the 2011 Revolution in Egypt, Latin American iconography reappeared, circulated and flourished. In 2012, Lebanese-Egyptian artist Bahia Shehab spray-painted poetry by Neruda in Cairo: 'You can cut all the flowers but you can't stop spring' ('Podrán cortar todas las flores, pero no podrá detener la primavera').[4] Neruda's iconic lines circulated on the streets of Cairo in Arabic as an emblem of the revolution; they read: *yumkinuka an tadhas al-wurūd lakinaka la tasṭati'a an tu'akhkhira al-rabī'*.[5] In 2012, Neruda's poem was especially apt and presaged revolution and renewal. In a poetry collection, dedicated to the 2011 Revolution in Egypt, *Irfa' ra'sak 'āliyan* (Hold your Head Up High, 2011), Hilmi Salim (Ḥilmī Sālim) (1951–2012), an Egyptian poet of the 1970s generation and a member of the experimental poetry group Ida'a 77 (Light 77), so called because it was founded in 1977, drew on Arab and Latin American literary, historical and political imagery. One particularly interesting poem was composed between February and May 2011. In his poem 'al-'askar' ('The Military'), Salim draws parallels to Spanish and Latin American military dictatorships. Both Chile's Pablo Neruda and Spain's Federico García Lorca (1898–1936), shot by Franco's forces in the Spanish Civil War, are invoked in the context of a brutal military history, as is President Salvador Allende, murdered in 1973 during the military coup led by Augusto Pinochet:

> We used to fear the military
> . . .
> For they are Neruda's murderers
> Who gunned down Allende with bullets of betrayal,
> And gunned down Lorca with bullets of betrayal. (2011: 30; my translation)

Mining relationships to Neruda and García Lorca, who met in Madrid when Neruda arrived in 1934, poets commonly associated with resistance to Latin American and Spanish dictatorships, Salim enfolds a global rather than merely local revolutionary archive in his poem. The poem reads a change in the perception of the military in Latin America and the Arab world more broadly (the coup in Chile and murder of García Lorca, on the one hand, and the more recent revolutionary moment in Egypt, on the other).[6] More recently, a wave of political unrest has swept the Arab world and Latin America from Lebanon, Iraq and Algeria to Chile, Bolivia and Colombia, circling back to that moment in which historical moments were read together.

Expanding exchange between Latin America and the Arab world has taken further turns. In recent years, travels and exchanges have grown more pronounced. Darwish's poem traces further routes between Palestine and Latin America and the expansion of Latin American travel literature to the Arab world (as in works by Abad, Rey Rosa and Ruy Sánchez, examined in Chapters 1 and 2). Latin American writers of Arab origin have begun to write about return to the Arab world (retracing the routes of Arab migrations in the nineteenth century). These memoirs and chronicles have contributed to a growing body of Latin American literature with ties to the Arab world. In 2013, Lina Meruane (b. 1970), a Chilean writer of Palestinian origin, published *Volverse Palestina* (Becoming Palestine), a chronicle that migrates between Chile and Palestine. In *Volverse Palestina*, Meruane recounts her trip to Palestine in 2012 to trace the origins of her family name and a history of her family's migration from Beit Jala to Chile, her 'return' borrowed from her father's near-return to his country of origin.[7] Palestinian migration to Chile and chronicles of return open up avenues for further study.

In the past decade efforts to redress the limits of comparative literature have spurred more scholarship that expands the linguistic and geographic borders of the field.[8] Martí proposed a literary model as early as 1877 that concerns directions of comparison that have been central to this book. In 1877, Martí, then in exile in Guatemala, proposed a magazine, *Revista Guatemalteca* (*Guatemalan Magazine*), that never came to fruition (López 2009: 227). Its purpose was to bring together cultural production from Guatemala, the Americas and Europe, making Guatemalan, and Latin American, production known beyond Latin America (López 2009: 229, 227). Alfred J. López reads the prescience of 'Martí's model for an explicitly transatlantic, and implicitly global, comparative literary and cultural study . . . then and now' (2009: 229). Martí's transcontinentalism furnished a model of a fully transcontinental comparative literature.

This book has focused on neglected links between Latin America and the Arab world. It has proposed a transcontinental comparative framework for reading Latin American and Arabic literatures and has read the legacy of a Third World solidarity that extended to cultural exchange. As I have shown, some of the ties between these two important world literatures can be read within new horizontalist frameworks. In *From the Tricontinental to the Global South*, Anne Garland Mahler traces the roots of the global South in the Tricontinental:

> much of the erasure of the Tricontinental's legacy can be attributed to the way that the field of postcolonial studies has focused on the national contexts represented at Bandung and has employed a definition of postcoloniality that largely elides both Latin America as well as oppressed populations within wealthy countries like the United States. In response, new modes of critical analysis are emerging such that we are witnessing a shift within contemporary scholarship from the center-periphery and colonizer-colonized model of postcolonial theory to horizontalist critical approaches, like the Global South. (2018: 243)

I extend Mahler's reading of the neglect of Tricontinentalism to a model that reads Latin America and the Arab world. In this regard, tricontinental solidarities inspired a model of transcontinental literature that depends on historical links. In some cases, these include the global South, a history of migration and an Orientalist tradition. Latin American and Arab writers, in some cases, have revived tricontinental solidarities and cemented historical ties. While I trace the comparative study of Latin American and Arabic literatures to what Mahler describes as Tricontinentalism in 'horizontalist critical approaches' (2018: 244), comparisons are also deeply rooted in the writers' itineraries and literary influences. I should note that in focusing on the importance of Bandung and the Non-aligned Movement's 'tricontinentalism' to reading comparatively Latin American and Arabic literatures, I am not reading its relevance into each text, but only when it fits clearly into works that engage directly with Third World solidarity or networks.

This book acknowledges important contributions to the comparative study of Latin America and the Arab world and has sought to provide avenues for further comparatism that brings together two world literatures. The central concern of this book has been to examine exchanges between

Latin America and the Arab world within Third Worldist networks. Another concern has been to read Arabic literature within a transcontinental comparative framework, with literatures in the global South, as well as within world literature where it is rarely considered, and to make Arabic literature visible in comparative scholarship.

As we have seen, exchanges between Latin America and the Arab world show that, first, literary ties have sprung from a long tradition of Orientalism, interconnected with *The Thousand and One Nights*. Second, some of the ties between Arabic and Latin American literatures are inflected by a legacy of Third Worldist networks and Tricontinentalism. Like the literary influences examined in Chapter 4, examples from Arabic literature engage with a largely overlooked history of Third World liberation struggles and Tricontinentalism.

Connections between Latin America and the Arab world are far from exhaustive. This book has examined literary ties in examples from Arabic and Latin American literatures, and further scholarship will uncover other exchanges, such as, for example, relations between Cuba and the Arab world: Martí's Orient and further Arab-Cuban ties.[9] Literature, literary movements and cultural events have travelled between Latin America and the Arab world. Travel, political movements and translation are likely to animate comparative study.

As the examples noted above show, exchanges are transcontinental and bidirectional. First, they trace how Arab writers have addressed or begun to travel to Latin America and how works that are little known and local have travelled. Second, they show how a new wave of Latin American writers has returned to the Arab world in the new millennium. Arab and Latin American writers have created circuits encompassing Medellín, Cairo, Havana, Beirut, Baghdad, Buenos Aires and Tangier and extended routes between Egypt, Iraq, Lebanon, Chile, Mexico and Cuba.

Notes

Introduction

1. The 1881–82 ʻUrābī revolution in Egypt erupted against European domination, the Ottoman Empire and Turco-Circassian dominance of the army. On 9 September 1881, Colonel Aḥmad ʻUrābī, army officers and civilians marched to ʻAbdīn Palace to demand from Khedive Tawfiq a constitution and the restoration of the army to 18,000 soldiers (Cole 1999: 235). The British bombarded Alexandria in July 1882. ʻUrābī's army was defeated at al-Tal al-Kabīr on 13 September 1882, which began the British occupation of Egypt to protect British interests in the Suez Canal. For fuller examination of the 1881–82 revolution, see Cole (1999). For a detailed discussion of Martí's chronicle on Egypt, see Menéndez Paredes (2007), especially 'El cronista Cubano de la rebellion egipcia de 1881' ('The Cuban Chronicle of the Egyptian Rebellion of 1881'), 298–306.
2. See Martí's *Obras completas* (2016). Hereafter cited by volume and page number. Unless otherwise noted, all translations are my own.
3. Aníbal González likens scenes in Martí's chronicles to 'dioramas' in which he conjures events with a rhetorical 'flourish' (2007: 36).
4. For scholarship on Martí's relationship to the Arab and Muslim Orient, see Azougarh (1998). On Martí's Orient, see Rodríguez Drissi (2019).
5. I quote from Anne Fountain's translation, a bilingual edition of *Versos sencillos*. The Spanish reads: 'Yo sé de Egipto y Nigricia, / Y de Persia y Zenophonte' (2005: 24). In 1891, in a letter, Martí writes: '[el] Cairo, que es la tierra a donde hemos de hacer el primer viaje de recreo mi hijo y yo' (7: 396) ('Cairo, which is the land to which my son and I should make our first trip').

6. See, for example, *Versos sencillos* (2005): Moorish architecture (52–3), 'al ojo moro' ('Moorish eye') (54–5), Agar ('a Moorish girl, Agar' [Hagar]) (104–5).
7. In 'Musa traviesa' ('Mischievous Muse'), his mischievous muse, his son, drags a 'paño árabe' ('Arab cloth'); plays with an 'ónice árabe' ('Arab onyx'); and lastly, enfolds the poetic speaker's dusty, old books in the Arab cloth. See Tyler Fisher's translation of 'Musa traviesa' in *Ismaelillo* (2007: 15–25). Other poems are replete with allusions: 'Haschish' (1875); 'La perla de la mora', in *La edad de oro* (The Golden Age), where the Moor of Tripoli casts a pearl in the sea (Menéndez Paredes 2007: 298); and 'Árabe', in which the speaker longs for the Moor's freedom, tent and horse: 'Sin pompa falsa oh árabe!, saludo / Tu libertad, tu tienda y tu caballo' (16: 243).
8. For an interesting examination of the links between Cuba's Oriente, the Eastern province known for its revolutionary history (1868–1959), and his Arab Orient, an emblem of anti-colonial struggle, see Rodríguez Drissi (2019: 172). Rodríguez Drissi notes that the Orient 'becomes implicitly conflated with the island's Oriente, so that to speak of the Moor is also to speak of those Cubans (as *Santiagueros* were traditionally called) who at the time were fighting for independence in the east' (2019: 174).
9. See José Martí's 'Los moros en España' and 'España en Melilla' in *Obras completas*, vol. 5 (2016: 333–5, 335–7). See Aidi (2017: 28). On cultural links between Latin America and the Arab world, see Aidi (2005). On 'Moorish "Morisco" or Sephardi "converso" lineage' in Latin American literature, see Shohat (2013: 54). On Moorish, Arab and Islamic themes in Cuban literature, see Rodríguez Drissi (2014).
10. For the relationship of Egypt and Cuba, see Heikal (1973: ch. 12). For Cuba's admiration and interest in Egypt during the Suez crisis, see Vélez (2016: 60).
11. For an example of diplomatic and historical ties, see Balloffet (2018). Balloffet, noting the travel of Argentine president Juan Péron's political writings to Egypt, observes: 'the [1952] Revolution opened new paths of circulation between Argentina and Egypt for Arabic translations' (2018: 560). See also Vélez (2016).
12. I focus on literature in Spanish and Arabic. Lusophone literature is beyond the scope of this study.
13. See a special issue of *NACLA Report on the Americas*, 'The Latin East', devoted to the 'Pink Tide' or comparisons between Latin America and the Middle East (2018). The special issue traces several connections: Iraqi Kurds'

longstanding interest in Latin American revolutionaries and literature in the struggle for Kurdish independence; the importance of Latin American *testimonio* literature for Palestinian prisoners; the influence of Latin American writers, notably Borges and García Márquez, on Iraqi intellectuals; violence in Latin America and the Middle East; the influence of the Palestinian struggle on Puerto Rican activism for independence from the United States; the Palestinian press in Chile; pro-Assad mobilisation in the Syrian-Lebanese community in Argentina; and Peruvian-Syrian poet Farid Matuk's solidarity with Palestine. On Middle East-Latin American ties in the Cold War, see also a special dossier of 'Pushing Boundaries: New Directions in Contemporary Latin America-Middle East History' (2019). For recent scholarship on Latin American writers of Arab heritage, see *Arab Latin America*, a special issue of *Review: Literature and Arts of the Americas* (2019).

14. On the relations of Pink Tide countries in Latin America with the Arab world, see Velasco, Dahi, Antoon and Weiss (2018).
15. See, for example, Stites Mor (2014) on the Argentine Left's solidarity with the Palestinian struggle.
16. On Lebanese and Syrian migration to Southern California through Latin America, for example, see Gualtieri (2019). On migration from the Levantine Middle East to Argentina from the mid-twentieth to the twenty-first century, see Balloffet (2020).
17. On Arab migration to Latin America – Argentina, Bolivia, Brazil, Colombia, Haiti, Honduras and Mexico – see Klich and Lesser (1998a).
18. For an examination of the burgeoning of Orientalist imagery in Latin American literature and how references to 'the Arab' and 'the Orient' in Domingo F. Sarmiento's *Facundo o Civilización y barbarie* (*Facundo or Civilisation and Barbarism*) played a role in the elaboration of an Argentine national identity, see Civantos (2006). On the role of North Africa in the elaboration of an Orientalist Argentine discourse in the nineteenth and twentieth centuries, see Gasquet (2015).
19. See Civantos (2006) and López-Calvo (2007).
20. For fuller discussion of Argentine Orientalist literature 1873–1950, see Gasquet (2015).
21. On Sarmiento's travel essay about his travels to Algeria in *Viajes por Europa, África y América*, see Civantos (2006: 42–8).
22. I am indebted to Alexandra Ortiz Wallner for drawing my attention to Enrique Gómez Carrillo's travel literature.

23. On the centrality of Egypt to solidarity networks with Asia, Africa and South America, see Abou-El-Fadl (2020).
24. On the Bandung and Tricontinental Conferences, see Young (2016: 191) and Prashad (2007: part 1).
25. For a compelling study of the cultural production of the Tricontinental and the roots of the global South in the Tricontinental, see Mahler (2018).
26. On the cultural cold war in Cairo and Beirut, and the publication of Latin American and Arabic journals sponsored by the CIA's Congress for Cultural Freedom, *Mundo Nuevo* and *Ḥiwār*, respectively, in the 1950s and 1960s, see Holt (2018).
27. On other Cuban, Chilean, Colombian, Mexican, Ecuadorean, Argentine and Uruguayan writers of Arab origin, see Civantos (2017b).
28. The notable Syrian-born Palestinian translator of Gabriel García Márquez's novels into Arabic, Saliḥ 'Almānī, translated a pantheon of Latin American literature by Jorge Luis Borges, Mario Vargas Llosa and Isabel Allende. Shadi Rohana, a Palestinian Mexico-based translator, has translated works by Uruguayan novelist Eduardo Galeano. He also translated Mexican writer José Emilio Pacheco's *Las batallas en el desierto* (Battles in the Desert, 1981) into Arabic in 2016 and Lina Meruane's *Volverse Palestina* (Becoming Palestine, 2014) in 2021.
29. See Ette and Pannewick's *ArabAmericas* (2006) for Latin American and Arab authors who have contributed to connections between Latin America and the Arab world: Lebanese Elias Khoury, Mexican Verónica Murguía and Alberto Ruy Sánchez, Brazilian Alberto Mussa, Palestinian-American Nathalie Handal, and Colombian Luis Fayad.
30. For an examination of Argentine Orientalist and Arab Argentine immigrant literature, see Civantos (2006). For notable recent edited collections that explore connections between the Americas and the Middle East, see Alsultany and Shohat (2013) and Amar (2014). See also Karam (2007) and Alfaro-Velcamp (2006).
31. For an expansion of the purview of the Arabic novel, linguistically and geographically, to span novels by Arab immigrants in Latin America, see Hassan (2017b: 4). See, for example, the chapters devoted to the development of the Arabic novel in Latin American countries: Civantos, 'Argentina and Hispano-America', 501–22; Hassan, 'Brazil', 543–56; and El Attar, 'Chile', 589–602.
32. The only monograph on Arab Latin American literature is Civantos's *Between*

Argentines and Arabs. For a study of al-Andalus in Arab and Latin American literatures and a rare look at Arabic literature, see Civantos (2017a).

33. A handful of articles have devoted attention to Arabic literature and the Cold War. On Arabic journals in the Cold War, see Holt (2013) and Creswell (2019: 32–51). On Afro-Asian networks in 1968–90s that pre-date the foundation of postcolonial studies in the US, see Halim (2012).
34. See Mahler (2018).
35. See Alsultany and Shohat (2013).
36. See Lionnet and Shih (2005b).

Chapter 1

1. In a talk delivered at the Casa de América in Madrid in 2010, Abad observed: 'I lived in Boston and Berlin, spent periods of time in Turin and Cairo' (2014a: 74).
2. For expanding scholarship on the connections between Latin America and the Arab world, see Ette and Pannewick (2006b), Civantos (2006) and Alsultany and Shohat (2013).
3. See Tinajero (2003). On Argentine Orientalism, particularly the ways in which Arab and non-Arab Argentine writers employed the Orient and the Oriental, see Civantos (2006).
4. On Arab migration to Latin America, see Zabel (2006a).
5. Citations are from the Spanish edition and Gregory Rabassa's translation. Hereafter cited by page number.
6. Ottmar Ette and Friederike Pannewick call Santiago Nasar 'possibly the best-known Latin-American Arab in world literature' (2006a: 7).
7. For critical attention to the Arab character in *Crónica de una muerte anunciada*, see Ette (2006), El Attar (2013) and Civantos (2018).
8. See García Márquez (1980: 1–3, 5, 6).
9. See Ette (2006: 229–32) and Civantos (2018: 173).
10. Citations are from the Spanish edition and Gregory Rabassa's translation. Hereafter cited by page number.
11. In her examination of the novel, El Attar makes an argument for Santiago Nasar's Palestinian origins: she points out 'his family name – the Nasars. Besides being one of the most common among Palestinian families in Latin America, this name evokes the city of Nazareth' (2013: 262).
12. On the true events that inspired *Crónica de una muerte anunciada*, see Bell-Villada (2010: 206).

13. García Márquez (1980: 1). Unless otherwise noted, all translations are my own.
14. Yamil Shaium and Nahir Miguel's names were also later added to the typescript of *Crónica de una muerte anunciada*. See García Márquez (1980: 91–2, 99, 103, 107).
15. By his own account, Abad first met García Márquez in Santiago de Cuba soon after the publication of his harsh review of García Márquez's *Noticia de un secuestro* (*News of a Kidnapping*, 1996) in *El Espectador*. In his review, he expressed ethical reservations about a chronicle of the Medellín drug cartel's kidnapping of a Bogotá elite that overlooked Colombians of humble origins. García Márquez was reportedly offended but graciously thanked Abad for the criticism. Thereafter he invited Abad to write a column for *Cambio*, a magazine he co-founded in Colombia. As Abad notes, 'I came to love him and admire him very much. We had a great relationship (*una gran relación*) although the beginning was terrible' (Seoane 2020). In his obituary of García Márquez, he writes, 'he was our Homer, who wrote the founding sagas of our real and imaginary history'. See Abad (2014b).
16. For the relationship of *Crónica de una muerte anunciada* to *El olvido que seremos*, see the review by Tremlett (2010).
17. I quote from Héctor Abad Faciolince's *El olvido que seremos* and Anne McLean's English translation.
18. Abad addresses his uncertain Arab origins in his introduction to the Arabic translation of *El olvido que seremos*. See Abad (2014d).
19. Conversation with Héctor Abad Faciolince on 25 June 2014.
20. Abad, a regular contributor to and co-editor of Colombia's national newspaper *El Espectador*, traces how Europe became a centre of commerce 'because the wisdom of the Egyptians, the Arabs, the Indians, Chinese, indigenous Americans . . . circulated and settled throughout its territory'. See Abad (2014c).
21. *El olvido que seremos* was translated into Arabic in 2014.
22. Conversation with Héctor Abad Faciolince on 25 June 2014.
23. Abad chose to travel to Egypt to write a travelogue-novel.
24. The series, with around eight books, includes travelogues by Chilean Roberto Bolaño and Guatemalan Rodrigo Rey Rosa.
25. Conversation with Héctor Abad Faciolince on 25 June 2014.
26. *Oriente empieza en El Cairo* does not appear in any critical study of Abad's works. See, for example, the entry on Héctor Abad Faciolince in

Raymond Williams's comprehensive *Columbia Guide to the Latin American Novel since 1945* that lists it as *Oriente comienza en el Cairo* but does not survey it.

27. See the entry on Héctor Abad Faciolince in Raymond Williams's *Columbia Guide to the Latin American Novel since 1945* (2007: 77).
28. A notable omission is Enrique Gómez Carrillo's 'La vida callejera de El Cairo' in *La sonrisa de la esfinge: sensaciones de Egipto* (The Smile of the Sphinx: Sensations of Egypt, 1913).
29. For an overview of the importance of French Orientalists and *The Thousand and One Nights* to Guatemalan Enrique Gómez Carrillo and Nicaraguan Rubén Darió, see Azougarh (1998: 14).
30. On Latin American Orientalism, see Hubert (2012: 47).
31. For an examination of Orientalism in Argentine literature, see Gasquet (2015). On the Far East in modern Hispanic American literature, where Orientalism differs from European imperial representations of the Middle East, see Tinajero (2003).
32. Subsequent parenthetical citations are to Héctor Abad Faciolince's *Oriente empieza en El Cairo*. Unless otherwise noted, all translations are my own.
33. I use the notion of a 'real Orient' here in the sense noted by Said in *Orientalism* in his commentary on Nerval's regret that his dream of the Orient, or Egypt, would become a memory: 'Memory of the modern Orient disputes imagination, sends one back to the imagination as a place preferable, for the European sensibility, to the real Orient' (1978: 100–1).
34. I quote from Francis Steegmuller's English translation of Flaubert's *Notes de voyage*.
35. *El callejón de los milagros* (1995) is also a Mexican cinematic adaptation of Mahfouz's *Zuqāq al-midaqq* (*Midaq Alley*).
36. The narrator frequently consults Twain's *The Innocents Abroad* on his trip and notes the American traveller's laborious climb of the pyramids when he himself is at the pyramids.
37. A review of the novel appeared in the biweekly newspaper of Egypt's Socialist Labour Party, *al-Sha'b*, on 28 April 2000. Ḥaydar's novel tells the story of two Iraqi leftists in exile in 1970s Algeria. The columnist Muḥammad 'Abbās lambasted the novel – ironically published in 1983 but reissued in a modern Arabic series by Egypt's Ministry of Culture in 2000 – and alleged that it was virulently anti-Islamic. He accused the author and the Ministry of Culture of blasphemy. An unprecedented riot at Egypt's Islamic University

of al-Azhar ensued and al-Azhar banned the novel for offending religion and public morality. On the Ḥaydar Ḥaydar controversy, see Rodenbeck (2000). The source also appears in the list of works Abad appended to *Oriente*. For a detailed analysis of the Ḥaydar Ḥaydar controversy and surrounding debates, see Hafez (2000) and Allan (2016: ch. 1).

38. See Abad (2018b).

Chapter 2

1. On Argentine Domingo Sarmiento's evocations of the Orient in *Facundo o Civilización y barbarie* (*Facundo or Civilisation and Barbarism*, 1845), see Spence (2007). On the chronicles of Guatemalan Enrique Gómez Carrillo, notably *De Marsella a Tokio: sensaciones de Egipto, la India, la China y el Japón* (1906), and Nicaraguan Rubén Darío's *Cuentos y crónicas* (1918), see Ortiz Wallner (2012). On Argentine Roberto Arlt's travels to Morocco in 1935, see Majstorovic (2006). Furthermore, Cuban Severo Sarduy travelled to Morocco and Tunisia; see Park (2010: 172).
2. On Tangier as a transit to Africa and Europe, as well as the Americas, in literature, including Sarduy's 'Tanger' and Rey Rosa's *La orilla africana*, see Ette (2018).
3. Rey Rosa published *El tren a Travancore (Cartas Indias)* in *Tres novelas exóticas*, a collection that includes *Lo que soñó Sebastián* (What Sebastian Dreamed, 1994), a novella set in Guatemala's Peten jungle, and *La orilla africana.*
4. See Majstorovic (2015: 204).
5. See Majstorovic (2015: 203–5).
6. On Paul Bowles's relationship to Morocco, see Edwards (2011).
7. See Guerrero (2002: 104) and Gray's interview with Rey Rosa (2007: 164).
8. For a notable study on Rey Rosa in English, see Brickhouse (2016).
9. See Rey Rosa and Esposito (2015).
10. See Rey Rosa and Esposito (2015).
11. For an interview with Rey Rosa, see Sánchez (2008).
12. On the theme of violence in Rey Rosa's novels, see Goldman (2013).
13. See Rey Rosa and Esposito (2015).
14. See Posadas's interview with Rey Rosa (2005).
15. Unless otherwise noted, all English citations are from Jeffrey Gray's translation of *La orilla africana*.
16. See Rey Rosa and Esposito (2015).

17. On the forms of the exchange of the owl in *La orilla africana*, see García (2009: 41).
18. I owe this insight to Alexandra Ortiz Wallner.
19. Citations are from Jeffrey Gray's English translation of *Fábula asiática.*
20. I quote from Andrew Hurley's translation of 'El Aleph'.
21. See Benlabah (2004).
22. *Los nombres del aire* was translated into Arabic by Fatiha Benlabah and published in Essaouira by Editorial Aliseos (Lahrech 1998).
23. Unless otherwise noted, all English citations are from Mark Schafer's translation of *Los nombres del aire.*
24. See Lahrech (1998).

Chapter 3

1. For further discussion of Arab and Latin American relations in world literature, see Hassan (2012, 2013).
2. Rasheed El-Enany notes that Mahfouz 'admits to reading Marquez' – *Cien años de soledad* was published in Arabic in 1980 – in Gamal al-Ghitani's *Najīb Maḥfūẓ yatadhakkar*. El-Enany also draws attention to Mahfouz's short story collections, *Ra'ayt fīma yarā al-nā'im* (I Saw in a Dream, 1982) and *Al-Tanẓīm al-sirrī* (The Secret Organization, 1984), in which 'dreams, visions and the interweaving of the realistic and the fantastic' are evocative of García Márquez's magical realism (1993: 242, 212).
3. Unless otherwise noted, all translations are my own. The first Arabic translation of *Cien años de soledad* from Spanish by Sulaymān al-'Attār appeared in 1979–80.
4. For further discussion of Mahfouz's novel as a political allegory, see Ghazoul (1996).
5. I quote from Edith Grossman's translation of *Vivir para contarla.*
6. I quote from Denys Johnson-Davies's English translation of *Layālī alf layla.* Subsequent parenthetical references are to the English translation, followed by the Arabic edition.
7. My citations are from Gregory Rabassa's English translation of *Cien años de soledad.* Citations from the English translation are followed by the Spanish edition.
8. I quote from Peter Theroux's English translation of *Awlād ḥāratinā*. Citations from the English translation are followed by the Arabic edition.
9. See Echevarría (1984).

10. Said's 'Foreword' of Khoury's *Little Mountain* was reprinted in *Reflections on Exile and Other Essays*.
11. See Zoellner (2019).
12. I quote from Humphrey Davies's English translation of an excerpt from *The Assembly of Secrets* and Khoury's *Majma' al-asrār*. Hereafter cited by page number.
13. An unpublished draft of 'al-Kitāba wa-l-Alam' ('Writing and Pain'), kindly shared by Khoury. It appeared thereafter in *Bidāyāt* (2019).
14. Unless otherwise noted, all translations are my own.
15. This is also an allusion that is reworked and expanded in Khoury's recent novel, *Awlād al-ghītū – ismī Ādam* (*Children of the Ghetto – My Name Is Adam*).
16. See Khoury's interview with Creswell (2017).
17. For an examination of the Arabic translation of Spanish descriptions of Santiago Nasar, see Civantos (2018: 177, 185).
18. The Arabic reads:

    'كان نحيلاً شاحباً له حاجبان عربيّان وشعر أجعد ورثه عن أبيه'.

19. I have adapted Civantos's translation (2018: 177). I have retained the repetition of conjunctions in the first sentence and rendered 'naḥilan' to 'slim' in order to retain the echo of Gregory Rabassa's rendering of the description of Santiago Nasar in *Chronicle of a Death Foretold*. The description of Santiago Nasar in *Crónica de una muerte anunciada* reads: 'y era esbelto y pálido, y tenía los párpados árabes y los cabellos rizados de su padre' (13) ('he was slim and pale and had his father's Arab eyelids and curly hair' (5)).
20. Cited in Paula Haydar's preface to her translation of Khoury's *Mamlakat al-ghurabā'* (*The Kingdom of Strangers*, 1993).

Chapter 4

1. Unless otherwise noted, all translations are my own.
2. I quote from Michelle Hartman's English translation of *Al-Riḥla*.
3. In the 'Translator's Note', Michelle Hartman points to how Ashour's memoir approaches 'Third World solidarity', which she has sought to retain in her translation: 'I have . . . tried to remain true to Third World solidarity politics of the 1970s, where African Americans and Egyptians were part of a larger worldwide struggle against racism and imperialism' (2018: 149).
4. For a fuller examination of Radwa Ashour's *Al-Riḥla*, see Abdel Nasser (2017: ch. 6).

5. See also a recent translation of García Márquez's journalism – little known in Arabic – whose style permeates his reportage in *Relato de un náufrago* and *La aventura de Miguel Littín, Bilā quyūd: maqālāt saḥafiyya 1974–1995* (Without Shackles: Journalistic Articles 1974–1995).
6. On historical and diplomatic ties between Argentina and Egypt in the 1950s, see Balloffet (2018).
7. Another celebrated play is *Laylat mawt Jivāra al-'aẓīm* (The Night Guevara the Great Died, 1972) by Egyptian playwright Mikhail Ruman (Mīkhāīl Rummān). For a compelling study of translations of Che Guevara in Arabic literature, see Morsi (2019).
8. On how Egyptian writers have been able to follow the 'vogue for Latin American' and other literatures, see Jacquemond (2008: 121).
9. On Ibrahim's study in Moscow, see Malas and Litvin (2016).
10. Ibrahim read Brazilian writer Jorge Amado in prison. See Ibrahim's prison memoir *Yawmīyyāt al-Wāḥāt* (literally, Notes from the Oases Prison) (*Notes from Prison*, 2004). *Yawmīyyāt al-Wāḥāt* also recounts the story of the years he spent in prison (1959–64) through a diary.
11. The Dhofar revolution convulsed the Sultanate of Oman from 1965 to 1975 in Dhofar, in southern Oman on the Oman-Yemen border. In 1965 Dhofar tribesmen, supported by South Yemen, rose against Sultan Sa'id bin Taimur. The revolution was defeated by Britain, Oman and Iran in 1975. On the Dhofar revolution, see Takriti (2013). The Omani revolution began in and belonged to an age of 'pan-Arabism, Bandung, and tricontinentalism' (Takriti 2013: 1, 3). In the 1960s, Takriti notes, 'The new sources of inspiration for thought and practice were Cuba, Vietnam and China, as well as Arab arenas such as Algeria and Palestine' (2013: 3–4).
12. The translation of the epigraph is my own.
13. On the archival in *Warda*, see Aboul-Ela (2018).
14. Subsequent parenthetical references are to Hosam Aboul-Ela's English translation of *Warda*, followed by the Arabic edition.
15. See Sonallah Ibrahim's interview (Colla 2011).
16. Ibrahim's sources, appended to *Warda*, include Ernesto Che Guevara's *Complete Works*, published in Arabic by Dār al-Farābī and Dār Dimashq (1982), and I. Lavretsky's *Ernesto Che Guevara* (1976).
17. On guerrilla and militant narratives in Central American Cold War literature, see Esch (2020).
18. On extreme masculinity in armed conflict, see Esch (2018: 22).

19. Ibrahim has noted about *1970*: 'The idea is, who is Gamal Abdel Nasser? What were his motives?' See Ibrahim's interview with Guyer (2017).
20. All references are to Samah Selim's 2006 English translation *Memories of a Meltdown*, followed by the Arabic edition.
21. Makhzangi's introduction to 'Moscow Queues' (included in *Memories of a Meltdown*) is omitted from the Arabic edition.
22. The result was Littín's documentary *Acta general de Chile* (1986). García Márquez notes in his introduction to *La aventura de Miguel Littín*: 'El resultado fue una película de cuatro horas para la televisión y otra de dos horas para el cine, que empieza a proyectarse . . . en todo el mundo' (1986a: 6) ('The result was a four-hour film for television and a two-hour feature for movie theaters . . . around the world' (1986b: xxix)).
23. On Makhzangi's experimentation with the '*uqsūsa*', see Jacquemond (2008: 218).
24. In Syrian filmmaker Mohamad Malas's Moscow diary about his friend Sonallah Ibrahim in his memoir *Madhāq al-balaḥ* (*The Flavour of Dates*, 2011), he recalls in 1973 'a long conversation about revolutions and conspiracies, about Dhofar and about Aden' (Malas and Litvin 2016: 218).

Chapter 5

1. *Waḥdaha shajarat al-rummān* (literally, The Pomegranate Alone) was translated by the author into English as *The Corpse Washer* (2013). I quote from Antoon's self-translated novel, followed by the Arabic edition.
2. On relationships to Latin American literature in Arabic literature, see also Antoon (2017).
3. The author is known in Arabic as Jabbār Yāsīn (so his name appears in print).
4. Christina Civantos examines the evocation of intercultural dialogue modelled on al-Andalus in two Arabic reworkings of 'La busca de Averroes': Moroccan Abdelfattah Kilito's 'Du balcon d'Averroès' ('On Averroes's Balcony', 2007) and Iraqi Jabbar Yussin Hussin's 'Yawm Bwinus Ayris' ('The Day in Buenos Aires', 2000). In Kilito's 'Du balcon d'Averroès', the narrator also muses on an enigmatic phrase, spoken by Averroes, in a dream. See Civantos (2017a: ch. 1).
5. Personal communication from Jabbar Yussin Hussin, 13 March 2020.
6. See Bouchardeau (2001).
7. Citations are from the Spanish edition (in *Cuentos completos*), followed by the English translation.

8. On Borges and the Orient, see Younes (1994).
9. Citations are from the French edition, followed by the English translation.
10. For an examination of literary allusions to Borges in *L'Enfant de sable*, see Fayad (1993).
11. On Orientalism and exoticisation in *L'Enfant de sable*, see El Younssi (2014).
12. I quote from Randa Jarrar's English translation of 'The Day in Buenos Aires', followed by the Arabic edition.
13. Hussin uses the name Ibn Rushd in his story. I use the name Ibn Rushd to differentiate between his character and Borges's.
14. The poet Abū al-'Alā al-Ma'arrī (973–1057), born in Ma'arrat al-Nu'mān (now Syria), is one of the greatest poets in classical Arabic literature.
15. Personal communication from Jabbar Yussin Hussin, 13 March 2020.
16. The title of 'La busca de Averroes' that appears in Hussin's story in Arabic is 'Miḥnat Ibn Rushd' ('Averroes's Ordeal') instead of 'Baḥth Ibn Rushd' ('Averroes's Search'), the standard Arabic translation of Borges's story, or 'Ḥīrat Ibn Rushd' ('Averroes's Dilemma'), as Hussin has also referred to the story in *El Aleph* (*The Aleph*, 1949) (personal communication from Jabbar Yussin Hussin, 13 March 2020). See Borges (1987).
17. Nancy Berg observes that 'Ibn Rushd dreams of an anachronistic encounter with Borges' (2010: 152).
18. Personal communication from Jabbar Yussin Hussin, 13 March 2020.
19. On Borges's introduction of Averroes in Spanish literature, see Berg (2010: 159).
20. I quote from the English translation of 'The Messenger from Mexico', featured in *Banipal*.
21. Citations are from a French manuscript kindly shared by Hussin. Both the published version and the manuscript of 'Le songe de l'officier américain' are cited in the bibliography.
22. See Darwish (2007). On Darwish's poem, see Abdel Nasser (2017: 164).
23. Berg observes that Borges's story introduces Ibn Rushd to Spanish readers and notes the way through which he is 'also returned to al-Andalus' (2010: 148).
24. *The Madman of Freedom Square* was originally published in English, then in edited form in Arabic in 2012, and was banned in Jordan.
25. See Blasim's interview with Holland (2014), and Yassin-Kassab (2017).
26. See Litvin and Sellman (2016).
27. Hassan Blasim's short story collection *The Iraqi Christ* and debut novel *God*

99 won the English PEN Writers in Translation award in 2012 and 2019 respectively. *The Iraqi Christ* won the 2014 Independent Foreign Fiction Prize.

28. See a review of new writing from the Arab world by Yassin-Kassab (2010).
29. Personal communication from Hassan Blasim, 8 March 2020.
30. See Litvin and Sellman (2016).
31. I quote from Jonathan Wright's English translation of *The Iraqi Christ*, followed by the Arabic edition. Blasim has published two short story collections in English: *The Madman of Freedom Square* (2009) and *The Iraqi Christ* (2013). Both collections were reissued in the US edition *The Corpse Exhibition* (2014). I quote from the Arabic edition of *The Corpse Exhibition, Ma'raḍ al-juthath*, which includes both collections *Majnūn sāḥat al-ḥurriyya* (*The Madman of Freedom Square*) and *al-Masīḥ al-'Irāqī* (*The Iraqi Christ*).
32. See Yassin-Kassab (2017).
33. I quote from Jonathan Wright's English translation, followed by the Arabic edition.
34. For a review of Blasim's *The Iraqi Christ*, see Mcgregor (2013).
35. Personal communication from Hassan Blasim, 8 March 2020.
36. Personal communication from Hassan Blasim, 26 May 2020.
37. Fuentes also published fantastic short stories, *Los días enmascarados* (The Masked Days, 1954).
38. For a review of *The Corpse Exhibition*, see Kipen (2014).

Epilogue

1. A final version of Darwish's poem appeared under the title 'Fī Bayt Ritsus' ('In Ritsos's Home') in the London-based pan-Arab newspaper *Al-Hayat* in 2001, though he had originally read the poem in Jordan in 1997. However, the poem was reprinted in his collection *Lā ta'tadhir 'amma fa'alt* (*Don't Apologize for What You've Done*, 2003) under the title 'Ka-Ḥāditha ghāmiḍa' ('Like a Mysterious Incident'). Citations are from Fady Joudah's English translation in the bilingual anthology *The Butterfly's Burden*. See also Darwish's poem 'Maḥmūd Darwīsh: Qaṣidatān' ('Mahmoud Darwish: Two Poems') (2001).
2. See Darwish (2009).
3. See Darwish (2009).
4. My citations of Neruda's poem and Mark Eisner's translation are from Eisner (2018).

5. This was soon after the Port Said Stadium massacre on 1 February 2012, following the first anniversary of Egypt's 2011 Revolution.
6. For fuller discussion of the moment in which the poem appeared, see Abdel Nasser (2016: 114–15).
7. On Meruane's *Volverse Palestina*, see Abdel Nasser (2018).
8. On hemispheric American comparative practice, see, for example, Spitta and Parkinson Zamora (2009); for a critique of the Eurocentrism of comparative literature, see López (2009).
9. For scholarship in this direction, see Rodríguez Drissi (2014, 2019) and Morsi (2018).

Bibliography

Abad Faciolince, Héctor (1998), *Fragmentos de amor furtivo*, Bogotá: Alfaguara.

_____ (2002), *Oriente empieza en El Cairo*, Bogotá: Alfaguara.

_____ (2006), *El olvido que seremos*, Bogotá: Planeta.

_____ (2013), *Oblivion: A Memoir*, trans. Anne McLean and Rosalind Harvey, Exeter: Old Street Publishing.

_____ (2014a), 'The Bastard's Pride', *Review: Literature and Arts of the Americas*, 47, no. 1, 74–80.

_____ (2014b), 'Gabriel García Márquez, in memoriam', *El Espectador*, 19 April, <https://www.elespectador.com/opinion/gabriel-garcia-marquez-memoriam-columna-487657> (last accessed 14 March 2022).

_____ (2014c), 'An Idea of Europe', trans. Kieran Tapsell, *El Espectador*, 4 May, <https://johnmenadue.com/hector-abad-faciolince-an-idea-of-europe> (last accessed 14 March 2022).

_____ (2014d), 'Introduction', in *Al-Nisyān*, trans. Mark Jamāl, Cairo: al-'Arabī Publishing, pp. 3–5.

_____ (2014e), *Al-Nisyān*, trans. Mark Jamāl, Cairo: al-'Arabī Publishing.

_____ (2014f), personal interview, 25 June.

_____ (2015a), *La oculta*, Madrid: Alfaguara.

_____ (2015b), 'La persistente curiosidad', interview by Juan Fernando Ospina, *Bacanika*, 5 February, <https://www.bacanika.com/articulo/la-persistente-curiosidad.html> (last accessed 14 March 2022).

_____ (2018a), *The Farm*, trans. Anne McLean, New York: Archipelago Books.

_____ (2018b), *Al-Sharq yabda' fī al-Qāhira*, trans. Muḥammad al-Fūlī, Cairo: Sefsafa Publishing House.

Abdel Nasser, Tahia (2011), 'al-Archīf al-'Arabī li-l-Wāqi'iyya al-Siḥriyya', *Alif: Journal of Comparative Poetics*, 31, 185–214.

_____ (2016), 'Revolutionary Poetics and Translation', in Mona Baker (ed.), *Translating Dissent: Voices from and with the Egyptian Revolution*, London: Routledge, pp. 107–22.

_____ (2017), *Literary Autobiography and Arab National Struggles*, Edinburgh: Edinburgh University Press.

_____ (2018), 'Palestine and Latin America: Lina Meruane's *Volverse Palestina* and Nathalie Handal's *La estrella invisible*', *Journal of Postcolonial Writing*, 54, no. 2, 239–53.

Abou-El-Fadl, Reem (2020), 'Beyond Pan-Arabism: Suez and Afro-Asian Solidarity in Abdel Nasser's Egypt', *Jadaliyya*, October, <https://www.jadaliyya.com/Details/41860> (last accessed 14 March 2022).

Aboul-Ela, Hosam (2018), *Domestications: American Empire, Literary Culture, and the Postcolonial Lens*, Evanston, IL: Northwestern University Press.

Ahmad, Aijaz (1987), 'Jameson's Rhetoric of Otherness and the "National Allegory"', *Social Text*, 17, 3–25.

Aidi, Hisham (2005), '"Let Us Be Moors": Islam, Race, and "Connected Histories"', *Souls*, 7, no. 1, 36–51.

_____ (2017), 'Juan Goytisolo: Tangier, Havana and the Treasonous Intellectual', *Middle East Report*, 282, 19–31.

Al-Ghitani, Gamal (ed.) (1987), *Najīb Maḥfūẓ yatadhakkar*, 3rd edn, Cairo: Akhbār al-yawm.

Al-Masri, Khaled (2018), 'An Enchanted Ring and a Dung Beetle: Contaminated Borders in Hassan Blasim's Nightmarish Narratives', *Middle Eastern Literatures*, 21, nos. 2–3, 115–33.

Alfaro-Velcamp, Theresa (2006), 'Immigrant Positioning in Twentieth-Century Mexico: Middle Easterners, Foreign Citizens, and Multiculturalism', *Hispanic American Historical Review*, 86, no. 1, 61–92.

_____ (2007), *So Far from Allah, So Close to Mexico: Middle Eastern Immigrants in Modern Mexico*, Austin: University of Texas Press.

Allan, Michael (2016), *In the Shadow of World Literature: Sites of Reading in Colonial Egypt*, Princeton: Princeton University Press.

Allen, Esther (2002), 'Abdala', in *José Martí: Selected Writings*, ed. and trans. Esther Allen, New York: Penguin, pp. 3–7.

Almond, Ian (2004), 'Borges the Post-Orientalist: Images of Islam from the Edge of the West', *Modern Fiction Studies*, 50, no. 2, 435–59.

Alsultany, Evelyn and Ella Shohat (eds) (2013), *Between the Middle East and the Americas: The Cultural Politics of Diaspora*, Ann Arbor: University of Michigan Press.

Amar, Paul (ed.) (2014), *The Middle East and Brazil: Perspectives on the New Global South*, Bloomington and Indianapolis: Indiana University Press.

Antoon, Sinan (2010), *Waḥdaha shajarat al-rummān*, Beirut: al-Mu'assassa al-'Arabiyya li-l-Dirāsāt wa-l-Nashr.

_____ (2013), *The Corpse Washer*, trans. Sinan Antoon, New Haven: Yale University Press.

_____ (2017), 'Reading César Vallejo in Arabic', *Middle East Research and Information Project*, 284/285, <https://merip.org/2018/04/reading-cesar-vallejo-in-arabic> (last accessed 14 March 2022).

Ashfeldt, Lane (2015a), 'Literary Defiance: An Interview with Hassan Blasim', *World Literature Today*, 89, no. 1, 10–12.

_____ (2015b), 'Translating Hassan Blasim: A Conversation with Jonathan Wright', *World Literature Today*, 89, no. 1, <https://www.worldliteraturetoday.org/2015/january/translating-hassan-blasim-conversation-jonathan-wright-lane-ashfeldt> (last accessed 14 March 2022).

Ashour, Radwa (2015), *Al-Riḥla: Ayyām ṭāliba miṣriyya fī Amrīka*, Cairo: Dār al-Shurūq.

_____ (2018), *The Journey: Memoirs of an Egyptian Woman Student in America*, trans. Michelle Hartman, Northampton, MA: Olive Branch Press.

Awaad, Hala Abdelsalam (2015), '*La orilla africana* y la búsqueda de identidad', in Noureddine Achiri, Álvaro Baraibar and Felix K. E. Schmelzer (eds), *Actas del III Congreso Ibero-Africano de Hispanistas*, Pamplona: Biblioteca Áurea Digital, pp. 121–37.

Azougarh, Abdesalam (1998), 'Martí orientalista', *Casa de las Américas*, 210, 12–20.

Badawi, M. M. (1975), *A Critical Introduction to Modern Arabic Poetry*, Cambridge: Cambridge University Press.

Bahoora, Haytham (2015), 'Writing the Dismembered Nation: The Aesthetics of Horror in Iraqi Narratives of War', *Arab Studies Journal*, 23, no. 1, 184–208.

Baker, Mona and Sameh Fekry Hanna (2009), 'Arabic Tradition', in Mona Baker and Gabriela Saldanha (eds), *Routledge Encyclopedia of Translation Studies*, 2nd edn, London: Routledge, pp. 317–37.

Bakhtin, M. M. (1981), *The Dialogic Imagination: Four Essays*, ed. Michael

Holquist, trans. Caryl Emerson and Michael Holquist, Austin: University of Texas Press.

_____ (1984), *Problems of Dostoevsky's Poetics*, ed. and trans. Caryl Emerson, Minneapolis: University of Minnesota Press.

Balloffet, Lily Pearl (2018), 'Argentine and Egyptian History Entangled: From Perón to Nasser', *Journal of Latin American Studies*, 50, no. 3, 549–77.

_____ (2020), *Argentina in the Global Middle East*, Palo Alto: Stanford University Press.

Balloffet, Lily, Fernando Camacho Padilla and Jessica Stites Mor (2019), 'Pushing Boundaries: New Directions in Contemporary Latin America-Middle East History', *Jahrbuch für Geschichte Lateinamerikas Anuario de Historia de América Latina*, 56, 1–14.

Behdad, Ali (1994), *Belated Travelers: Orientalism in the Age of Colonial Dissolution*, Durham, NC: Duke University Press.

Bell-Villada, Gene H. (2010), *García Márquez: The Man and his Work*, Chapel Hill: University of North Carolina Press.

Ben Jelloun, Tahar (1985), *L'Enfant de sable*, Paris: Éditions du Seuil.

_____ (1987), *The Sand Child*, trans. Alan Sheridan, London: Quartet Books.

Benlabah, Fatiha (2004), 'Alberto Ruy Sánchez ou le Voyage de Retour', <http://www.angelfire.com/ar2/libros/FATIHA.html> (last accessed 14 March 2022).

Berg, Nancy E. (2010), 'When Ibn Rushd Met Borges', *Journal of Arabic Literature*, 41, 148–59.

Blasim, Hassan (2009), *The Madman of Freedom Square*, trans. Jonathan Wright, London: Comma Press.

_____ (2013), *The Iraqi Christ*, trans. Jonathan Wright, London: Comma Press.

_____ (2014), *The Corpse Exhibition and Other Stories of Iraq*, trans. Jonathan Wright, New York: Penguin.

_____ (2015), 'Writer Hassan Blasim on Magic, Horror, and his Journey on Foot to Europe', *Ruya Foundation*, 10 December, <https://ruyafoundation.org/en/2015/12/hassan-blasim> (last accessed 14 March 2022).

_____ (2016), 'Introduction', trans. Jonathan Wright, in Hassan Blasim (ed.), *Iraq +100*, New York: Tom Doherty Associates, pp. 7–13.

_____ (2017), *Ma'raḍ al-juthath*, 2nd edn, Milan: Almutawassit Books.

Bolaño, Roberto (2011), *Between Parentheses*, trans. Natasha Wimmer, New York: New Directions.

Borges, Jorge Luis [1962] (1970), 'Averroes's Search', trans. James E. Irby, in

Donald A. Yates and James E. Irby (eds), *Labyrinths, Selected Stories and Other Writings*, New York: Penguin, pp. 180–8.

_____ (1987), 'Baḥth Ibn Rushd', *Al-Marāyā wa al-matāhāt*, trans. Ibrāhīm al-Khaṭīb, Casablanca: Dār Tubqāl li-l-Nashr, pp. 21–7.

_____ (1998), 'El Aleph', in *Collected Fictions*, trans. Andrew Hurley, New York: Penguin, pp. 274–86.

_____ (2011), *Cuentos completos*, New York: Vintage Español.

Bouchardeau, François (2001), 'Du Tigre à La Loire: Livres d'exil', *Le Monde diplomatique*, February, <https://www.monde-diplomatique.fr/2001/02/BOUCHARDEAU/1866> (last accessed 14 March 2022).

Brickhouse, Anna (2016), 'Unsettling World Literature', *PMLA*, 131, no. 5, 1361–71.

Byrne, Jeffrey James (2016), *Mecca of Revolution: Algeria, Decolonization, and the Third World Order*, New York: Oxford University Press.

Camayd-Freixas, Erik (2013a), 'Introduction: The Orientalist Controversy and the Origins of Amerindian Culture', in Erik Camayd-Freixas (ed.), *Orientalism and Identity in Latin America: Fashioning Self and Other from the (Post) Colonial Margin*, Tucson: University of Arizona Press, pp. 1–18.

_____ (ed.) (2013b), *Orientalism and Identity in Latin America: Fashioning Self and Other from the (Post)Colonial Margin*, Tucson: University of Arizona Press.

Camus, Albert (1942), *L'étranger*, Paris: Éditions Gallimard.

Carpentier, Alejo (1995), 'The Baroque and the Marvelous Real', trans. Tanya Huntington and Lois Parkinson Zamora, in Lois Parkinson Zamora and Wendy B. Faris (eds), *Magical Realism: Theory, History, Community*, Durham, NC: Duke University Press, pp. 89–108.

_____ (2017), 'Preface', in *The Kingdom of this World*, trans. Pablo Medina, New York: Farrar, Straus and Giroux, pp. xiii–xx.

Chasteen, John Charles (1996), 'Introduction', in Angel Rama, *The Lettered City*, ed. and trans. John Charles Chasteen, Durham, NC: Duke University Press, pp. vii–xiv.

Civantos, Christina (2006), *Between Argentines and Arabs: Argentine Orientalism, Arab Immigrants, and the Writing of Identity*, Albany: State University of New York Press.

_____ (2015), 'The View from Beyond: Diaspora and Intertextuality in Ilyās Khūrī's *Majma' al-Asrār*', *Journal of Arabic Literature*, 46, 193–215.

_____ (2017a), *The Afterlife of al-Andalus: Muslim Iberia in Contemporary Arab and Hispanic Narratives*, Albany: State University of New York Press.

_____ (2017b), 'Argentina and Hispano-America', in Waïl S. Hassan (ed.), *The Oxford Handbook of Arab Novelistic Traditions*, New York: Oxford University Press, pp. 501–22.

_____ (2018), 'Orientalism and the Narration of Violence in the Mediterranean Atlantic: Gabriel García Márquez and Elias Khoury', in Kerry Bystrom and Joseph R. Slaughter (eds), *The Global South Atlantic*, New York: Fordham University Press, pp. 165–85.

Cole, Juan R. I. (1999), *Colonialism and Revolution in the Middle East: Social and Cultural Origins of Egypt's 'Urabi Movement*, Cairo: American University in Cairo Press.

Colla, Elliott (2011), 'The Imagination as Transitive Act: An Interview with Sonallah Ibrahim', *Jadaliyya*, 12 June 2011, <https://www.jadaliyya.com/Details/24087/The-Imagination-as-Transitive-Act-an-Interview-with-Sonallah-Ibrahim> (last accessed 14 March 2022).

Cooper, Brenda (1998), *Magical Realism in West African Fiction: Seeing with a Third Eye*, New York: Routledge.

Corona, Ignacio and Beth E. Jörgensen (eds) (2002), *The Contemporary Mexican Chronicle: Theoretical Perspectives on the Liminal Genre*, Albany: State University of New York Press.

Creswell, Robyn (2017), 'Elias Khoury, The Art of Fiction', *The Paris Review*, 223, 21–50.

_____ (2019), *City of Beginnings: Poetic Modernism in Beirut*, Princeton: Princeton University Press.

Dalmau, Miguel (2000), 'Engimas y transparencias', *Revista de libros de la Fundación Caja Madrid*, 43–4, 52.

Damrosch, David (2003), *What Is World Literature?*, Princeton: Princeton University Press.

Darwish, Mahmoud (2001), 'Maḥmūd Darwīsh: Qaṣidatān', *Al-Hayat*, 3 August, <https://www.sauress.com/alhayat/31099928> (last accessed 14 March 2022).

_____ (2004), *Lā ta'tadhir 'amma fa'alt*, Beirut: Riad El-Rayyes.

_____ (2007), 'Like a Mysterious Incident', in *The Butterfly's Burden*, trans. Fady Joudah, Port Townsend: Copper Canyon Press, pp. 307–11.

_____ (2009), 'Dhāhibūn īla al-qaṣīda – īla Bāblū Nīrūda', *Al-Ḥiwār al-Mutamaddin*, 2732, <http://www.ahewar.org/debat/show.art.asp?aid=180589&r=0> (last accessed 14 March 2022).

De la Torre, Roberto (2011), review of *The Secret Gardens of Mogador: Voices of the Earth*, by Alberto Ruy Sánchez and Rhonda Dahl Buchanan, *Chasqui*, 40, no. 1, 219–20.

Echevarría, Roberto González (1984), '"*Cien años de soledad*": The Novel as Myth and Archive', *MLN*, 99, no. 2, 358–80.

Edwards, Brian T. (2011), 'The Moroccan Paul Bowles', *Michigan Quarterly Review*, 50, no. 2, 191–209.

Efthimiatou, Sophia and Elias Khoury (2013), 'Elias Khoury: Interview', *Granta*, <https://granta.com/interview-elias-khoury> (last accessed 14 March 2022).

Eisner, Mark (2018), 'What We Can Learn from Neruda's Poetry of Resistance', *The Paris Review*, <https://www.theparisreview.org/blog/2018/03/26/pablo-nerudas-poetry-of-resistance> (last accessed 14 March 2022).

El-Enany, Rasheed (1993), *Naguib Mahfouz: The Pursuit of Meaning*, London: Routledge.

El Attar, Heba (2006), 'Diálogo latinoamericano-árabe: desde el multi-e interculturalismo hacia la Multipolaridad', *Hispania*, 89, no. 3, 574–84.

_____ (2013), 'Turcophobia or Turcophilia: Politics of Representing Arabs in Latin America', in Ella Shohat and Evelyn Alsultany (eds), *Between the Middle East and the Americas: The Cultural Politics of Diaspora*, Ann Arbor: University of Michigan Press, pp. 252–63.

_____ (2017), 'Chile', in Waïl S. Hassan (ed.), *The Oxford Handbook of Arab Novelistic Traditions*, New York: Oxford University Press, pp. 589–602.

El Younssi, Anouar (2014), 'An Exoticized World Literature: Ben Jelloun at the Two Shores of the Mediterranean', *Alif: Journal of Comparative Poetics*, 34, 225–50.

Esch, Sophie (2018), *Modernity at Gunpoint: Firearms, Politics, and Culture in Mexico and Central America*, Pittsburgh: University of Pittsburgh Press.

_____ (2020), 'Uneven Battles: Central American Cold War Literature', in Andrew Hammond (ed.), *The Palgrave Handbook of Cold War Literature*, Cham: Palgrave Macmillan, pp. 451–70.

Ette, Ottmar (2006), 'Chronicle of a Clash Foretold? ArabAmerican Dimensions and Transareal Relations in Gabriel García Márquez and Elias Khoury', in Ottmar Ette and Friederike Pannewick (eds), *ArabAmericas: Literary Entanglements of the American Hemisphere and the Arab World*, Frankfurt: Vervuert and Madrid: Iberoamericana, pp. 215–60.

_____ (2016), *Transarea: A Literary History of Globalization*, trans. Mark W. Person, Berlin: De Gruyter.

_____ (2018), 'TransArea Tangier: The City and the Literatures of the World', in Gesine Müller, Benjamin Loy and Jorge Locane (eds), *Re-Mapping World Literature: Writing, Book Markets, and Epistemologies between Latin America and the Global South*, Berlin and Boston: De Gruyter, pp. 283–321.

Ette, Ottmar and Friederike Pannewick (2006a), 'The American Hemisphere and the Arab World. Introduction', in Ottmar Ette and Friederike Pannewick (eds), *ArabAmericas: Literary Entanglements of the American Hemisphere and the Arab World*, Frankfurt: Vervuert and Madrid: Iberoamericana, pp. 7–18.

_____ (eds) (2006b), *ArabAmericas: Literary Entanglements of the American Hemisphere and the Arab World*, Frankfurt: Vervuert and Madrid: Iberoamericana.

Fadda-Conrey, Carol N. (2006), 'The Passage from West to South: Arabs between the Old and New World', in Darcy A. Zabel (ed.), *Arabs in the Americas: Interdisciplinary Essays on the Arab Diaspora*, New York: Peter Lang, pp. 19–28.

Farah, Paulo Daniel (2017), 'South-South Solidarity and the Summit of South American-Arab Countries', *Middle East Research and Information Project*, 284/285, <https://merip.org/2018/04/south-south-solidarity-and-the-summit-%E2%80%A8of-south-american-arab-countries> (last accessed 14 March 2022).

Faris, Wendy B. (1995), 'Scheherazade's Children: Magical Realism and Postmodern Fiction', in Lois Parkinson Zamora and Wendy B. Faris (eds), *Magical Realism: Theory, History, Community*, Durham, NC: Duke University Press, pp. 163–90.

_____ (2004), *Ordinary Enchantments: Magical Realism and the Remystification of Narrative*, Nashville: Vanderbilt University Press.

Fayad, Luis (2006), 'Lebanese Migration to the Americas', in Ottmar Ette and Friederike Pannewick (eds), *ArabAmericas: Literary Entanglements of the American Hemisphere and the Arab World*, Frankfurt: Vervuert and Madrid: Iberoamericana, pp. 111–21.

Fayad, Marie (1993), 'Borges in Tahar Ben Jelloun's *L'Enfant de sable*: Beyond Intertextuality', *The French Review*, 67, no. 2, 291–9.

Fernández Parilla, Gonzalo (2013), 'Translating Modern Arabic Literature into Spanish', *Middle Eastern Literatures*, 16, no. 1, 88–101.

Flaubert, Gustave (1972), *Flaubert in Egypt: A Sensibility on Tour*, ed. and trans. Francis Steegmuller, New York: Penguin.

Flores, Ronald (2008), 'The Enigmatic Drifter', *The Latin American Review of Books*, 64, <http://www.latamrob.com/the-enigmatic-drifter> (last accessed 14 March 2022).

Franco, Jean (1999), *Critical Passions: Selected Essays*, ed. Mary Louise Pratt and Kathleen Newman, Durham, NC: Duke University Press.

_____ (2002), *The Decline and Fall of the Lettered City: Latin America in the Cold War*, Cambridge, MA: Harvard University Press.

Fuentes, Carlos (1976), *Terra Nostra*, trans. Margaret Sayers Peden, Funks Grove, IL: Dalkey Archive Press.

_____ (1982), *Los dias enmascarados*, Mexico City: Biblioteca ERA.

_____ (1991), *The Death of Artemio Cruz*, trans. Alfred MacAdam, New York: Farrar, Straus and Giroux.

_____ (1999), *The Buried Mirror: Reflections on Spain and the New World*, Boston: Mariner Books.

García, Claudia (2009), 'Territorialidad fantasmática y periferias: una lectura de *La orilla africana*, de Rodrigo Rey Rosa', *A Contracorriente: Una revista de historia social y literatura de América Latina*, 6, no. 2, 21–45.

García Márquez, Gabriel (1966), *Cien años de soledad*, TS, Gabriel García Márquez Collection, Harry Ransom Center, Austin.

_____ (1967), *Cien años de soledad*, New York: Vintage Español.

_____ (1970), *The Story of a Shipwrecked Sailor*, trans. Randolph Hogan, London: Penguin Books.

_____ (1980), *Crónica de una muerte anunciada*, TS, Box 7, Folder 5, Series 1: Literary Activities, 1948–2009, Subseries A. Long Works, 1948–2007, Gabriel García Márquez Collection, Harry Ransom Center, University of Texas at Austin.

_____ (1981), *Crónica de una muerte anunciada*, TS, Gabriel García Márquez Collection, Harry Ransom Center, University of Texas at Austin.

_____ (1982), *Chronicle of a Death Foretold*, trans. Gregory Rabassa, New York: Penguin.

_____ (1986a), *La aventura de Miguel Littín: clandestino en Chile*, Barcelona: Plaza & Janés Editores, S.A.

_____ (1986b), *Clandestine in Chile: The Adventures of Miguel Littín*, trans. Asa Zatz, New York: New York Review of Books.

_____ (1993), *Crónica de una muerte anunciada*, Barcelona: Random House Mondadori.

_____ (2002), *Vivir para contarla*, New York: Vintage Español.

_____ (2003), *Living to Tell the Tale*, trans. Edith Grossman, New York: Alfred A. Knopf.

_____ (2007), *One Hundred Years of Solitude*, trans. Gregory Rabassa, New York: Penguin.

_____ (2010), *Relato de un náufrago*, New York: Vintage Español.

_____ (2018), *Bilā quyūd: maqālāt saḥafiyya 1974–1995*, trans. Heba El Attar and Jihan Hamid, Beirut: Dār al-Farābī.

García Usta, Jorge (1997), 'Árabes en Macondo', *Deslinde*, 21, 122–39.

Gasquet, Axel (2015), *El llamado de Oriente: Historia cultural del orientalismo argentino (1900–1950)*, Buenos Aires: Eudeba.

_____ (2020), *Argentinean Literary Orientalism: From Esteban Echeverría to Roberto Arlt*, trans. José I. Suárez, Cham: Palgrave Macmillan.

Ghazoul, Ferial (1996), *Nocturnal Poetics: The Arabian Nights in Comparative Context*, Cairo: American University in Cairo Press.

Gleijeses, Piero (1996), 'Cuba's First Venture in Africa: Algeria, 1961–1965', *Journal of Latin American Studies*, 28, no. 1, 159–95.

Goldman, Francisco (2013), 'Rodrigo Rey Rosa', trans. Ellie Robins, *Bomb*, 125, 70–6.

Gómez Carrillo, Enrique (1917), *La sonrisa de la esfinge*, Madrid: Casa Editorial Galleja.

González, Aníbal (2007), *A Companion to Spanish American Modernismo*, Rochester, NY: Boydell and Brewer.

Gray, Jeffrey (2007), 'Placing the Placeless: A Conversation with Rodrigo Rey Rosa', *A Contracorriente: Una revista de historia social y literatura de América Latina*, 4, no. 2, 160–86.

_____ (2013), 'Afterword: Rodrigo Rey Rosa and Tangier', in Rodrigo Rey Rosa, *The African Shore*, trans. Jeffrey Gray, New Haven: Yale University Press, pp. 139–46.

Gualtieri, Sarah M. A. (2019), *Arab Routes: Pathways to Syrian California*, Palo Alto: Stanford University Press.

Guerrero, Gustavo (2002), 'Conversación con Rodrigo Rey Rosa', *Cuadernos Hispanoamericanos*, 624, 103–8.

Guyer, Jonathan (2017), 'Plight of an Arab Intellectual', *The Cairo Review of Global Affairs*, <https://www.thecairoreview.com/q-a/plight-of-an-arab-intellectual> (last accessed 14 March 2022).

Hafez, Sabry (1994), 'Jadaliyyat al-Binya al-Sardiyya al-Murakkaba fī Layālī Shahrāzād wa Najīb Maḥfūẓ', *Fuṣūl*, 13, no. 2, 20–70.

_____ (2000), 'The Novel, Politics and Islam', *New Left Review*, 5, 117–41.

Halim, Hala (2012), '*Lotus*, the Afro-Asian Nexus, and Global South Comparatism', *Comparative Studies of South Asia, Africa, and the Middle East*, 32, no. 3, 563–83.

Harding, Jeremy (2006), 'Jeremy Harding Goes to Beirut to Meet the Novelist Elias Khoury', *London Review of Books*, 28, no. 22, 16 November, <https://www.lrb.co.uk/the-paper/v28/n22/jeremy-harding/jeremy-harding-goes-to-beirut-to-meet-the-novelist-elias-khoury> (last accessed 14 March 2022).

Hartman, Michelle (2018), 'Translator's Note', in Radwa Ashour, *The Journey: Memoirs of an Egyptian Woman Student in America*, trans. Michelle Hartman, Northampton, MA: Olive Branch Press, pp. 147–9.

Hassan, Waïl S. (2012), 'Jorge Ahmad', *Comparative Literary Studies*, 49, no. 3, 395–404.

_____ (2013), 'Which Languages?', *Comparative Literature*, 65, no. 1, 5–14.

_____ (2017a), 'Brazil', in Waïl S. Hassan (ed.), *The Oxford Handbook of Arab Novelistic Traditions*, New York: Oxford University Press, pp. 543–56.

_____ (ed.) (2017b), *The Oxford Handbook of Arab Novelistic Traditions*, New York: Oxford University Press.

_____ (2018), 'Carioca Orientalism: Morocco in the Imaginary of a Brazilian *Telenovela*', in Kerry Bystrom and Joseph R. Slaughter (eds), *The Global South Atlantic*, New York: Fordham University Press, pp. 274–94.

_____ (2020), 'Humberto de Campos and Brazilian "Arab" Texts', in Waïl S. Hassan and Rogério Lima (eds), *Literatura e (I)Migração no Brasil/Literature and (Im)Migration in Brazil*, Rio de Janeiro: Makunaima, pp. 122–38.

Hatzky, Christine and Jessica Stites Mor (2014), 'Latin American Transnational Solidarities: Contexts and Critical Research Paradigms', *Journal of Iberian and Latin American Research*, 20, no. 2, 127–40.

Hawwārī, Salāḥ al-Dīn (2009), *Shu'arā' al-mahjar al-janūbī*, Beirut: Dār wa Maktabat al-Hilāl.

Haydar, Paula (1996), 'Preface', in Elias Khoury, *The Kingdom of Strangers*, trans. Paula Haydar, Fayetteville: University of Arkansas Press, pp. v–viii.

Heikal, Mohamed (1973), *The Cairo Documents: The Inside Story of Nasser and his Relationships with World Leaders, Rebels, and Statesmen*, New York: Doubleday & Company, Inc.

Holland, Jessica (2014), 'A Nightmare of Violence and Terror' (interview with Hassan Blasim), *Guernica*, 1 May, <https://www.guernicamag.com/a-nightmare-of-violence-and-terror> (last accessed 14 March 2022).

Holt, Elizabeth M. (2013), '"Bread or Freedom": The Congress for Cultural Freedom, the CIA, and the Arabic Literary Journal *Ḥiwār* (1962–1967)', *Journal of Arabic Literature*, 44, no. 1, 83–102.

_____ (2018), 'Cairo and the Cultural Cold War for Afro-Asia', in Chen Jian, Martin Klimke, Masha Kirasirova, Mary Nolan, Marilyn Young and Joanna Waley-Cohen (eds), *The Routledge Handbook of the Global Sixties: Beyond Protest and Nation-Building*, London: Routledge, pp. 480–93.

Hubert, Rosario (2012), 'Rewriting Travel Literature: A Cosmopolitan Critique of Exoticism in Contemporary Latin American Fiction', in Ignacio López-Calvo (ed.), *Peripheral Transmodernities: South-to-South Dialogues between the Luso-Hispanic World and 'the Orient'*, Newcastle: Cambridge Scholars Publishing, pp. 42–61.

Hudson, Rex A. (ed.) (2010), *Colombia: A Country Study*, Washington, DC: Library of Congress.

Hussin, Jabbar Yussin (Jabbār Yāsīn) (2000), *Le lecteur de Baghdad: contes et nouvelles*, trans. Mustapha Oulmane and Luc Barbulesco, Paris: Atelier du Gué.

_____ (2004), 'al-'Irāqiyūn sayu'īdūn binā' burj Bābil al-thaqāfī', *Al-Madā*, 15 May, <https://almadapaper.net/sub/05-112/p09.htm> (last accessed 14 March 2022).

_____ (2006), 'El sueño del oficial americano', trans. Alberto Román, in David Lida (ed.), *El Gringo a través del espejo*, Mexico City: Cal y Arena, pp. 13–22.

_____ (2007a), 'The Day in Buenos Aires', trans. Randa Jarrar, in Samantha Schnee, Alane Salierno Mason and Dedi Felman (eds), *Words Without Borders: The World Through the Eyes of Writers*, New York: Anchor, pp. 113–19.

_____ (2007b), 'Le songe de l'officier américain', *Brèves*, 81.

_____ (2009), 'The Language of Parchment: Excerpt from a Novel *The Messenger from Mexico*', trans. Lulu Norman, *Banipal*, 34, 129–33.

_____ (2010), 'El mensajero de México', trans. Mariano Sánchez Ventura, in Alberto Manguel (ed.), *Sol Jaguar: Antología de cuentos sobre México*, Mexico City: Fondo de Cultura Económica, pp. 134–41.

_____ (2017a), *Al-Qāri' al-Baghdādī*, Cairo: Bayt al-Yasmīn li-l Nashr wa-l-Tawzī'.

_____ (2017b), 'Rasūl Mexico', trans. 'Āṭif Muḥammad 'Abd al-Majīd, *Al-Hilāl al-Yawm*, 22 April, <https://www.darelhilal.com/News/67154.aspx> (last accessed 4 April 2022).

_____ (2020), 'Le songe de l'officier américain', manuscript shared by the author, 26 March.

Hutcheon, Linda (1989), 'Modern Parody and Bakhtin', in Gary Saul Morson and Caryl Emerson (eds), *Rethinking Bakhtin: Extensions and Challenges*, Evanston, IL: Northwestern University Press, pp. 87–103.

Ibn Ḥazm, 'Alī ibn Aḥmad (1953), *The Ring of the Dove*, trans. A. J. Arberry, London: Luzac & Co.

_____ (2004), *Ṭawq al-ḥamāma fī al-ulfa wa-al-ullāf*, Beirut: Dār al-Jīl li-l-Nashr wa-l-Ṭibā'a wa-l-Tawzī'.

Ibrahim, Sonallah (1980), *Najmat Aghusṭus*, 3rd edn, Beirut: Dār al-Farābī.

_____ (1992), *Dhāt*, Cairo: Dār al-Mustaqbal al-'Arabī.

_____ (2001), *Zaat*, trans. Anthony Calderbank, Cairo: American University in Cairo Press.

_____ (2003), *Amrīkānlī*, Cairo: Dār al-Thaqāfa al-Jadīda.

_____ (2005), *Yawmīyyāt al-Wāḥāt*, Cairo: Dār al-Mustaqbal al-'Arabī.

_____ (2011), *al-Jalīd*, Cairo: Dār al-Thaqāfa al-Jadīda.

_____ (2013), *That Smell and Notes from Prison*, trans. Robyn Creswell, New York: New Directions.

_____ (2014a), *Birlīn 69*, Cairo: Dār al-Thaqāfa al-Jadīda.

_____ (2014b), *Warda*, 4th edn, Cairo: Dār al-Thaqāfa al-Jadīda.

_____ (2017), *1967*, Cairo: Dār al-Thaqāfa al-Jadīda.

_____ (2019), *Ice*, trans. Margaret Litvin, London: Seagull Books.

_____ (2020), *1970*, Cairo: Dār al-Thaqafa al-Jadīda.

_____ (2021), *Warda: A Novel*, trans. Hosam Aboul-Ela, New Haven: Yale University Press.

Jacquemond, Richard (2008), *Conscience of the Nation: Writers, State, and Society in Modern Egypt*, trans. David Tresilian, Cairo: American University in Cairo Press.

_____ (2009), 'Translation Policies in the Arab World: Representations, Discourses and Realities', *The Translator*, 15, no. 1, 1–21.

_____ (2014), 'Les flux de traduction de et vers l'arabe', *Bibliodiversity – Translation and Globalization*, 9–16.

Jameson, Fredric (1986), 'On Magic Realism in Film', *Critical Inquiry*, 12, no. 2, 301–25.

Jarrar, Randa (2007), 'Translator's Note', in Jabbar Yussin Hussin, 'The Day in Buenos Aires', in Samantha Schnee, Alane Salierno Mason and Dedi Felman (eds), *Words Without Borders: The World Through the Eyes of Writers*, New York: Anchor Books, p. 112.

Jayyusi, Salma Khadra (1977), *Trends and Movements in Modern Arabic Poetry*, Leiden: E. J. Brill.

Kafka, Franz (1961), *Metamorphosis and Other Stories*, London: Penguin.

Kanafani, Ghassan (2013), *Rijāl fī al-shams*, Limassol, Cyprus: Rimal Books.

Karam, John Tofik (2007), *Another Arabesque: Syrian-Lebanese Ethnicity in Neoliberal Brazil*, Philadelphia: Temple University Press.

Khoury, Elias (1994), *Majma' al-asrār*, Beirut: Dār al-Ādāb.

_____ (1998), *Bāb al-shams*, Beirut: Dār al-Ādāb.

_____ (2004–5), 'Al-Riwāya, al-Riwā'ī wa-l-Ḥarb', *Al-Abḥāth*, 52–3, 73–87.

_____ (2005), *Gate of the Sun*, trans. Humphrey Davies, London: Vintage Books.

_____ (2006a), *The Assembly of Secrets*, trans. Humphrey Davies, *Words without Borders*, <https://www.wordswithoutborders.org/article/from-the-assembly-of-secrets> (last accessed 14 March 2022).

_____ (2006b), 'Literature and Emigration', in Ottmar Ette and Friederike Pannewick (eds), *ArabAmericas: Literary Entanglements of the American Hemisphere and the Arab World*, Frankfurt: Vervuert and Madrid: Iberoamericana, pp. 101–10.

_____ (2009a), 'Elias Khoury in Beirut Review', *Prague Writers' Festival*, 15 January, <http://www.pwf.cz/archivy/texts/interviews/elias-khoury-in-beirut-review_1794.html> (last accessed 14 March 2022).

_____ (2009b), 'Elias Khoury: Interview from Banipal', *Prague Writers' Festival*, 15 January, <http://www.pwf.cz/archivy/texts/interviews/elias-khoury-interview-from-banipal_1796.html> (last accessed 14 March 2022).

_____ (2016), *Awlād al-ghītū – ismī Ādam*, Beirut: Dār al-Ādāb.

_____ (2019a), 'al-Kitāba wa-l-Alam', *Bidāyāt*, 22, <https://www.bidayatmag.com/node/985> (last accessed 14 March 2022).

_____ (2019b), 'al-Kitāba wa-l-Alam', manuscript shared by the author, 1 March.

_____ (2019c), *Najmat al-baḥr*, Beirut: Dār al-Ādāb.

Kilito, Abdelfattah (2007), 'Du balcon d'Averroès', *Le Cheval de Nietzsche*, Casablanca: Éditions Le Fennec, pp. 155–79.

Kipen, David (2014), review of *The Corpse Exhibition* by Hassan Blasim, *The New York Times*, 28 January, <https://www.nytimes.com/2014/01/29/books/the-corpse-exhibition-stories-about-a-war-torn-life.html?_r=0> (last accessed 14 March 2022).

Klengel, Susanne and Alexandra Ortiz Wallner (eds) (2016), *Sur/South: Poetics and Politics of Thinking Latin America/India*, Madrid: Iberoamericana.

Klich, Ignacio and Jeffrey Lesser (eds) (1998a), *Arab and Jewish Immigrants in Latin America: Images and Realities*, London: Routledge.

_____ (1998b), 'Introduction: Images and Realities of Arab and Jewish Immigrants in Latin America', in Ignacio Klich and Jeffrey Lesser (eds), *Arab and Jewish Immigrants in Latin America: Images and Realities*, London: Routledge, pp. vii–xiv.

Kushigian, Julia A. (1991), *Orientalism in the Hispanic Literary Tradition: In Dialogue with Borges, Paz, and Sarduy*, Albuquerque: University of New Mexico Press.

Lahrech, Oumama Aouad (1998), 'Alberto Ruy Sánchez y Mogador: Puente colgante entre las dos orillas del Atlántico', <http://www.angelfire.com/ar2/libros/Oumamogador.html> (last accessed 14 March 2022).

Lee, Christopher (ed.) (2019), *Making a World after Empire: The Bandung Moment and its Political Afterlives*, Athens: Ohio University Press.

Lee, Christopher J. and Anne Garland Mahler (2020), 'The Bandung Era, Non-alignment and the Third-Way Literary Imagination', in Andrew Hammond (ed.), *The Palgrave Handbook of Cold War Literature*, Cham: Palgrave Macmillan, pp. 183–202.

Leeuwen, Richard Van (2004), 'The Cultural Context of Translating Arabic Literature', in Said Faiq (ed.), *Cultural Encounters in Translations from Arabic*, Toronto: Multilingual Matters, pp. 14–25.

Lionnet, Françoise and Shu-mei Shih (2005a), 'Introduction: Thinking Through the Minor, Transnationally', in Françoise Lionnet and Shu-mei Shih (eds), *Minor Transnationalism*, Durham, NC: Duke University Press, pp. 1–23.

_____ (eds) (2005b), *Minor Transnationalism*, Durham, NC: Duke University Press.

Litvin, Margaret and Johanna Sellman (2016), 'Hassan Blasim, interviewed by Margaret Litvin and Johanna Sellman', *Tank*, 69, <http://tankmagazine.com/issue-69/talk/hassan-blasim> (last accessed 14 March 2022).

López, Alfred J. (2007), 'Introduction: The (Post) Global South', *The Global South*, 1, no. 1, 1–11.

_____ (2009), 'Hugo Meltzl and That Dangerous American Supplement; or, A Tale of Two 1877s', *Comparative Literature*, 61, no. 3, 220–30.

López Baralt, Luce (1988), 'El Simurg de Alberto Ruy Sánchez', *Vuelta*, 135,

58–61, <https://letraslibres.com/vuelta/el-simurg-de-alberto-ruy-sanchez> (last accessed 4 April 2022).

López-Calvo, Ignacio (ed.) (2007), *Alternative Orientalisms in Latin America and Beyond*, Newcastle: Cambridge Scholars Publishing.

_____ (2010a), 'Introduction', in Ignacio López-Calvo (ed.), *One World Periphery Reads the Other: Knowing the 'Oriental' in the Americas and the Iberian Peninsula*, Newcastle: Cambridge Scholars Publishing, pp. 1–15.

_____ (ed.) (2010b), *One World Periphery Reads the Other: Knowing the 'Oriental' in the Americas and the Iberian Peninsula*, Newcastle: Cambridge Scholars Publishing.

_____ (ed.) (2012), *Peripheral Transmodernities: South-to-South Dialogues between the Luso-Hispanic World and 'the Orient'*, Newcastle: Cambridge Scholars Publishing.

_____ (2020), 'Magical Realism and the "Boom" of the Latin American Novel', in Christopher Warnes and Kim Anderson Sasser (eds), *Magical Realism and Literature*, Cambridge: Cambridge University Press, pp. 101–16.

López-Calvo, Ignacio and Nicholas Birns (2020), 'Magical Realism in the Context of the Cold War Cultural Intervention', in Andrew Hammond (ed.), *The Palgrave Handbook of Cold War Literature*, Cham: Palgrave Macmillan, pp. 225–43.

Luzárraga, Raquel (2005), 'Entrevista a Rodrigo Rey Rosa', *Maga. Revista Panameña de Cultura*, 57–8, 109–14.

Mcgregor, Steven (2013), 'The Iraqi Christ, by Hassan Blasim – Review', *The Spectator*, 25 May, <https://www.spectator.co.uk/article/the-iraqi-christ-by-hassan-blasim---review> (last accessed 14 March 2022).

McGuirk, Bernard (1987), 'Free-play of Fore-play: The Fiction of Non-consummation: Speculations on *Chronicle of a Death Foretold*', in Bernard McGuirk and Richard Cardwell (eds), *Gabriel García Márquez: New Readings*, New York: Cambridge University Press, pp. 169–89.

McManus, Anne-Marie (2017), 'Between Solidarity and Pleasure: An Interview on World Literature with Elias Khoury', *Journal of World Literature*, 2, no. 3, 394–407.

Mahfouz, Naguib (1986), *Awlād ḥāratinā*, Beirut: Dār al-Ādāb.

_____ (1994), 'Alf Layla Aḥāṭat bi-l-Ḥaḍāra al-Sharqiyya', *Fuṣūl*, 13, no. 2, 377–85.

_____ (1995), *Arabian Nights and Days*, trans. Denys Johnson-Davies, Cairo: American University in Cairo Press.

_____ (1996), *Children of the Alley*, trans. Peter Theroux, Cairo: American University in Cairo Press.

_____ (2006), *Layālī alf layla*, Cairo: Dār al-Shurūq.

_____ (2014), *Zuqāq al-midaqq*, 5th edn, Cairo: Dār al-Shurūq.

Mahler, Anne Garland (2018), *From the Tricontinental to the Global South: Race, Radicalism, and Transnational Solidarity*, Durham, NC: Duke University Press.

Majstorovic, Gorica (2006), 'From Argentina to Spain and North Africa: Travel and Translation in Roberto Arlt', *Iberoamericana. América Latina – España – Portugal*, 21, 109–15.

_____ (2015), 'Narrative Unmoored: Photography, Orientalism, and Geopolitics in Roberto Arlt's "La cadena del ancla"', *Symposium: A Quarterly Journal in Modern Literatures*, 69, no. 4, 203–13.

_____ (2017), 'Cosmopolitan Critique and the "Atlantic" Arlt', *Atlantic Studies*, 14, no. 1, 99–111.

Makhzangi, Mohamed (1998), *Laḥaẓāt gharaq jazīrat al-ḥūt*, Cairo: al-Hay'a al-'Āmma li Quṣūr al-Thaqāfa.

_____ (2006), *Memories of a Meltdown: An Egyptian between Moscow and Chernobyl*, trans. Samah Selim, Cairo: American University in Cairo Press.

Malas, Mohamad and Margaret Litvin (2016), 'Portrait of a Friend: Sonallah Ibrahim', *Alif: Journal of Comparative Poetics*, 36, 201–25.

Manguel, Alberto (2007), 'Jabbar Yussin Hussin', trans. Samantha Schnee, in Samantha Schnee, Alane Salierno Mason and Dedi Felman (eds), *Words Without Borders: The World Through the Eyes of Writers*, New York: Anchor Books, pp. 111–12.

Martí, José (1997), *Versos sencillos/Simple Verses*, trans. Manuel A. Tellechea, Houston: Arte Público Press.

_____ (2002), *José Martí: Selected Writings*, ed. and trans. Esther Allen, New York: Penguin.

_____ (2005), *Versos sencillos*, trans. Anne Fountain, Jefferson, NC: McFarland and Company, Inc.

_____ (2007), *Ismaelillo*, trans. Tyler Fisher, San Antonio: Wings Press.

_____ (2011a), *Abdala*, in *Obras completas*, vol. 18, Havana: Editorial de Ciencias Sociales, pp. 11–24.

_____ (2011b), 'España en Melilla', in *Obras completas*, vol. 5, Havana: Editorial de Ciencias Sociales, pp. 335–7.

_____ (2011c), 'Los moros en España', in *Obras completas*, vol. 5, Havana: Editorial de Ciencias Sociales, pp. 333–5.

_____ (2011d), 'La revuelta en Egipto. – Interesante problema', in *Obras completas*, vol. 14, Havana: Editorial de Ciencias Sociales, pp. 113–17.

_____ (2016), *Obras completas*, Edición Crítica, vols. 1–24, Havana: Centro de Estudios Martianos.

Martin, Gerald (1987), 'On "Magical" and Social Realism in García Márquez', in Bernard McGuirk and Richard Cardwell (eds), *Gabriel García Márquez: New Readings*, New York: Cambridge University Press, pp. 95–116.

_____ (2008), *Gabriel García Márquez: A Life*, New York: Vintage.

Mehrez, Samia (1994), *Egyptian Writers between History and Fiction: Essays on Naguib Mahfouz, Sonallah Ibrahim, and Gamal al-Ghitani*, Cairo: American University in Cairo Press.

_____ (2008), *Egypt's Culture Wars: Politics and Practice*, London: Routledge.

Menéndez Paredes, Rigoberto (2007), *Los Árabes en Cuba*, Havana: Publicaciones de la Oficina del Historiador de la Ciudad.

_____ (2011), *Árabes de cuentos y novelas: el inmigrante árabe en el imaginario narrativo latinoamericano*, Madrid: Huerga y Fierro.

Meruane, Lina (2014), *Volverse Palestina*, Barcelona: Penguin.

Monsiváis, Carlos (2002), 'On the Chronicle in Mexico', in Ignacio Corona and Beth E. Jörgensen (eds), *The Contemporary Mexican Chronicle: Theoretical Perspectives on the Liminal Genre*, Albany: State University of New York Press, pp. 25–35.

Moretti, Franco (1996), *Modern Epic: The World-System from Goethe to García Márquez*, trans. Quintin Hoare, New York: Verso.

_____ (2000), 'Conjectures on World Literature', *New Left Review*, 1, 54–68.

_____ (2003), 'More Conjectures', *New Left Review*, 20, 73–81.

_____ (2005), 'World-Systems Analysis, Evolutionary Theory, "Weltliteratur"', *Review (Fernand Braudel Center)*, 28, no. 3, 217–28.

_____ (2013), *Distant Reading*, London: Verso.

Morsi, Eman (2018), 'Let Them Eat Meat: The Literary Afterlives of Castro's and Nasser's Dietary Utopias', in Chen Jian, Martin Klimke, Masha Kirasirova, Mary Nolan, Marilyn Young and Joanna Waley-Cohen (eds), *The Routledge Handbook of the Global Sixties: Between Protest and Nation-Building*, London: Routledge, pp. 564–74.

_____ (2019), 'Cuba in Arabic and the Limits of Third World Solidarity', *The Global South*, 13, no. 1, 145–77.

Negm, Ahmad Fuad (2011), 'Jivāra māt', *Al-Adab al-'Arabī*, 18 May, <http://

adab-arabi.blogspot.com/2011/05/blog-post_955.html?m=1> (last accessed 14 March 2022).

Nerval, Gérard de (2013), *Journey to the Orient*, trans. Conrad Elphinstone, Plimmerton: Antipodes Press.

_____ (2020), *Voyage en Orient*, Paris: Philaubooks.

Nijland, C. (1989), 'The Fatherland in Arab Emigrant Poetry', *Journal of Arabic Literature*, 20, no. 1, 57–68.

Nijland, C. and Shafiq al-Ma'luf (1987), 'A "New Andalusian" Poem', *Journal of Arabic Literature*, 17, 102–20.

Ortiz Wallner, Alexandra (2012), *El arte de ficcionar: la novela contemporánea en Centroamérica*, Frankfurt: Vervuert and Madrid: Iberoamericana.

_____ (2013), 'Rodrigo Rey Rosa', in Will H. Corral, Juan E. De Castro and Nicholas Birns (eds), *The Contemporary Spanish-American Novel: Bolaño and After*, London: Bloomsbury, pp. 136–41.

Ostle, R. C. (1992), 'The Romantic Poets', in M. M. Badawi (ed.), *Modern Arabic Literature*, Cambridge: Cambridge University Press, pp. 82–131.

Padilla, Fernando Camacho and Eugenia Palieraki (2019), '*Hasta Siempre*, OSPAAAL!', *NACLA Report on the Americas*, 51, no. 4, 410–21.

Park, Paula (2010), 'Staging Absence: Severo Sarduy's Fictive Orientalism in *From Cuba with a Song*', in Ignacio López-Calvo (ed.), *One World Periphery Reads the Other: Knowing the 'Oriental' in the Americas and the Iberian Peninsula*, Newcastle: Cambridge Scholars Publishing, pp. 172–87.

Pastor, Camila (2017), *The Mexican Mahjar: Transnational Maronites, Jews, and Arabs under the French Mandate*, Austin: University of Texas Press.

Pelayo, Rubén (2001), *Gabriel García Márquez: A Critical Companion*, Westport, CT: Greenwood Press.

Polit Dueñas, Gabriela (2013), *Narrating Narcos*, Pittsburgh: University of Pittsburgh Press.

Posada-Carbo, Eduardo and Louise Fawcett (1998), 'Arabs and Jews in the Development of the Colombian Caribbean 1850–1950', in Ignacio Klich and Jeffrey Lesser (eds), *Arabs and Jewish Immigrants in Latin America: Images and Realities*, London: Routledge, pp. 57–79.

Posadas, Claudia (2005), 'Una escritura sin precipitaciones. Entrevista con Rodrigo Rey Rosa', *Espéculo. Revista de Estudios Literarios*, 29, <http://www.ucm.es/info/especulo/numero29/reyrosa.html> (last accessed 14 March 2022).

Prashad, Vijay (2007), *The Darker Nations: A People's History of the Third World*, New York: New Press.

Pratt, Mary Louise (2008), *Imperial Eyes: Travel Writing and Transculturation*, London: Routledge.

Prestholdt, Jeremy (2012), 'Resurrecting Che: Radicalism, the Transnational Imagination, and the Politics of Heroes', *Journal of Global History*, 7, no. 3, 506–26.

Quesada, Catalina (2013), 'Héctor Abad Faciolince', in Will H. Corral, Juan E. De Castro and Nicholas Birns (eds), *The Contemporary Spanish-American Novel: Bolaño and After*, London: Bloomsbury, pp. 212–19.

Rama, Ángel (1996), *The Lettered City*, ed. and trans. John Charles Chasteen, Durham, NC: Duke University Press.

Rey Rosa, Rodrigo (1989), *Dust on her Tongue*, trans. Paul Bowles, San Francisco: City Lights Books.

_____ (1996), *El cojo bueno*, Madrid: Alfaguara.

_____ (2004), *The Good Cripple*, trans. Esther Allen, New York: New Directions Books.

_____ (2010), *La orilla africana*, 2nd edn, Guatemala City: F&G Editores.

_____ (2013), *The African Shore*, trans. Jeffrey Gray, New Haven: Yale University Press.

_____ (2014), *Severina*, trans. Chris Andrews, New Haven: Yale University Press.

_____ (2016a), *Fábula asiática*, Barcelona: Alfaguara.

_____ (2016b), *Tres novelas exóticas*, Mexico City: Alfaguara.

_____ (2019), *Chaos, A Fable*, trans. Jeffrey Gray, Seattle: AmazonCrossing.

Rey Rosa, Rodrigo and Scott Esposito (2015), 'Interview with Rodrigo Rey Rosa', *The White Review*, <http://www.thewhitereview.org/interviews/interview-with-rodrigo-rey-rosa> (last accessed 14 March 2022).

Rodenbeck, Max (2000), 'Witch Hunt in Egypt', *The New York Review*, 16 November, <https://www.nybooks.com/articles/2000/11/16/witch-hunt-in-egypt> (last accessed 14 March 2022).

Rodríguez Drissi, Susannah (2014), 'Cuban *à l'Arab*: Exile and *lo Cubano* in Jesús Díaz's "El pianista árabe"', in Jorge Duany (ed.), *Un pueblo disperse: Dimensiones sociales y culturales de la diaspora cubana*, Valencia: Aduna Vieja, pp. 259–80.

_____ (2019), 'Call Him Ismael: Martí's *Oriente* and the Arab World', *Review: Literature and Arts of the Americas*, 52, no. 2, 170–6.

Ruy Sánchez, Alberto (1992), *Mogador: The Names of the Air*, trans. Mark Schafer, San Francisco: City Lights Books.

_____ (1996), *Los nombres del aire*, Mexico City: Alfaguara.

_____ (1997), 'Shadow and Light in the Desert', trans. Mark Schafer, *Review: Literature and Arts of the Americas*, 30, no. 55, 62–6.

_____ (2000), 'Writing on the Body's Frontiers', trans. Michelle Suderman, *Studies in the Literary Imagination*, 33, no. 1, 65–72.

_____ (2006), 'The Nine Gifts that Morocco Gave Me', in Ottmar Ette and Friederike Pannewick (eds), *ArabAmericas: Literary Entanglements of the American Hemisphere and the Arab World*, Frankfurt: Vervuert and Madrid: Iberoamericana, pp. 261–73.

Said, Edward W. (1978), *Orientalism*, New York: Penguin.

_____ (1989), 'Foreword', in Elias Khoury, *Little Mountain*, trans. Maia Tabet, New York: Picador, pp. ix–xxi.

_____ (2000), *Reflections on Exile and Other Essays*, Cambridge, MA: Harvard University Press.

Sālim, Ḥilmī (2011), *Irfa' ra'sak 'āliyan*, Cairo: al-Hay'a al-Miṣriyya al-'Āmma li-l-Kitāb.

Samamé, María Olga (2003), 'Transculturación, identidad y alteridad en novelas de la inmigración Árabe hacia Chile', *Revista signos*, 36, no. 53, 51–73.

Sánchez, Escarlata (2008), '"Belles étrangères": escritores de Guatemala', *Puente de las Artes*, 3 December, <http://www1.rfi.fr/actues/articles/108/article_9999.asp> (last accessed 14 March 2022).

Schulman, Ivan A. (2013), 'Narrating Orientalisms in Spanish American Modernism', in Erik Camayd-Freixas (ed.), *Orientalism and Identity in Latin America: Fashioning Self and Other from the (Post)Colonial Margin*, Tucson: University of Arizona Press, pp. 95–107.

Sellman, Johanna (2018), 'A Global Postcolonial: Contemporary Arabic Literature of Migration to Europe', *Journal of Postcolonial Writing*, 54, no. 6, 751–65.

Seoane, Andrés (2020), 'Héctor Abad Faciolince: "Los diarios son el sustituto del psicoanalista y del confessor"', *El Cultural*, 13 March, <https://elcultural.com/hector-abad-faciolince-los-diarios-son-el-sustituto-del-psicoanalista-y-del-confesor> (last accessed 14 March 2022).

Shohat, Ella (2013), 'The Sephardi-Moorish Atlantic: Between Orientalism and Occidentalism' in Evelyn Alsultany and Ella Shohat (eds), *Between the Middle East and the Americas: The Cultural Politics of Diaspora*, Ann Arbor: University of Michigan Press, pp. 42–62.

Shohat, Ella and Evelyn Alsultany (2013), 'The Cultural Politics of "the Middle East" in the Americas: An Introduction', in Evelyn Alsultany and Ella Shohat (eds), *Between the Middle East and the Americas: The Cultural Politics of Diaspora*, Ann Arbor: University of Michigan Press, pp. 3–41.

Slemon, Stephen (1995), 'Magic Realism as Postcolonial Discourse', in Lois Parkinson Zamora and Wendy B. Faris (eds), *Magical Realism: Theory, History, Community*, Durham, NC: Duke University Press, pp. 407–26.

Smyth, Tim (2013), 'Review of *The Iraqi Christ* by Hassan Blasim', *The Quarterly Conversation*, 11 June, <http://quarterlyconversation.com/the-iraqi-christ-by-hassan-blasim> (last accessed 14 March 2022).

Spence, Julie King (2007), 'Of Bedouins and Gauchos: Orientalism in Argentina', in Ignacio López-Calvo (ed.), *Alternative Orientalisms in Latin America and Beyond*, Newcastle: Cambridge Scholars Publishing, pp. 182–91.

Spitta, Silvia and Lois Parkinson Zamora (2009), 'Introduction: The Americas, Otherwise', *Comparative Literature*, 61, no. 3, 189–208.

Spivak, Gayatri Chakravorty (2009), 'Rethinking Comparativism', *New Literary History*, 40, no. 3, 609–26.

Starkey, Paul (2016), *Sonallah Ibrahim: Rebel with a Pen*, Edinburgh: Edinburgh University Press.

Stites Mor, Jessica (2014), 'The Question of Palestine in the Argentine Political Imaginary: Anti-Imperialist Thought from Cold War to Neoliberal Order', *Journal of Iberian and Latin American Research*, 20, no. 2, 183–97.

_____ (2019), 'Rendering Armed Struggle: OSPAAAL, Cuban Poster Art, and South-South Solidarity at the United Nations', *Jahrbuch für Geschichte Lateinamerikas (Anuario de Historia de América Latina)*, 56, 42–65.

Tageldin, Shaden M. (2014), 'The Place of Africa, in Theory', *Journal of Historical Sociology*, 27, no. 3, 302–23.

Takriti, Abdel Razzaq (2013), *Monsoon Revolution: Republicans, Sultans, and Empires in Oman, 1965–1976*, Oxford: Oxford University Press.

Tinajero, Araceli (2003), *Orientalismo en el modernismo hispanoamericano*, West Lafayette, IN: Purdue University Press.

Tremlett, Giles (2010), '*Oblivion: A Memoir* by Héctor Abad Faciolince – Review', *The Guardian*, 27 November, <http://www.theguardian.com/books/2010/nov/27/oblivion-memoir-hector-abad-review> (last accessed 14 March 2022).

Twain, Mark (2010), *The Innocents Abroad or The New Pilgrim's Progress*, London: Wordsworth.

Velasco, Alejandro, Omar Dahi, Sinan Antoon and Laura Weiss (2018), 'The Latin East', *NACLA – Report on the Americas*, 50, no. 1, 1–7.

Vélez, Federico (2016), *Latin American Revolutionaries and the Arab World: From the Suez Canal to the Arab Spring*, New York: Routledge.

Warnes, Christopher and Kim Anderson Sasser (eds) (2020), *Magical Realism and Literature*, Cambridge: Cambridge University Press.

West-Pavlov, Russell (ed.) (2018), *The Global South and Literature*, Cambridge: Cambridge University Press.

Williams, Raymond Leslie (2007), *The Columbia Guide to the Latin American Novel since 1945*, New York: Columbia University Press.

Wood, Michael (1998), *Children of Silence: On Contemporary Fiction*, New York: Columbia University Press.

Yassin-Kassab, Robin (2010), 'Beirut 39: New Writing from the Arab World', *The Guardian*, 12 June, <https://www.theguardian.com/books/2010/jun/12/beirut-new-writing-arab-world> (last accessed 14 March 2022).

_____ (2013), '*The Iraqi Christ* by Hassan Blasim – Review', *The Guardian*, 20 March, <https://www.theguardian.com/books/2013/mar/20/iraqi-christ-hassan-blasim-review> (last accessed 14 March 2022).

_____ (2017), '"This Is Only the Beginning of the Crisis": Iraqi Author Hassan Blasim on Refugees, War and Futurism', 5 January, <http://www.thenational.ae/arts-life/the-review/this-is-only-the-beginning-of-the-crisis-iraqi-author-hassan-blasim-on-refugees-war-and-futurism#page2> (last accessed 14 March 2022).

Younes, Ebtehal (1994), 'Athar al-Turāth al-Sharqī wa *Alf layla wa layla* fī Ru'yat al-'Ālam 'ind Burkhis', *Fuṣūl*, 13, no. 1, 348–74.

Young, Robert J. C. (2005), 'Postcolonialism: From Bandung to the Tricontinental', *Historein*, 5, 11–21.

_____ (2016), *Postcolonialism: An Historical Introduction*, Chichester: Wiley Blackwell.

_____ (2018), 'Disseminating the Tricontinental', in Chen Jian, Martin Klimke, Masha Kirasirova, Mary Nolan, Marilyn Young and Joanna Waley-Cohen (eds), *The Routledge Handbook of the Global Sixties: Between Protest and Nation-Building*, London: Routledge, pp. 517–47.

Zabel, Darcy A. (ed.) (2006a), *Arabs in the Americas: Interdisciplinary Essays on the Arab Diaspora*, New York: Peter Lang.

_____ (2006b), 'Introduction: The Arab Diaspora in the Americas: Latin America, the United States, and Canada', in Darcy A. Zabel (ed.), *Arabs in the Americas: Interdisciplinary Essays on the Arab Diaspora*, New York: Peter Lang, pp. 1–15.

Zamora, Lois Parkinson (1995), 'Magical Romance/Magical Realism: Ghosts in U.S. and Latin American Fiction', in Lois Parkinson Zamora and Wendy B. Faris (eds), *Magical Realism: Theory, History, Community*, Durham, NC: Duke University Press, pp. 497–550.

Zamora, Lois Parkinson and Wendy B. Faris (1995), 'Introduction: Daiquiri Birds and Flaubertian Parrot(ie)s', in Lois Parkinson Zamora and Wendy B. Faris (eds), *Magical Realism: Theory, History, Community*, Durham, NC: Duke University Press, pp. 1–11.

Zoellner, Tom (2019), 'What Is Good in Man Is Love: An Interview with Elias Khoury', *Los Angeles Review of Books*, 18 February, <https://lareviewofbooks.org/article/what-is-good-in-man-is-love-an-interview-with-elias-khoury> (last accessed 14 March 2022).

Index

Abad Faciolince, Héctor, 23–56
Angosta, 41
Asuntos de un hidalgo disoluto (*The Joy of Being Awake*), 41
Basura (*Garbage*), 38, 41
El olvido que seremos (*Oblivion: A Memoir*), 13, 24, 38–42, 54
Fragmentos de amor furtivo (*Fragments of Furtive Love*), 40
and García Márquez, 170n
La oculta (*The Farm*), 24, 39
Oriente empieza en El Cairo (*The Orient Begins in Cairo*), 12, 23–5, 27–30, 39–58
Abu Dhabi Authority for Culture and Heritage, 12
Africa, 57–77
Afro-Asian People's Solidarity Organization (AAPSO), 11, 126
Ahmad, Aijaz, 26
al-Andalus, 6–7, 22, 70–4, 137–50, 175n
al-Azhar, 52–3, 171–2n
Algeria, 3, 6, 10, 43, 112, 121–2, 144n, 162, 171n
and Cuba, 10
Algerian National Liberation Front (FLN), 10
Algerian War of Independence (1954–62), 3, 10, 121
al-Ghitani, Gamal, 79
Algiers, 33
Al-Hayat newspaper, 178n
allegory, 2, 80–89, 94, 101, 149
Allen, Sturé, 88
Allende, Salvador, 114–15, 122, 161
All-Russian State Institute of Cinematography, 118
ʿAlmānī, Sāliḥ, 168n
al-Mutannabī, Abu al-Ṭayyib, 135
al-Rābiṭa al-Adabiyya (the Literary Union), 7
al-Sayyab, Badr Shakir, 12
'alternative' Orientalism, 8, 29
al-'Uṣba al-Andalusiyya (the Andalusian League), 7
Amado, Jorge, 118, 175n
Ocavaleiro de esperanca or *Vida de Luís Carlos Prestes* (*The Knight of Hope* or *The Life of Luis Carlos Prestes*), 122
American University in Cairo, 88
Antoon, Sinan, 135–6
Waḥdaha shajarat al-rummān (*The Corpse Washer*), 135
Arab migration to Colombia, 30–8
Arab migration to Europe, 136–7
Arab migration to Latin America, 3–8, 14–20, 27–44, 104, 130, 162
The Arabian Nights see *The Thousand and One Nights*
Arabic and world literature, 135–58
Argentina, 7, 29, 83
Argentine Orientalism, 8
Arlt, Roberto
África, 58
Aguafuertes españolas (*Spanish Etchings*), 8, 58
Aguafuertes gallegas (*Galician Etchings*), 58
Artes de México magazine, 69
Ashour, Radwa, 114–15, 174n
Al-Riḥla: Ayyām ṭāliba miṣriyya fī Amrīka (*The Journey: Memoirs of an Egyptian Woman Student in America*), 114–15
Aṣlān, Ibrahīm, 52–3
Asturias, Miguel Angel, 12

Badawi, M. M., 7
Baghdad, 135–58, 164
Mongol invasion of (1258), 139, 149
Bakhtin, Mikhail, 47–8, 80, 85, 95, 97–8
Bandung Conference, 9, 10, 121, 123
Behdad, Ali, 60
'belated Orientalism', 60
Bell-Villada, Gene H., 35–6, 94

Ben Barka, Mehdi, 124
Ben Bella, Ahmed, 10
Ben Jelloun, Tahar, 141–2
  L'Enfant de sable (*The Sand Child*), 141–2
Berlin, 60n, 133, 151
bin Taimur, Sultan Saʿid, 121, 175n
Blasim, Hassan, 135–7
  'Alf sikkīn wa sikkīn' ('A Thousand and One Knives'), 152–3, 156
  al-Masīḥ al-'Irāqī (*The Iraqi Christ*), 150, 152–8, 178n
  The Corpse Exhibition, 155
  Iraq +100, 156
  'Kawābīs Kārlus Fwintis' ('The Nightmares of Carlos Fuentes'), 135–58
  Majnūn sāḥat al-ḥurriyya (*The Madman of Freedom Square*), 135–58
  PEN Writers in Translation award, 150–1, 177–8n
  'Shāḥinat Berlin' (The Truck to Berlin'), 151
Bolaño, Roberto, 151
Bolivia, 123, 162
Boom novels, 4, 13, 38, 41, 115
Borges, Jorge Luis
  dreams of, 135–58
  'El libro de arena' ('The Book of Sand'), 149
  Islamic Orient, 16, 28, 41, 51
  'La busca de Averroes' ('Averroes's Search'), 137–47, 150, 176n, 177n
  magical realism, 8
  translations, 12, 118
Bouhired, Djamila, 122
Bowles, Paul, 57, 61–2, 67–8, 69
Brazil, 6–8, 29
Brazilian Orientalism, 8
Britain
  Dhofar revolution (1965–76), 121, 175n
  imperialism, 1–8, 159, 174n
  Orientalism, 28, 30, 50, 54
Bseiso, Muin, *Ma'sāt Jivāra* (*Guevara's Tragedy*), 117
Burton, Richard, 52

Cabral, Amilcar, 11
Calvino, Italo, 151–2
Camus, Albert, *L'Étranger* (*The Stranger*), 109–10, 112
capitalism, 86, 120, 124
Cardenal, Ernesto, *La revolución perdida* (*The Lost Revolution*), 124
carnivalesque, 80, 85–6, 94–5
Carpentier, Alejo, *El reino de este mundo* (*The Kingdom of This World*), 82–3
Carrillo, Enrique Gómez, *La sonrisa de la esfinge: sensaciones de Egipto* (*The Smile of the Sphinx: Sensations of Egypt*), 8, 57
Castro, Fidel, 9, 121, 122
Castro, Raúl, 9
censorship, 52–3, 171–2n
centre-periphery model, 17–18
Cervantes, Miguel de, *Don Quixote*, 14, 117
Chahine, Youssef, 146
Chasseboeuf Volney, Constantin-François de, *Voyage en Syrie at en Égypte* (*Travels through Syria and Egypt in the Years 1783, 1784, and 1785*), 51
Chennai, 58
Chernobyl explosion, 126–33
Chile, 64, 114–16, 122–8, 159–62
China, 139, 175n
Civantos, Christina, 29, 34, 106, 110, 140–1, 146–7, 168n, 168–9n, 174n, 176n
Cold War, 3, 6, 9, 10, 115–16, 120, 129, 133
Colección Año O, 40, 55
Colombia, 162
  García Márquez, Gabriel, 79
  La Violencia (1948–58), 39, 106
  Majma' al-asrār, 102–13
  Oriente empieza en El Cairo, 23–56
  strike (1928), 95
communism, 89, 121–2, 129
Communist Party, 119, 121
Comparative Literature, 5, 15–17, 24–5, 162
Congo, 117, 122, 124, 130
consumerism, 119–20, 124, 132–3
'contact zones', 59
Córdoba, 138–47
Cortázar, Julio, 104, 148, 155
Crónicas, 102–12
Cuba
  and Algeria, 10
  and Egypt, 9
  influence on Dhofar revolution (1965–76), 175n
  internationalism, 3, 10
  Martí, José, 2, 6, 164
  and the Orient, 166n
  Warda, 114–26
Cuban Missile Crisis, 10
Cuban Revolution 1959, 3, 9, 10, 122, 125
Cuban War of Independence, 2–3

Damrosch, David, 17–18
Darío, Rubén, 8, 57
Darwish, Mahmoud, 150, 159–60
  'Dhāhibūn īla al-qaṣīda - īla Bāblū Nīrūda' ('On the way to the poem – to Pablo Neruda'), 160
  'Fī Bayt Ritsus' ('In Ritsos's Home'), 159–60, 177–8n
  'Ka-Ḥāditha ghāmiḍa', 177–8n
  Lā ta'tadhir 'amma fa'alt (*Don't Apologize for What You've Done*), 178n
decolonisation movements, 3, 116, 119–26
Delacroix, Eugène, *Femmes d'Alger dans leur appartement* (Women of Algiers in their Apartment), 72
Dhofar Liberation Front, 120, 123, 125

Dhofar revolution (1965–76), 119–26, 175n, 176n
diaries, 114–34
DuBois, Shirley Graham, 116–17

Egypt
and Cuba, 9
Guevara, Che, 3, 114–26, 134
Israeli-British-French attack, 3
Layālī alf layla, 78–101
Makhzangi, Mohamed, 126
Martí, José, 6, 159
nationalism, 80
Oriente empieza en El Cairo, 23–5, 39–56
translations, 117
ʿUrābī revolution, 1–2, 165n
War of Attrition (1969–70), 126
Egyptian Higher Council for Culture, 118
Egyptian Ministry of Culture, 52–3, 171–2n
Egyptian Revolution (2011), 160–1, 179n
El callejón de los milagros (The Alley of Miracles), 13
El Espectador newspaper, 170n
El Quaderno Verbo de Che, 124
El Salvador, 124
Eltit, Diamela, 12
Ette, Ottmar, 16, 37–8, 72, 113
ArabAmericas: Literary Entanglements of the American Hemisphere and the Arb World, 14
Eurocentric Orientalism, 8, 33–4, 37–8, 66
Eurocentrism, 17
exotic literature, 61–5, 115
exoticism, 29, 35–8, 42, 46, 48–9, 54, 58, 60–77, 142
experimentalism, 150–8

Fanon, Frantz, 11, 26
Far East, 28–9, 171n
Faris, Wendy B., 83–5, 90–1, 99
Fayad, Luis, 12
Flaubert, Gustave, 23, 38, 41–4, 46, 48–50, 53–4
Notes de voyage, 42–3, 49–50
France, 66, 121, 124, 138, 149
Franco, General Francisco, 161
Franco, Jean, 83–4, 88
The Decline and Fall of the Lettered City, 83
French Orientalism, 72
Fuentes, Carlos
'buried mirror', 14–15
'cultural authority', 103
'Kawābīs Kārlus Fwintis', 156
Khoury compared with, 104
La muerte de Artemio Cruz (*The Death of Artemio Cruz*), 155
magical realism, 137
nightmares of, 135–58
Terra Nostra, 135
translations, 12
Fuṣūl: Journal of Literary Criticism, 87

García Márquez, Gabriel, 23–56
Abad and, 170n
in Arabic, 78–113
Cien años de soledad (*One Hundred Years of Solitude*), 23–4, 26, 30–2, 34, 38, 78–101, 115
Crónica de una muerte anunciada (*Chronicle of a Death Foretold*), 27–9, 32–9, 54–6, 79–80, 102–13, 170n, 174n
'cultural authority', 103
El amor en los tiempos del cólera (*Love in the Time of Cholera*), 115
El otoño del patriarca (*The Autumn of the Patriarch*), 51
La aventura de Miguel Littín: clandestino en Chile (*Clandestine in Chile: The Adventures of Miguel Littín*), 115–16, 128–9, 175n
La mala hora (*In Evil Hour*), 23
Macondo, 81–102
magical realism, 136, 152
Noticia de un secuestro (*News of a Kidnapping*), 170n
Relato de un náufrago (*The Story of a Shipwrecked Sailor*), 115, 126–7
reportage, 118, 132–3
translations, 12, 118, 168n
Tricontinental magazine, 11
tricontinentalism, 16
Vivir para contarla (*Living to Tell the Tale*), 33, 90
Ghazoul, Ferial, 91–2
global South, 17–18
Gonzales, Antonius, *Le Voyage en Egypte du Père Antonius Gonzales, 1665–1666* (*Father Antonius Gonzales's Journey to Egypt, 1665–1666*), 51
Goytisolo, Juan, *Crónicas sarracinas*, 42
The Guardian, 151
Guatemala, 57–63, 63–4, 124, 162
guerrilla literature, 124
Guevara, Che
Algeria, 10
in Cairo, 119–26
Complete Works, 175n
diaries, 114–34
Egypt, 3, 9
Guerrilla Warfare, 123, 125
'A Treatise on the State of Global Revolution', 124
Gutiérrez, Alberto 'Korda' Díaz, *Guerrillero Heroico* (*Heroic Guerilla*), 116

Hartman, Michelle, 174n
Hatoum, Milton, 12

Ḥaydar, Ḥaydar, *Walīma li-a'shāb al-baḥr* (*A Banquet for Seaweed*), 52–3, 171n
Hispanic literature, 12
Hispanic Orientalism, 28–30, 71
Holguín, Andrés, *Notas egipcias* (*Egyptian Memoirs*), 42, 51
horizontal Orientalism, 70–1, 77
horizontalism, 17, 18, 163
horror and fantasy, 150–8
Hussin, Jabbar Yussin, 135–8
  Al-Qāri' al-Baghdādī (*The Reader of Baghdad*), 137–58
  'El mensajero de México' ('The Messenger from Mexico'), 148–9
  Le lecteur de Baghdad, 138, 141, 149
  'Le songe de l'officier américain' ('The Dream of the American Soldier'), 149–50
  'Yawm Bwinus Ayris' ('The Day in Buenos Aires'), 137–58, 176n
Hutcheon, Linda, 48

Ibn Arabi, 73, 75
Ibn Hazm, *Ṭawq al-ḥamāma fī al-ulfa wa al-ullāf* (*The Ring of the Dove: A Treatise on the Art and Practice of Arab Love*), 72–4
Ibn Rushd, 138–50, 157, 177n
Ibrahim, Sonallah, 119
  1970, 125–6, 134
  al-Jalīd (*Ice*), 118, 119
  Amrīkānlī, 119
  Bīrlīn 69 (*Berlin 69*), 119
  Dhāt (*Zaat*), 119–20, 125, 133
  and Guevara, 175n
  Malas and, 176n
  Najmat Aghusṭus (*August Star*), 133
  read Amado, 175n
  Warda, 115–16, 118–26, 133–4
iconoclasm, 118–19
Ida'a 77, 161
illegal migration, 150–8
imperialism, 124, 162
  American, 119
  'contact zones', 59
  Latin American iconography, 115–16
  magical realism, 85–6
  Martí, José, 162
  Martí's Orientalism, 1–3, 6
  Non-Aligned Movement, 9
  Orientalism, 28–9, 47, 171n
  Tageldin, Shaden, 18
  Third World solidarity, 143
  Tricontinental Conference 1966, 10–11, 123–4
Infante, Guillermo Cabrera, 9
L'Institut du Monde Arab, 138
International Prize for Arabic Fiction, 13
internationalism, 3–5, 8–10, 15–18, 125–6

Iran, 150–1, 175n
Iran–Iraq war, 135
Iraq, 122, 135–58, 162
  US invasion of (2003), 7, 135, 138, 149
Islamic Orient, 140–1
Istanbul, 68

Jacquemond, Richard, 117
Jameson, Fredric, 26, 84
Joudah, Fady, 178n

Kafka, Franz, *Metamorphosis*, 151–2
Kalima, 12
Kanafani, Ghassan, 151
  Rijāl fī al-shams (*Men in the Sun*), 151
Khoury, Elias
  Alf layla wa layla, 108
  al-Jabal al-ṣaghīr (*Little Mountain*), 103
  'al-Riwāya, al-Riwā'i wa-l-Ḥarb' ('The Novel, the Novelist, and War'), 108
  al-Wujūh al-bayḍā' (*White Masks*), 103
  Awlād al-ghītū - ismī Ādam (*Children of the Ghetto – My Name Is Adam*), 103
  Bāb al-shams (*Gate of the Sun*), 103
  'Elias Khoury, the Art of Fiction', 78
  Ka'annaha nā'ima (*As Though She Was Sleeping*), 108
  Majma' al-asrār (*The Assembly of Secrets*), 79–80, 102–13
  translations, 12
Kiev, 118, 126–32
Kilito, Abdelfattah, 'Du balcon d'Averroès' ('On Averroes's Balcony'), 176n
Kipling, Rudyard, *Letters of Travel*, 43, 51
Klengel, Susanne, *Sur/South*, 18
Kushigian, Julia, 71
  Orientalism in the Hispanic Literary Tradition, 28

Latin American iconography, 114–34, 160–1
Latin American Orientalism, 8, 15, 27–30, 57–9
Lebanese Civil War (1975–90), 6–7, 80, 102–13, 160
Lebanon, 30, 162
Lehmann, Paul, 47
'lettered', 4, 124
Lionnet, Françoise, 26
Liscano, Carlos, 12
Littín, Miguel, 12
  Acta general de Chile, 176n
  adventures, 114–34
Llosa, Mario Vargas, *La fiesta del Chivo* (*The Feast of the Goat*), 51
López, Alfred J., 162
López Baralt, Luce, 72
López-Calvo, Ignacio, 29
  Alternative Orientalisms in Latin America and Beyond, 8

Lorca, Federico García, 161
Lumumba, Patrice, 122

magical realism, 78–114
  Abad and, 41
  Arabisation of, 20–1, 91, 101–2
  Blasim, Hassan, 135–6, 150–8
  Borges, Jorge Luis, 8
  Cien años de soledad, 26
  Los nombres del aire, 72
  politics of, 83–4
  translations, 115
Mahfouz, Naguib
  al-Azhar, 53
  al-Thulāthiyya (Cairo Trilogy), 80–1
  Awlād ḥāratinā (*Children of the Alley*), 80, 94–8
  Ḥāra, 94–8
  Layālī alf layla (*Arabian Nights and Days*), 78–101
  Malḥamat al-ḥārafīsh (*The Epic of Harafish*), 80
  Najīb Maḥfūẓ yatadhakkar (*Naguib Mahfouz Remembers*), 78–9
  Nobel Prize, 80–1, 103
  Zuqāq al-midaqq (*Midaq Alley*), 13, 50, 81
Mahler, Anne Garland, 11, 16, 17, 18
  From the Tricontinental to the Global South: Race, Radicalism and Transnational Solidarity, 17, 163
Makhzangi, Mohamed, 118
  'The Four Seasons of Chernobyl', 126–34
  Laḥaẓāt gharaq jazīrat al-ḥūt (*Memories of a Meltdown: An Egyptian between Moscow and Chernobyl*), 115–16, 118–19, 126–34
  'Moscow Queues', 126–34
Malas, Mohamad, *Madhāq al-balaḥ*, 176n
Manguel, Alberto, 148
Martí, José
  Abdala, 2
  crónica, 159
  Cuba, 6
  'Escenas Europeas' ('European Vignettes'), 1–2
  Guatemala, 162
  Ismaelillo (*Little Ishmael*), 2, 166n
  'La revuelta en Egipto. – Interesante problema' ('The Revolt in Egypt. – An Interesting Problem'), 1, 159
  'Los moros en España', 2–3
  mestiza, 83
  Orient, 164
  'Seamos moros!', 2–3
  Versos sencillos (*Simple Verses*), 1, 2, 165n
Martin, Gerald, 30–1, 82–3, 86
mashru' al-alf kitab, Thousand Book Project, 117
McGuirk, Bernard, 35
Mehrez, Samia, 86–7
Meruane, Lina, 12
  Volverse Palestina (*Becoming Palestine*), 162
mestiza, 70–1, 73, 77, 83
Mexico, 57, 69–77, 148–9
  and Morocco, 59, 76–7
migration
  illegal, 150–8
  see also Arab migration
Minor Transnationalism, 26
modernismo, 8, 42
Monterroso, Augusto, 12
Moors, 2–3, 14–15, 70–1, 166n
Moretti, Franco, 17, 136–7
  Modern Epic, 25–6
Morocco, 2–3, 57–77
  and Mexico, 59, 76–7
Mrabet, Mohammed, 68
Mussa, Alberto, 12

NACLA Report on the Americas, 166–7n
Nassar, Raduan, 12
Nasser, Gamal Abdel, 9, 121, 122, 125–6
National Translation Project, 118
nationalism, 1–2, 80, 121–2
Negm, Ahmad Fuad, 'Jivāra māt' ('Guevara is Dead'), 114
Neruda, Pablo, 12, 135, 150, 159–61
Nerval, Gérard de, 23, 38, 42, 45–50, 53, 55, 171n
  Voyage en Orient, 43, 47
networks, 4–21, 24, 26–7, 36–8, 55, 79, 104–6, 113, 137, 163–4
Nicaragua, 6, 124
nightmare realism, 152–6
Non-Aligned Movement, 9, 10, 123
North Africa, 57–77
Nubia, 2

Oman, 118, 119–26, 134, 175n
Open Door consumerism, 87, 120
La Opinion Naciónal newspaper, 1
Organization of Solidarity of the Peoples of Africa, Asia, and Latin America (OSPAAAL), 10–11, 117, 123, 124
Orient
  Abad, 27–8
  in Cairo, 38–54
  Civantos, Christina, 34
  Islamic, 140–1
  in Latin America, 27–30
  and Oriente, 166n
  'real', 171n
Orientalism, 3–4, 7–8, 27–30
  alternative, 8, 29
  Argentine, 8
  belated, 60
  Brazilian, 8
  Crónica de una muerte anunciada, 34–8, 79–80, 113

Eurocentric, 8, 28–9, 34, 42–4, 55
French, 72
Hispanic, 28–30, 71
horizontal, 70–1, 77
'La busca de Averroes', 140–1, 145–7
Latin American, 8, 15, 27–30, 57–9
Los nombres del aire, 72, 76–7
Majma' al-asrār, 102–3, 106
Martí, José, 2–3
Oriente empieza en El Cairo, 39–56
'peripheral', 8
South-South, 7–8, 28–9
Tricontinentalism, 163–4
Ortiz Wallner, Alexandra, 61, 67
Sur/South, 18
Other, 38, 43, 54, 60, 65–6, 109, 112
otherness, 34–5, 38, 66, 141, 147–8
Ottoman Empire, 4, 18, 30–1, 35, 165n

Palestine, 6, 103, 117, 119, 122, 162, 167n
Palestine Liberation Organization (PLO), 6, 124, 160
pan-Africanism, 9, 18, 115
Pannewick, Friederike, 16
ArabAmericas: Literary Entanglements of the American Hemisphere and the Arab World, 14
parody, 41–2, 47–9, 50, 54, 55
Pastor, Camila, *The Mexican Mahjar*, 70
Paz, Octavio, 28
peripheral literature, 25–30
'peripheral' Orientalism, 8
Péron, Juan, 166n
Pink Tide, 6, 166–7n
Pinochet, Augusto, 114–15, 127–8, 161
Poe, Edgar Allan, 151
Port Said Stadium massacre (2012), 179n
Portuguese colonialism, 69, 72, 77
postcolonial studies, 5, 11–19, 84–5, 161, 163, 169n
Pratt, Mary Louise, *Imperial Eyes*, 59

Qaboos, Sultan, 123

Rama, Ángel, *La ciudad letrada* (*The Lettered City*), 4
'real Orient', 171n
repetition, 107–8, 111
reportage, 115–16, 118, 126–34
Revista Guatemalteca magazine, 162
Rey Rosa, Rodrigo, 57–77
El cojo bueno (*The Good Cripple*), 62–4
El tren a Travancore (Cartas Indias) (*The Train to Travancore*), 58
Fábula asiática (*Chaos, A Fable*), 68–9
La orilla africana (*The African Shore*), 57, 60–70, 76–7
Severina, 62
Tangier, 12
Tres novelas exóticas (Three Exotic Novels), 60–1
Ritsos, Yannis, 159–60
Ruman, Mikhail, *Laylat mawt Jivāra al-'aẓīm* (*The Night Guevara the Great Died*), 175n
Ruy Sánchez, Alberto, 57–77
En los labios del agua, 69
Essouira, 12
Los nombres del aire (*Mogador: The Names of the Air*), 71–6
'The Nine Gifts that Morocco Gave Me', 69, 70
Quinteto de Mogador (*Mogador Quintet*), 69–77
'Shadow and Light in the Desert', 57
'Writing on the Body's Frontiers', 71, 75

Sábato, Ernesto, 12
Sadat, Anwar, 86–7, 93–4, 96
Said, Edward
'After Mahfouz', 81, 103
Egypt, 86
Eurocentric Orientalism, 44
Mahfouz, Naguib, 80–1, 113
Nerval, Gérard de, 46–7
Orientalism, 28, 29, 171n
repetition, 108
translations, 12
Salim, Hilmi, 'al-'askar' ('The Military'), 161
Sandinista Revolution (1970s–1980s), 124
Sandinistas, 6
Sarduy, Severo, 9, 28
El Cristo de la rue Jacob (*Christ on the Rue Jacob*), 57–8
'Tanger', 57
Sarmiento, Domingo Faustino
Facundo o Civilización y barbarie (*Facundo or Civilisation and Barbarism*), 43
Viajes por Europa, África y América (*Travels in Europe, Africa and America*), 8, 43, 58
Scheherazade, children of, 78–113
semi-peripheral literature, 24–7
Shih, Shu-mei, 26
Shohat, Ella, 14
Shu'ūn Filasṭiniyya journal (*Palestinian Affairs*), 160
Sorbonne occupation 1968, 124
South-South
comparison, 18
exchanges, 5, 8, 25, 117
model, 16
relationship, 71, 77
solidarity, 55–6
South-South Orientalism, 7–8, 28–9
Soviet Union, 118–19, 126–34
Spain
Abad Faciolince, Héctor, 40, 50
colonialism, 2–3, 59–77
crónica, 32

Spain (*cont.*)
  Moors, 14
  Morocco, 20, 59–77
  Orientalism, 29
  translations, 13, 103
Spivak, Gayatri Chakravorty, 'Rethinking Comparativism', 17
Stites Mor, Jessica, 9, 117
Suez Canal, 121
surrealism, 151–8
Syrian Civil War 2011, 7, 124
Syro-Lebanese poets, 7

Tageldin, Shaden, 18
Tangier, 57–77
Tel Quel, 57
Thackeray, William Makepeace, *Notes on a Journey from Cornhill to Grand Cairo*, 43, 50
Thelwell, Michael, 116–17
Third World
  decolonisation movements, 3
  liberation movements, 9
  literature, 104
  revolutionary movements, 122, 125, 133–4
  solidarity, 42–3, 162–3, 174n
Third Worldism
  Ashour, Radwa, 115–16
  networks, 5–6, 11, 13, 15–16, 27, 163–4
  Oriente empieza en El Cairo, 46–7, 49, 53, 54–5
  Warda, 118–19
The Thousand and One Nights, 78–113, 135–58
  Abad Faciolince, Héctor, 40, 44
  Antoon, Sinan, 135
  Borges, Jorge Luis, 28
  Cien años de soledad, 38
  García Márquez, Gabriel, 113
  Laḥaẓāt gharaq jazīrat al-ḥut, 129
  Layālī alf layla, 14
  Orient, 8, 50–1
  Orientalism, 164
  Oriente empieza en El Cairo, 47–51
transcontinental literature, 23–56
transcontinentalism, 18, 159–66
translations, 12–13, 115, 160
  ʿAlmānī, Sāliḥ, 168n
  Blasim, Hassan, 137, 150–1
  Boom novels, 115
  El olvido que seremos, 40–1
  García Marquéz, Gabriel, 53
  Hussin, Jabbar Yussin, 139
  Khoury, Elias, 103–4
  Laḥaẓāt gharaq jazīrat al-ḥūt, 134
  Oriente empieza en El Cairo, 53, 55
  Said, Edward, 81
  The Thousand and One Nights, 52
  Warda, 134
  'Yawm Bwinus Ayris', 146–7
transnational solidarity, 9, 115–16
  travel literature, 12, 57–8, 162
Tricontinental, 10–11, 134
Tricontinental Bulletin, 11
Tricontinental Conference 1966, 10–11, 120, 123–4
Tricontinentalism, 16, 122, 124, 125, 163–4
Tripartite Aggression (1956), 121
Trujillo, Rafael, 51
turco, 31, 35, 37, 110
Turner-Kitab, 13
Twain, Mark, 38, 50–1
  The Innocents Abroad, 41–3, 171n

Ukraine, 126–33
UNESCO, *Index translationum*, 117–18
United Nations General Assembly 1960, 9
University of Massachusetts at Amherst, 114–17
ʿUrābī Pasha, Colonel Aḥmad, 1–2, 165n
ʿUrābī revolution in Egypt, 1–2, 165n
US invasion of Iraq 2003, 7, 135, 138, 1

Vietnam, 117, 119, 122–3, 175n
violence, 63–4, 76
  Blasim, Hassan, 136–8, 151–6
  Colombia, 39–41, 48, 52
  Fábula asiática, 68
  Guatemala, 61–4, 68
  La orilla africana, 60–4
  Layālī alf layla, 76, 92, 96, 99
  Majma' al-asrār, 106
  Morocco, 63–4
  NACLA Report on the Americas, 166–7n
  unreal, 156
  Waḥdaha shajarat al-rummān, 135
voyage en Orient, 19, 23, 42; *see also* Nerval, Gérard de

Wharton, Edith, *In Morocco*, 42, 51
women, 46–8, 70–2, 75–7, 119–20, 125, 141–3, 144–5
  unveiling, 47–8, 143

Yemen, 117, 119, 121–2, 130, 133, 175n
Young, Robert J. C., 10, 16
  Postcolonialism: An Historical Introduction, 114
Yousef, Saadi, 135

Zamora, Lois Parkinson, 16, 82, 99, 156–7
Zaydān, Jurjī, 135

EU representative:
Easy Access System Europe
Mustamäe tee 50, 10621 Tallinn, Estonia
Gpsr.requests@easproject.com

www.ingramcontent.com/pod-product-compliance
Lightning Source LLC
Chambersburg PA
CBHW070353240426
43671CB00013BA/2481
9781399507134